Research on Terrorism
Trends, Achievements & Failures

G000270995

Editor
Andrew Silke

Foreword
Bruce Hoffman

Routledge
Taylor & Francis Group

LONDON AND NEW YORK

First published in 2004 in Great Britain by
Routledge
2 Park Square, Milton Park, Abingdon, Oxon, OX14 4RN

270 Madison Ave, New York NY 10016

Website: www.routledge.com

Routledge is an imprint of the Taylor & Francis Group

Transferred to Digital Printing 2009

British Library Cataloguing in Publication Data

Research on Terrorism: trends, achievements and failures. –
(Routledge series on political violence)
1. Terrorism 2. Terrorism – Research – Methodology
I. Silke, Andrew
303.6ɘ25ɘ072

ISBN 0-7146-5311-X (hbk)
ISBN 0-7146-8273-X (pbk)
ISSN 1365-0580

Library of Congress Cataloging-in-Publication Data

Research on terrorism: trends, achievements, and failures / editor, Andrew Silke; foreword,
Bruce Hoffman.
p. cm. (Routledge series on political violence, ISSN 1365-0580)
Includes bibliographical references and index.
1. Terrorism – Research. I. Silke, Andrew. II. Series.
HV6431.T496 2003
303.6ɘ25ɘ072 – dc22

2003062610

Typeset in 11/13pt Adine 401 by Routledge

4

£8

8

RESEARCH ON TERRORISM
Trends, Achievements and Failures

Contents

List of Illustrations   vii

List of Tables   ix

About the Editor   xi

About the Contributors   xii

Foreword
Bruce Hoffman   xvii

1 An Introduction to Terrorism Research   ᴅᴏɴᴇ
   Andrew Silke   1

2 The Case for Firsthand Research   ᴅᴏɴᴇ
   John Horgan   30

3 The Devil You Know: Continuing Problems   ᴅᴏɴᴇ
   with Research on Terrorism
   Andrew Silke   57

4 Weapons of Mass Destruction Terrorism Research:
   Past and Future
   Gavin Cameron   72

5 Everything That Descends Must Converge:
   Terrorism, Globalism and Democracy
   Leonard Weinberg and William Eubank   91

6 Terrorism and Knowledge Growth:
   A Databases and Internet Analysis
   Avishag Gordon   104

7 What Do We Know About the Substitution
   Effect in Transnational Terrorism?
   Walter Enders and Todd Sandler   119

8 Conflict Theory and the Trajectory of
Terrorist Campaigns in Western Europe
Leonard Weinberg and Louise Richardson 138

9 Breaking the Cycle: Empirical Research DONE
and Postgraduate Studies on Terrorism
Frederick Schulze 161

10 The Road Less Travelled: Recent Trends in DONE
Terrorism Research
Andrew Silke 186

11 Redefining the Issues: The Future of Terrorism ?
Research and the Search for Empathy
Gaetano Joe Ilardi 214

Index 229

List of Illustrations

3.1. Methods in Terrorism Research, 1995–99   62

3.2. Statistical Analysis in Terrorism Research, 1995–2000   66

3.3. Comparing the Use of Statistical Analysis in
Social Science Research, 1995–99   67

6.1. Comparing the Level of International Terrorist
Incidents with Publications on Terrorism
(Monographs and Articles), 1979–98   107

6.2. Number of Terrorism-Related Journals in Circulation   110

6.3. The Growth in Terrorism Publications   111

7.1. All Incidents   129

7.2. Individuals Killed   129

7.3. Proportions of Incidents Involving Casualties and Deaths   130

7.4. Assassinations   131

List of Tables

3.1. Sources of Research Data on Terrorism   60
5.1. Relationship between Waves of Democratization and
      Level of Globalization   98
6.1. Growth of Terrorism Literature in the Social Science
      Databases   109
6.2. Knowledge Growth and the Use of Statistics   114
6.3. The Growth of Terrorism Monographs and Government
      Reports in Online Databases, 1980–2001   115
10.1. Basic Trends in Publishing   190
10.2. The Most Prolific Authors in the Major Terrorism
      Journals, 1990–99   192
10.3. The Professional Backgrounds of Authors   193
10.4. Trends in the Professional Backgrounds of Authors   194
10.5. Significant Changes in the Backgrounds of Authors   195
10.6. Country of Residence of Authors   196
10.7. Trends in the Country of Residence of Authors   197
10.8. Significant Changes in Country of Residence of Authors   198
10.9. Country Focus of Articles   199
10.10. Country Focus of Articles: Changes Over Time   201
10.11. World Region Focus of Articles, 1990–99   202
10.12. World Region Focus of Articles: Changes Over Time   203
10.13. Group Focus of Articles, 1990–99   204
10.14. Terrorist-Type Focus of Articles, 1990–99   206
10.15. Terrorist-Type Focus of Articles: Changes Over Time   206

About the Editor

Dr Andrew Silke (BSc Hons, AFBPsS, PhD) has a background in forensic psychology and has worked both in academia and for government. He has published extensively on terrorists and terrorism in journals, books and the popular press, and his most recent book on the subject was *Terrorists, Victims and Society: Psychological Perspectives on Terrorism and its Consequences*, published by Wiley (2003). He is an Honorary Senior Research Associate of the Centre for the Study of Terrorism and Political Violence at the University of St Andrews and is a Fellow of the University of Leicester. His work has taken him to Northern Ireland, the Middle East and Latin America. He is a member of the International Association for Counterterrorism and Security Professionals and serves on the United Nations Roster of Terrorism Experts.

E-mail: andrew_silke@yahoo.co.uk

About the Contributors

Dr Gavin Cameron, School of English, Sociology, Politics and Contemporary History, University of Salford, Salford, Greater Manchester, M5 4WT, United Kingdom.
Gavin Cameron is a lecturer in politics and military history at the University of Salford in England. His research focuses on terrorism using non-conventional weapons, and on strategies to counter this threat. His book, *Nuclear Terrorism: A Threat Assessment for the Twenty-first Century* (Palgrave) was published in 1999. He received his doctorate in International Relations from the University of St Andrews in Scotland, and has been a research fellow at the Center for Nonproliferation Studies in Monterey, California and at the Belfer Center for Science and International Affairs at Harvard University.

Dr Walter Enders, Department of Economics, Finance and Legal Studies, University of Alabama, Tuscaloosa, Alabama 37475, USA.
Walter Enders is the Lee Bidgood Professor of Economics at the University of Alabama. He received his doctorate in Economics from Columbia University in New York. His research focuses on time-series econometrics with a special emphasis on the dynamic aspects of terrorism. He has published articles in the *American Economic Review* (published by the American Economics Association), the *American Political Science Review* (published by the American Political Science Association) and the *Journal of Business and Economics Statistics* (published by the American Statistical Association). He has also published four books including: *Applied Time-Series Econometrics* and *RATS Handbook for Econometric Time-Series*.

Professor William Eubank, Department of Political Science, University of Nevada, Reno, NV 89557, USA.
William Eubank is an Associate Professor in the Department of Political Science at the University of Nevada. He and his co-author, Leonard Weinberg, have written extensively on the subject of political violence and terrorism. Their work includes tests of Hirshman's Exit Voice and Loyalty hypothesis, the relationship between political violence and

democratic structures, political culture and election systems. Besides his interest in terrorism, Eubank is interested in constitutionalism, voting, and statistics and choice theory.

Avishag Gordon, Computer Science Library, Technion, Haifa 32000, Israel.
Avishag Gordon is teaching in the Department of Library Science at Haifa University and has a Senior Librarian position in the Computer Science Library at the Technion – Israel Institute of Technology. Her main research interest is the integration of Library and Information research methods into terrorism research. She has academic degrees in Political Science, Jewish History, Mass Communication (MA) and Library Science (Diploma), and a Post-Master degree in Library and Information Science (CAS), and she is currently working on her PhD in Political Science.

Dr John Horgan, Department of Applied Psychology, University College Cork, Enterprise Centre, North Mall, Cork City, Republic of Ireland.
Dr John Horgan is a lecturer at the Department of Applied Psychology, University College, Cork, where he teaches courses on forensic psychology and the psychology of terrorism and political violence. His work on terrorism has been published in a variety of sources and his books include: *The Future of Terrorism* (2000) and *The Psychology of Terrorism* (2003), both with Max Taylor and published by Frank Cass (London).

Gaetano Ilardi, Security Intelligence Group, Victoria Police, Australia.
Gaetano Joe Ilardi is a police officer and intelligence analyst with the Security Intelligence Group, Victoria Police, Australia. He has extensive policing experience, especially in the areas of criminal and counterterrorist intelligence. A former board member of the Australian Institute of Professional Intelligence Officers (AIPIO), Gaetano is in the process of completing his PhD into the function of intelligence within terrorist organizations, in particular al Qa'eda and the IRA.

Professor Louise Richardson, Radcliffe Institute for Advanced Study, Harvard University, Fay House, 10 Garden Street, Cambridge, MA 02138, USA.
Louise Richardson is Executive Dean at the Radcliffe Institute for Advanced Study at Harvard University. Educated at Trinity College,

Dublin and Harvard University she joined the faculty of the Department of Government at Harvard University in 1989. A Political Scientist by training, Richardson has taught courses on international terrorism and terrorism movements at Harvard College and Harvard Law School, for which she has won a number of awards. She also teaches international security and international relations. Author of *When Allies Differ* (1996), she has written articles and chapters on British foreign and defence policy, security institutions and prospect theory, as well as international terrorism. Richardson is currently researching the patterns of terrorist violence. She is co-editor of the SUNY series on trajectories of terrorist violence.

Professor Todd Sandler, School of International Relations, University of Southern California, Von Kleinsmid Center 330, Los Angeles, CA 90089-0043, USA.

Todd Sandler is the Robert R. and Katheryn A. Dockson Chair of International Relations and Economics at the University of Southern California, Los Angeles. He has previously held the position of Distinguished Professor of Economics and Political Science at Iowa State University. His writings address public goods and externalities, defence and peace economics, environmental economics, foreign assistance and other topics. He has published papers on terrorism since 1983. His terrorism papers have appeared in the *American Economic Review*, *American Political Science Review, Journal of Law and Economics, International Studies Quarterly, Kyklos* and *Terrorism and Political Violence.* He has written: *Economic Concepts for the Social Sciences* (Cambridge University Press, 2001); *Global Challenges* (Cambridge University Press, 1997); and *Collective Action: Theory and Applications* (University of Michigan Press, 1992). He has co-written *The Theory of Externalities, Public Goods, and Club Goods*, 2nd edn (Cambridge University Press, 1996).

Frederick Schulze, Centre for the Study of Terrorism and Political Violence, University of St Andrews, Fife, KY16 9AL, Scotland.

Frederick Schulze is a postgraduate student in International Relations and a junior Research Associate at the Centre for the Study of Terrorism and Political Violence at the University of St Andrews in Scotland. His graduate work was in Social Sciences at Wesleyan University; after which he lectured in History at Central Connecticut University in New Britain, Connecticut. He is currently in the process of completing his dissertation on the interaction between the Christian Identity movement and the terrorist organization The Order.

Dr Andrew Silke (*see* About the Editor)

Professor Leonard Weinberg, Department of Political Science, University of Nevada, Reno, NV 89557, USA.

Leonard Weinberg is Foundation Professor of Political Science at the University of Nevada. Over the course of his career he has been a Fulbright senior research fellow for Italy, a visiting scholar at UCLA, a guest professor at the University of Florence, and the recipient of an H.F. Guggenheim Foundation grant for the study of political violence. He has also served as a consultant to the United Nations Office for the Prevention of Terrorism (Agency for Crime Control and Drug Prevention). For his work in promoting Christian–Jewish reconciliation, Weinberg received the 1999 Thornton Peace Prize. His books include: *The Democratic Experience and Political Violence* (Frank Cass, 2001, co-edited with David Rapoport); *The Emergence of a Euro-American Radical Right* (Rutgers University Press, 1998, co-edited with Jeffrey Kaplan); *The Revival of Right-Wing Extremism in the Nineties* (Frank Cass, 1997, co-edited with Peter Merkl); and *The Transformation of Italian Communism* (Transaction, 1995).

Foreword

Much attention has been focused on the intelligence failures that led to the tragic events of 11th September 2001. Surprisingly little attention, however, has been devoted to the academic failures. Although these were patently less consequential, they were no less significant: calling into question the relevance of much of the scholarship on terrorism during the years leading up to 9/11. That bin Laden and al-Qa'eda figured so inconspicuously in this literature is a reflection not just of a failure to anticipate or interpret emerging trends in terrorist violence but of an intellectual myopia that characterized the field.

Until 9/11, for example, the conventional wisdom was that terrorists would abjure from carrying out mass casualty attacks using conventional weapons and would shun CBRN (chemical, biological, radiological or nuclear) weapons simply because there was little reason for them to kill *en masse* when the death of a handful of persons often sufficed. In the case of CBRN, this logic was taken further with the argument that there were few realistic demands that terrorists could make by threatening the use of such indiscriminate weapons, and little that they could accomplish by using them that they could not achieve otherwise. In short, the prevalent belief was that terrorists remained more interested in publicity than in killing and therefore had neither the need nor the interest in annihilating large numbers of people.

By the mid-1990s, however, the appearance of new adversaries, with new motivations and new rationales, began to challenge the conventional wisdom. In particular, incidents like the 1993 bombing of the World Trade Center, where the terrorists sought to topple one of the 107-storey Twin Towers onto the other with the aim of killing 250,000 people; the 1995 sarin nerve gas on the Tokyo subway; the massive explosion at a US government office building in Oklahoma City a month later; the bombings of the American embassies in Kenya and Tanzania in 1998; and the litany of aborted or averted attacks that continued literally until the eve of the new century and would likely have produced similar incidents of carnage, called into question the view that the self-imposed constraints which hitherto had prevented terrorists either from employing CBRN or undertaking mass casualty attacks with less exotic weaponry were still applied. Those who advanced such views, moreover, were often dismissed sceptically or decried for over-reacting and scaremongering. Observing this debate, an outsider would be inclined to conclude that terrorism scholars were a surprisingly conservative breed: aloof to, or dismissive of, the more speculative products of their colleagues' analytical and predictive efforts.

On 9/11, of course, bin Laden wiped the slate clean of the conventional wisdom on terrorists and terrorism and, by doing so, ushered in a new era of conflict – as well as a new discourse about it. The publication of *Terrorism Research: Trends, Achievements and Failures* is therefore both a timely and welcome addition to the literature. As its title states, the volume's purpose is to assess the state of the field; to reflect on its successes and assess its failures. The Editor has accordingly assembled an enviable collection of 13 essays by 11 leading scholars in the field. They include well-known and well-established figures like Professors Leonard Weinberg, William Eubank, Walter Enders and Todd Sandler, who have been teachers and mentors to generations of students; as well as some of their former students, along with other emerging junior scholars. In combination, they represent among the most dynamic and forward-looking thinkers in the field today.

One key theme which runs through the book is the need for a better understanding of the motivations, thought processes, mindsets and historical consciousness of terrorists. This, the Editor and many of the volume's contributors argue, is essential if the field is to grow in new and beneficial directions, retain its relevance, and provide incisive and insightful analysis of what has become one of the most compelling security issues of our time. John Horgan hits the nail precisely on the head in his chapter, where he laments the 'almost total reliance on secondary and tertiary source material' and concomitant dearth of first-hand research. Brian Jenkins, a doyen of the field, if not one of its 'founding fathers', once compared terrorism analysts to Africa's Victorian-era cartographers. Just as the cartographers a century ago mapped from a distance a vast and impenetrable continent few of them had ever seen, most contemporary terrorism research is conducted far removed from, and therefore with little direct knowledge of, the actual terrorists themselves. Indeed, although one can find a literature replete with accounts of the historical origins and tactics of various groups, as well as conceptual frameworks for understanding theories and strategies of violent political change, few show any genuine, firsthand familiarity or direct understanding of the subjects of these scholarly inquiries.

Research on Terrorism: Trends, Achievements and Failures is an important contribution to the study of terrorism that comes at an especially critical time. It paints an effective and compelling portrait of the need for greater perspicacity, insight and originality in the field. Its message is clear: if the voice of the scholarly community is to be heard by those policy-makers responsible for defending against and fighting terrorism as well as for finding ways to resolve longstanding conflicts and to address the grievances and causes that result in terrorism, the scholarly work on this subject must be relevant, empirical, incisive, and truly informed.

Bruce Hoffman
RAND, 2003

An Introduction to Terrorism Research

ANDREW SILKE

> Of all men's miseries the bitterest is this,
> to know so much and to have control over nothing.
> Herodotus (484–432 BC)

TERRORISM IS being increasingly seen as one of the most serious, disturbing and damaging problems of life in our time. Research on terrorism is not abstract science; it involves real people with real lives which are ruined, changed and controlled by the processes under study. Organized and planned campaigns of violence do not happen within a vacuum and they are not driven by trivial or fleeting motivations which reside in, and are shared only by, the perpetrators. Terrorism is not the result of psychopathy or mental illness. After 30 years of research all that psychologists can safely say of terrorists is that their outstanding characteristic is their normality. Terrorism is not the work of madmen or devils, and to try and fight it on those terms is to fight it with a very mistaken concept of who your enemies are and why others may support and sympathise with them.

Research on terrorism has had a deeply troubled past. Frequently neglected and often overlooked, the science of terror has been conducted in the cracks and crevices which lie between the large academic disciplines. There has been a chronic shortage of experienced researchers – a huge proportion of the literature is the work of fleeting visitors: individuals who are often poorly aware of what has already been done and naïve in their methods and conclusions. Thus, while the volume of what has been written is both massive and growing, the quality of the content leaves much to be desired. So much is dross, repetitive and ill-informed. As Brian Jenkins commented sombrely after 9/11, 'we are deluged with material but still know too little'.[1]

And yet, there can be few topics in the social sciences which cry out louder for better understanding. The very word, 'terrorism', is charged with emotion and horror. Not surprisingly, here is a subject which provokes extreme perceptions in almost all who consider and think about it; perceptions which spill easily into beliefs about the actors behind the violence. Misconceptions and prejudices born in the wake of the amorality of terrorist acts – the suffering of victims and the wanton destruction of property – if pervasive enough go on to influence the policies used to combat terrorism and can have a powerful influence (and often a poor one) on official attitudes on how to deal with the terrorists. Providing policy-makers and the wider world with the findings of balanced and reliable research has long been recognised as essential to producing effective strategies and policies to counter and prevent terrorism.

At a time when there is an increasing sense of paranoia regarding terrorism, there is a strong need for balanced, expert and informed research into this subject. Good research can provide powerful tools for insight and guidance on what has become one of the most challenging problems of the modern age, yet good research has often been desperately lacking. This book aims to address the need to provide an up-to-date assessment of the state and nature of research on terrorism. In doing so, the chapters assembled here examine the key issues surrounding the conduct and application of terrorism research. The focus of this volume is ultimately to present a clear and succinct view of the key issues and problems facing terrorism research, and to look at recent trends in the research, at its strengths and weaknesses and at the impact it is having (or is failing to have) in a world after 9/11.

A FOCUS FOR STUDY

Most books on terrorism, and certainly almost all with an academic or research focus, start with a discussion on how terrorism is defined. Or, to be more accurate, they discuss the peculiar and long-running failure to reach an agreed definition. This common opening, seen again in this volume, is not a reflection that the various authors lack the necessary originality or imagination for novel segues into their respective tomes.

On the contrary, the constant retreat to such discussion is a reflection of the seriousness of the problem it represents.

The problem is a simple one: there is no widely agreed definition of terrorism. The solution, however, is elusive. Certainly many candidates for a universal definition have been proposed. Schmid and Jongman recorded 109 different definitions in their famous review in the mid-1980s, but an energetic compiler today would have little trouble gathering at least twice that number.[2] The various definitions range from the absurdly over-specified to the unacceptably over-general. James Poland observed that the debate over an acceptable definition is 'the most confounding problem in the study of terrorism',[3] and so relentless is the bickering that Shafritz, Gibbons and Scott concluded in the early 1990s that 'it is unlikely that *any definition* will ever be generally agreed upon'.[4]

Most of the veteran researchers and commentators seem to have agreed with the Shafritz assessment. While the debate remained as unresolved as ever, the topic to an extent was bypassed; and in the specialist journals, articles on 'the definition question' became rarer and rarer as everyone turned their energies to less contentious issues. The relative calm of recent years on this front then raised the point: 'Why is the question of defining terrorism important?' After all, most people have a general understanding of what terrorism is. Certainly within Western countries there exists a shared and common perception as to the types of activity which are regarded as terrorism and the types of groups which are described as terrorist organizations. Like pornography, the sense often is that while I might not be able to define it for you, I still know it when I see it. Why then should there be much concern about reaching formal definitions? Does this really make any difference to the way research in this area is carried out or how the lessons and insights from such study might be applied?

For some, the definition debate is a hugely wasteful quagmire, undeserving of the energy it has swallowed over the years. Many experienced commentators hold such opinions. Weary of the heated and largely fruitless debates of the 1970s and 1980s, they view the necessity of a shared definition with a jaundiced eye, and consider the research effort expended on such efforts would be better applied to other more amenable issues.

Yet, regardless of the uncomfortable failure to reach some level of success in defining terrorism, research cannot ignore the definition question indefinitely. This is not chasing definitions simply for the sake of definitions. Adams Roberts, the Oxford professor, made this point well when he reflected:

I do not share the academic addiction to definitions. This is partly because there are many words that we know and use without benefit of definition. 'Left' and 'right' are good examples, at least in their physical meaning. I sympathise with the dictionary editor who defines 'left' as 'the opposite of right' and then obliges by defining 'right' as 'the opposite of left'. A more basic reason for aversion to definitions is that in the subject I teach, international relations, you have to accept that infinite varieties of meaning attach to the same term in different countries, cultures and epochs. It is only worth entering into definitions if something hangs on them. In this case, something does.[5]

And Roberts is right, something does hang on how terrorism is defined. An agreed definition allows the research world to develop shared methods, approaches, benchmarks and appropriate topics for study.[6] Without a definition, the focus of the field is scattered and fragmented, and an unrealistic range of activities, phenomena and actors have been labelled as terrorist. Ariel Merari, an experienced Israeli researcher, argued that:

> Repeated occurances of the same phenomenon are the basis of scientific research. In the case of terrorism, however, there is hardly a pattern which allows generalizations. Clearly, the heterogeneity of the terroristic phenomena makes descriptive, explanatory and predictive generalizations, which are the ultimate products of scientific research, inherently questionable.

Confusion in research circles mirrors problems in the international response to terrorism. With strong differences in interpretation, governments respond to terrorism in very different ways and sometimes are prepared to tolerate and even support it. The result is that there are sporadic successes against terrorism in some times and places and profound failures elsewhere. A terrorist organization can be crushed in one country only to enjoy respite and a haven to reorganise and regroup in an adjoining state because of conflicting definitions. 'One man's terrorist is another man's freedom fighter', runs the cliché; but the phrase became a cliché because it so aptly described so many groups and so many conflicts.

Even nations which are strong allies in most other respects can show a sometimes surprising disjointedness in how they view terrorism. The government of the UK for example, has a very explicit definition of terrorism which has been set out in its Terrorism Act 2000. Terrorism is defined there as:

> The use of serious violence against persons or property, or the threat to use such violence, to intimidate or coerce a government, the public, or any section of the public for political, religious or ideological ends.

This definition is very similar to those used by the UK's close ally, the USA. This is not surprising as the UK definition was itself heavily influenced by the definition used by the US Federal Bureau of Investigation (FBI) which defines terrorism as:

> The unlawful use of force or violence against persons or property to intimidate or coerce a government or civilian population in furtherance of political or social objectives.

Such similarities in tone and phrases, can be seen to represent a growing international agreement on what constitutes terrorism, an argument reinforced by the fact that both the USA and the UK have proscribed a broadly very similar range of organizations using their respective counter-terrorism legislation. However, broad agreement between close allies should not lull one into the belief that there is widespread international consensus on what actions constitute terrorism, and which groups can be fairly described as terrorist organizations. Further, the manner in which even close allies interpret their legislation can be quite different.

For example, since 1997, the US Department of State has been publishing *Designations of Foreign Terrorist Organisations*. Once listed, a group is proscribed as a terrorist organization and it becomes illegal for individuals subject to US jurisdiction to provide funds or other support to them. The UK has followed this approach and introduced its own list of proscribed terrorist organizations in 2001. However, despite the similarities in how both countries define terrorism, the lists they produced were quite different. In fact, most of the organizations proscribed by the US were not proscribed by the UK.

There was some agreement. Thirteen organizations appeared on both lists, including groups such as al-Qa'eda, Hamas, the Abu Nidal Organisation, the Kurdish Worker's Party (PKK), the Basque Homeland and Liberty group (ETA) and Hizballah. However, the US list included 15 organizations which did not appear on the UK list; and the UK in turn proscribed eight organizations which had not been censured by the USA. Thus, even close allies with apparently similar interpretations of what constitutes terrorism, can display a surprisingly wide degree of variance when it comes to the specific organizations they officially class as 'terrorist'. The result is that there are many alleged terrorist organizations which can openly operate, recruit and raise funds in one of the two allied countries, but who would be arrested and imprisoned if they tried to do the same in the other.

If such discrepancies can emerge between close allies, how much more room for disagreement is there between more diverse regimes? The answer, not surprisingly, is quite a lot. Indeed, exactly this point was made very clear at a conference of the 57-member Organization of the Islamic Conference (OIC), held in April 2002. The delegates to the conference were unable to agree on a definition of terrorism, though they were able to voice consensus on what they thought it was *not*: namely that they rejected any attempt to link the Palestinian struggle with terrorism.

Some nations (for example, Malaysia) had originally attempted to define terrorism so as to include all attacks directed against civilians – including attacks which were carried out by Palestinian suicide bombers. Such an approach might not have been especially problematic at a conference of North American or Western European nations. The USA for example, has for a number of years included both Hamas and Islamic Jihad (two of the groups currently carrying out suicide attacks) on its list of proscribed terrorist organizations. Clearly agreeing with the American assessment, in March 2001, the UK government included both of these organizations in its first list of proscribed foreign terrorist groups (though as we have already seen there was inconsistency between the USA and the UK on a range of other groups). At the OIC however, Palestinian and other Middle East delegates strongly rejected such an assessment, arguing that the suicide bombers emerging from organizations such as Hamas were driven by frustration stemming from Israeli actions in the Occupied Territories.

In the end, no consensus on the definition of terrorism was possible, and the declaration which was finally presented to the delegates avoided defining terrorism entirely. Rather it stated instead that the 57 Islamic countries represented rejected:

> any attempts to link terrorism to the struggle of the Palestinian people … We reject any attempt to associate Islamic states or Palestinian and Lebanese resistance with terrorism.

The draft went on to stress that what needed to be addressed were the *causes* of terrorist conflict, including 'foreign occupation, injustice and exclusion'. The outcome of the conference clearly emphasized that even post-11 September, very divergent views on what constitutes terrorism do exist and these can be expected to have a profound impact on international efforts to combat terrorism.

What hope is there then of a widely agreed definition emerging? The prospects are not promising. Conor Gearty describes well some of the problems in reaching a common definition:

> These works [of political science] set out definitions which are based on a belief that terrorism is in essence no more than a partic-ular and discernible method of subversion: in other words, that it is a tactical use of violence against an established order, regardless of its moral worth. If it were possible to follow this line consis-tently, the subject would be relatively straightforward. There would be available a value-free basis for the examination of the actions of groups and individuals, which would allow conclusive determination as to whether their orientation brought them within the sphere of terrorism. Unfortunately, matters are not so simple. The major difficulty is that identifying a terrorist is not simply a matter of ticking off items on a checklist of violent attrib-utes. The label itself is inevitably value-laden. Its meaning is moulded by government, the media and in popular usage, not by academic departments. The word resonates with moral oppro-brium and as such is, as far as the authorities and others are concerned, far too useful an insult to be pinned down and controlled. The manipulators of language are no respecters of academic integrity, and, simply to keep up, political scientists who believe a definition is possible have had to broaden their attempts so extensively that the exercise becomes rather pointless.[7]

Alex Schmid, currently the head of the UN's Terrorism Prevention Branch, and someone who has long grappled with the definition problem, has argued that a workable definition could be built around defining them as war criminals.[8] Importantly, Schmid sees much of what is currently regarded as terrorism as being, in reality, legitimate acts of war. He argues that while there remains considerable ambiguity about what exactly constitutes war, there does exist broad international agreement about what actions count as war crimes. He contends that this agreement should be exploited when attempting to produce a broadly acceptable definition of terrorism. He says of terrorists:

> What makes them different from soldiers ... is that they do not carry their arms openly and they do not discriminate between armed adversaries and non-combatants. Since they do not fight by the rules of war they turn themselves into war criminals. Terrorism distinguishes itself from conventional and to some extent also from guerrilla warfare through the disregard for the principles of chivalry and humanity contained in the Hague Regulations and Geneva Conventions.[9]

Schmid comments further that:

> I believe that Western policy-makers would do well to choose a restricted legal definition of terrorism as 'peacetime equivalents of war crimes'. Such a definition might exclude some forms of violence and coercion (such as attacks on the military, hijackings for escape and destruction of property) currently labelled 'terrorism' by some governments. However, a narrow and precise definition of terrorism is more likely to find broad support than one that includes various forms of violent dissent and protest short of terrorist atrocities. Other, lesser forms of political violence (for example, against property) will still be illegal by national laws. However, terrorist offences could be considered federal crimes against humanity, requiring special treatment. If we have clarity on this front, nobody will be able to confuse terrorists and freedom fighters. 'Freedom fighters' who adhere to the rules of war should be given privileged treatment. 'Freedom fighters' targeting civilians, on the other hand, should be dealt with as war criminals. Extradition problems, which now arise out of different interpretations about who is a terrorist, could then disappear. The good motive (like the fight for self-determination, freedom and democracy) can then no longer exculpate the bad deed of violence against the unarmed, the disarmed and the neutral bystanders.[10]

While an agreed definition is probably as far off as ever, the needs of this volume require at least the bones of a framework for focus. A few of the chapters which follow will touch again on the subject of definition in their introductions, but overall, the volume follows the relatively concise outline provided by Martha Crenshaw, who described terrorism as 'a particular style of political violence, involving attacks on a small number of victims in order to influence a wider audience'.[11] The events of 11 September cruelly illustrated that 'small' is a relative term. There remains dissent as to which behaviours fit comfortably into this definition. Nevertheless, the focus of this volume is very much that of what could be described as 'insurgent' terrorism. This is essentially a strategy of the weak: the use of violence 'by groups with little numerical, physical or direct political power in order to effect political or social change.'[12] In practical terms, 'insurgent' terrorists tend to be members of small, covert groups engaged in an organized campaign of violence.

ISSUES AND GAPS

Ultimately much of what is written about terrorism and terrorists is repetitive, but it is strong in a number of other respects. Research has generally been very good at exploring the impact of conventional terrorist violence on wider society, particularly in the western world in areas like Northern Ireland and Oklahoma City.[13] There has also been some good work done on the direct victims of bombings, hijackings and other types of terrorist attacks.[14] However, surprisingly little research work of scientific merit has been conducted on the perpetrators of terrorist violence. The activities of terrorist groups, and the nature of their membership, have by and large been studiously ignored by social scientists. There are a few exceptions to this rule (usually involving prisoners), but in general the academic disciplines have not rushed to the study of terrorists. Very few published attempts have been made to systematically study terrorists outside of a prison setting or to study in a systematic manner the actual activities carried out as part of the terrorist campaigns. For a dramatic phenomenon of such intense interest to the media and wider world, such gaping holes in the literature are nothing short of stunning.

Due to reasons of personal safety, political sensitivity and perceived methodological difficulty, researchers have largely shied away from action and actor-based research, largely leaving those topics to a handful of individuals who encounter the terrorists as part of their professional work and for whom research is both a peripheral and generally sporadic activity (for example, prison psychiatrists). The inevitable result has been a very lopsided literature which says surprisingly little on some very important aspects of the subject.

In the wider literature on terrorism, the quality of research tends to become poorer the closer one moves to the actual terrorists and their activities. A few isolated studies have examined mental issues with regard to terrorists and even less have looked at the background life histories of terrorists. Extremely little research has looked in any detail at actual terrorist events and there is only a limited understanding as to the internal dynamics, patterns and relationships which underlie what happens during a terrorist incident. Further, the little research that does exist in this respect is almost entirely restricted to considerations of just one form of terrorism: hostage-taking.

These holes in the literature are well recognized. With regard to the important issue of terrorist events, Alaster Smith observed that in general most research has approached the subject:

> in terms of 'factual' details, such as numbers involved, locations and demands. What tends to have been lacking ... is a consideration of the way in which these events are carried out; that is, the range of behavioural styles which may be observed.[15]

Schmid and Jongman, in their famous review, gave details of over 6,000 works published on terrorism between 1968 and 1988 and virtually none tried to uncover in an empirical manner the patterns and relationships which exist in how terrorists carry out operations.[16] The limited work which had been conducted tended to lack depth and relied largely on journalistic analysis coupled with descriptive statistics.

The period following Schmid and Jongman's survey has not seen a vast improvement in the situation. Research on terrorism – and particularly research which emerges from the various event databases which are available – tends to be relatively good at answering questions as to the *who, when* and *where* of terrorist activity. Issues of *why* are not so solidly covered; and perhaps even more surprisingly the *how* of terrorist events is remarkably underexamined.

Research which can improve our understanding of the dynamics and patterns of terrorism is important for a number of reasons. Martha Crenshaw concluded that:

> Even the most extreme and unusual forms of political behaviour can follow an internal, strategic logic. If there are consistent patterns in terrorist behavior, rather than random idiosyncrasies, a strategic analysis may reveal them. *Prediction of future terrorism can only be based on theories that explain past patterns.* [emphasis added].[17]

Edward Mickolus – the doyen of event-based researchers – noted that when one adopts an 'events approach, one assumes that the *behaviors of terrorists are patterned*, and that the discovery of these patterns through even the simplest of statistical procedures can be helpful in combating terrorism'[emphasis his].[18] Good science is all about prediction. Yet terrorism studies have achieved little in this respect. Good research has the potential to reveal information on how terrorist groups are organised, equipped and trained. It can indicate strengths and deficiencies in the skills and experience of members. It can reveal variations (both temporal and geographical) between the calibre of membership. Most important of all, it can reveal vital information on how terrorists plan and prepare for operations and how they react to different circumstances and events both during and after incidents. Such insights are of potentially massive benefit to the police and other individuals who must respond to terrorist events and who are trying to prevent future events from taking place. Despite the potential benefits, very little research with the necessary rigour and focus has been carried out to make inroads on these critical issues.

By and large, terrorism literature is composed mainly of studies which rely on relatively weak research methods. This is not meant to be an overly harsh criticism. Research on terrorism is science carried out in the real world and on applied issues and such research is often not easily amenable to the more rigorous scientific approaches. The problem for terrorism studies, however, becomes more pronounced the closer the focus moves to the actual terrorists themselves. There is a heavy reliance on qualitative and journalistic approaches which lack the validity and reliability generally expected within mainstream social science research. The approaches tend to be quite good in describing the broader context of terrorism, but quantitative research on the subject is relatively rare. This is borne out by even the most cursory examination of the main journals in the field. As Chapter Ten in this volume shows, studies which are based on the use of statistical methods in analysing data are extremely uncommon. Statistical methods are extremely useful for looking at relationships and patterns and expressing these patterns with numbers.[19] Descriptive statistics describe patterns of behaviour, while inferential statistics use probabilistic arguments so that findings can be generalised with reliability from samples to wider populations. Inferential statistics reveal more about data but their use in terrorist research is rare. The unfortunate consequence is that most research work scores poorly in terms of validity and objectivity. Because the research tends to lack distinct and quantifiable data –

and because the analysis of such data when it does exist tends to be so limited – critics point out that the conclusions emerging from most terrorism research always need to be treated with a significant degree of scepticism. Not only do the methods ultimately mean that the findings exist under a pall of doubt, but – perhaps worse – the superficial level of analysis means that much important information is lost.

One unfortunate feature of this trend is that researchers and writers in the area have developed an enormous tolerance for poor research methods. This is partly due to a sympathetic understanding of the considerable difficulties posed by the subject matter, but this empathy has also had some rather invidious consequences. Indeed, it could be argued that there now exists in some quarters an almost latent hostility to studies which do attempt to produce quantitative data which is then subjected to rigorous analysis. Sadly, this situation has encouraged the field to stagnate with little overall progress being made in the past decade in terms of our understanding of terrorism.

This is partly a problem to do with the level of analysis employed; but it is also partly a problem of focus. Most studies on terrorism tend to take quite a wide view of the topic. They look at *all* of the activities of a terrorist group over its entire history,[20] or else they look at a more limited aspect of terrorism but consider a large number of different terrorist groups who are spread between a wide range of countries, cultures and time periods.[21] This has some advantages but it also has some important disadvantages. Aware of the potential pitfalls, Martha Crenshaw warned that attempting to combine a wide range of terrorist groups and activities into just one analysis effort risked producing conflicting and ambiguous results.[22] Terrorism is not a homogeneous activity. There is wide variation both in terms of the actors and in terms of the activities they engage in. Such variation means that any attempt to study all terrorist activity under one rubric must inevitably end in frustration. If it is to be fruitful, research which is concerned particularly with the *behaviour* of terrorists must have an applied focus. Fundamentally, it should not attempt to consider *all* terrorist activity under *all* situations. Rather the circumstances should be select, such as considering just one particular type of activity.

A DANGEROUS CREED?

Why are there so few terrorism researchers? Terrorism has always attracted considerable wider interest, yet this relatively high profile has never translated into large numbers of investigators prepared to study the subject. It remains to be seen if the events and aftermath of 11 September will change this significantly. Chapter Ten in this volume points out that, compared to other scientific fields which are focused on areas involving violence, terrorism attracts markedly fewer researchers.

There are a number of reasons for this long-term shortage of people working in the area. At one level, the amount of funding available for studies on terrorism has always been very limited. For long periods, there has been a chronic shortage of funds to carry out research and sponsor other types of academic activity, and this has acted as a major obstacle to potential researchers. Another factor is the very real concern many outsiders feel with regard to personal safety. Individuals feel that research on terrorism will be inherently dangerous to the investigator. Quite sensibly, people are generally in no rush to have their names added to the target lists of groups like the IRA or al-Qa'eda. Yet, how real is the level of danger to researchers in this area?

Certainly, there is a degree of risk and it would be irresponsible to claim otherwise. For example, in March 2003 it emerged that a neo-Nazi extremist group, Combat 18, had identified a list of researchers from a university web page. Indeed, included on this list were several of the contributors in this volume. Combat 18 posted a message on their internal web pages, noting the internet site which listed the researchers' details and stating that the link to that website takes you directly to 'the enemy'. Is it likely that anything would come of such a message? Probably not. But being referred to as 'the enemy' by groups with reputations for extreme violence is not a threat that most academics ever face. It is understandable that such concerns act as a disincentive for people to work in this area.

Yet, seasoned researchers generally regard threats like this as fairly incidental. This is not bravado or foolhardiness. For example, in their chapters in this volume, John Horgan and Fred Schulze both describe tense moments during field research on extremists (the IRA and right-wing American militias, respectively). Perhaps what is most remarkable though is that both researchers report that such situations were not common. John Horgan, for example, describes how his more intimidating encounters tended to be with members of the security forces rather than with terrorists and their supporters! Thus, the idea that research is inevitably highly dangerous and risky is mistaken. That said, it does have to be acknowledged that in the course of their work, some researchers have been threatened, harassed, attacked, injured and even killed because of their activities. Their property, homes and workplaces have been vandalized. Friends, family and colleagues have been threatened and victimized. These are certainly serious risks but their commonality is usually greatly overestimated by outsiders.

In general terms, there are two types of danger which can arise during the research process: the ambient and the situational.[23] *Ambient danger* arises simply from being in a dangerous setting in order to carry out research (for example, Brewer's study on routine policing in Northern Ireland put him in ambient danger as he spent a lot of time in the company of on-duty police officers, and on-duty police officers were a major target of terrorist and civil violence in Ulster[24]). *Situational danger* arises when the researcher's presence explicitly provokes hostility and aggression from others in the setting (for instance, asking the wrong type of questions may provoke a backlash from a violent subject). For example, Ellison reported that while he was conducting research on the police in Northern Ireland, he was physically assaulted by an irate police officer who believed that the PhD student had ulterior motives for carrying out the research.[25]

The possibility that the researcher may come into conflict with governments and the criminal justice system is also very real. Indeed, one survey found that 1 in 20 anthropologists report that they have been arrested by the police at one time or another while conducting research.[26] For example, Stephen Small was prosecuted by the London police even after they were made aware that he was a university researcher. Small was doing research on police–public relations and had been at a demonstration when he was arrested. Thankfully, the case against him eventually collapsed in court and he was not imprisoned, but the risk of arrest and imprisonment certainly exists for many researchers in this area.[27]

Governments can respond very harshly indeed if they do not like the tenor of research findings. A Scottish academic, Lesley McCulloch, was imprisoned in December 2002 for five months by Indonesian authorities. McCulloch was the author of a number of articles highlighting abuses and corruption within the Indonesian security forces, and she was coming close to completing a book critical of the Indonesian Army. Her imprisonment for a 'visa violation' was widely seen as government punishment for her research work. An even more serious case was the effort by the Apartheid government in South Africa to dupe Loyalist paramilitaries in Northern Ireland into trying to assassinate the Belfast-based academic, Adrian Guelke. Though shot several times by the would-be assassins at his home, Guelke survived and continued with his research efforts. Experiences like this certainly provide a cautionary note and help, in part, to explain the lack of long-term researchers in the area despite its very high profile.

While this aura of risk has probably hindered more than helped research efforts, for a few it may have actually increased the attraction of working in the area. Research on dangerous subjects and populations can have a powerful attraction for some potential researchers. To begin with, such studies are relatively rare, so it is easy for an investigator to make a significant impact. Also, the nature of such populations nearly always guarantee that the research produced will be of wide interest and relevance. Researchers themselves may find the work exciting and challenging and that it provides more rewards than 'standard' studies.

Still, the level of danger overall has probably been greatly exaggerated and sensationalized. If the field is to grow, a greater appreciation of the reality of the risks and benefits of working in this area is needed. In this volume, chapters such as those by John Horgan and Fred Schulze highlight the reality of trying to meet terrorists face-to-face, and show that it can be accomplished in a feasible and safe manner. As importantly, other contributions show how meaningful research can be carried out using readily accessible sources of data (such as the well-known ITERATE databases). Taken together, these different approaches offer productive and secure ways forward for terrorism research.

PERSPECTIVE, PERSPECTIVE, PERSPECTIVE

One of the more unusual books to be published about terrorism research in the 1990s was Edward Herman and Gerry O'Sullivan's, *The Terrorism Industry*.[28] It is doubtful whether any academic book written in the area has been quite as scathing of fellow researchers as this one. Indeed, the authors are so vitriolic in places, that neutral readers cannot help but wonder how fair such severe criticism could be? The central argument of the book is that a very substantial amount of research on terrorism is carried out solely for the benefit and interests of government. In itself, this is a fair assessment – governments are the primary sponsors of work in this area. This is especially true with regard to the US government who sponsor not only work of researchers based within the USA, but also fund a substantial proportion of researchers based in other countries.

However, in *The Terrorism Industry*, the two authors claim that, as a result, a lot of important research questions are quietly (but systematically) ignored because the answers may be too uncomfortable for the sponsoring government. Instead, it is argued, research efforts are focused on providing support and encouragement for the authorities' view both of the terrorist problem, and of the 'right' approach to tackling extremism. It is suggested that research and researchers who ask the awkward questions are frozen out of funding and thus find it difficult to carry out future work. In contrast, researchers who go along with the government line receive what little funding is available, and are able to establish and sustain the few specialist institutes and centres devoted to the analysis and study of terrorism.

To the complete outsider, Herman and O'Sullivan's thesis has the ring of a plausible conspiracy. Their claim that a very substantial amount of research on terrorism is seriously flawed and biased then becomes a cause of acute concern. Underneath the acidic comments of the text even seasoned commentators would concede that a valid point is being made. This is not to say that there *is* an international conspiracy to systematically censor and direct research on terrorism. Rather, it is an important reminder that one needs to be aware of the perspective of researchers and research institutes in order to better understand the probable flaws and strengths of work coming from different sources.

Let us take an example. The Israeli-based International Policy Institute for Counter-Terrorism (ICT) has a long-established record for conducting and publishing research on terrorism, particularly as it applies to the Arab–Israeli conflict. The output has included much genuinely useful and interesting work. The Institute though has (openly acknowledged) close ties to the Israeli government and military, and it is fair to say that most of its published work is sympathetic to both these sectors.

One example of this was a report published in July 2002 by Don Radlauer, entitled 'An Engineered Tragedy: Statistical Analysis of Casualties in the Palestinian-Israeli Conflict September 2000–June 2002'.[29] This report looked at casualties as a result of the most recent Intifada (which the report refers to as 'The al-Aqsa conflict'). The central argument of the study is that the casualties of this recent campaign of violence are often described in terms which are too simplistic and which paint a misleading and overly negative view of the Israeli role. Most reports of the al-Aqsa conflict simply note that (by 27 July 2002) the violence had claimed 1,551 Palestinian lives compared to 578 Israelis. To the wider world the Palestinians were dying three times faster than the Israelis and this has generally been interpreted as the result of heavy-handed and unjust policies on the part of the Israelis.

The ICT report tried to counter such perceptions and pointed out, for example, that not all Palestinian fatalities were the result of Israeli actions. Many alleged collaborators had been killed by the Palestinians themselves, and there have also been sporadic clashes between rival Palestinian groups which have resulted in deaths. Further, there have been a number of 'own goals' in which Palestinians have died when weapons they were making or carrying exploded prematurely; not to mention the fact that suicide bombers are also included in the list of Palestinian fatalities. Thus, the ICT argued, it was too simplistic to view the conflict as being quite as one-sided as the raw casualty totals seemed to portray.

This is certainly a valid point and it deserved to be made. The ICT, however, undermined such legitimate observations when the study then engaged in some rather questionable sleights of hand to try and make the casualty statistics even less critical of Israel. For example, they divided fatalities into two categories: combatants and non-combatants. However, the fact that ICT was able to put uniformed Israeli soldiers (who were carrying weapons) into the non-combatant category, began to encourage doubts about the overall picture they were trying to paint. The ICT claimed that nearly ten per cent of Israeli victims fell into this category. However, the harsh reality is that most neutral observers would have some serious (and warranted) difficulties about classing armed soldiers as non-combatants (especially given the wider context of an on-going serious domestic conflict).

There were other concerns with the ICT's push to increase the general innocence of Israeli victims compared to Palestinian casualties. The report drew attention to the fact that considerably more of the Israeli victims have been female (177 compared to 70 Palestinian females). The report also suggested that Israelis have suffered more elderly victims compared to the Palestinians: 172 Israeli 'non-combatants' killed were aged 40 or over, compared to 74 Palestinians of the same category. Such statistics certainly suggested that vulnerable sections of Israeli society were being disproportionately targeted for violence. The report, however, then became reluctant to provide such blunt descriptions of especially young victims. In dealing with statistics on child fatalities the report started to talk in terms of proportions: the proportion of all Israeli victims who were children *versus* the proportion of all Palestinian victims who were children. This was the only way that Israeli casualties could be viewed as apparently equivalent. But why did the ICT not focus attention on the actual figures (as opposed to proportions)? The study gives no reason for this. Amnesty International however reported that at around the time the ICT released their report, some 250 Palestinian children had by then been killed in the conflict, compared to just 72 Israeli children.[30] In other words, for every one Israeli child killed, 3.5 Palestinian children had also been killed. The ICT report, while happy to discuss such ratios with regard to female victims and victims over 40 (where more Israelis than Palestinians had died), did not follow the same pattern for child victims. Indeed, there is no discussion at all of the ratios or raw figures when it comes to child deaths. It is at least reasonable to suggest that the ICT preferred to talk in terms of proportions on this question, because a more straightforward reporting of child casualties (as for female and elderly victims) simply would not support the general argument the research was intended to make.

This is a pity. Had the ICT been more balanced in its presentation, it would have been easier to accept at face value the more general points the report was stressing. But in being so selective in the way it focused on different categories of victims, and in being suspiciously flexible in how it defined 'non-combatant', the research became too transparently partisan to be widely trusted.

Bias in reporting is not the reserve of politically hot subjects such as terrorism. For example, this has long been recognised as a serious problem in research looking at the links between cancer and smoking. Research funded by the tobacco industry has tended to find evidence which is ambivalent about the strength of the link, whereas research which has been funded by almost every other source has tended to find a strong link between smoking and various cancers.

Research on terrorism is almost entirely funded by one side in the terrorism equation: the government's. The exact source can differ. It may, for example, come directly from a department of government, or from military or law enforcement agencies; or it may derive from a government-supported scientific funding agency. But, whatever the route, most research on terrorism – its causes, its manifestations and its treatment – are paid for by government. If nearly all research on lung cancer was being paid for by tobacco companies, how confident would you – could you – feel about the findings? Tobacco-sponsored research has in general not enjoyed a good reputation for producing trustworthy findings and so it is only sensible to wonder: how has terrorism research been affected by the prolonged government dominance in funding?

Herman and O'Sullivan argued strenuously that government dominance had seriously corrupted terrorism studies and as a result entire swathes of literature were hopelessly prejudiced, biased and flawed. For them, huge chunks of research were in essence little more than pieces of State-sponsored propaganda. The situation may not be quite as bad as Herman and O'Sullivan made out but, in some cases, there is certainly at least a kernel of truth to their argument of collusion with government views and preferences. A topic as sensitive and controversial as terrorism will never be entirely free of such influence. In the interests of arriving at correct and reliable insights, students should always consider the agendas and the perspective of researchers in considering how to interpret and how much to rely on their conclusions and assessments. Ultimately, a degree of healthy reservation is a good trait in any attempt to read research on terrorism and terrorists.

COLD BLOOD

Brian Jenkins has a gift for providing the right phrase at the right time. He has been a consistently cogent writer on terrorism and in the wake of the 9/11 attacks, his writing yet again cut straight to a critical point. 'Cold blooded mass murder', he wrote, 'requires cold-blooded analysis, the careful selection of words to convey precise meaning uncluttered by emotional rhetoric.'[31] As he penned those words in October 2001, Jenkins recognised that it is much easier to condemn terrorism than it is to understand it. In dealing with extreme violence of any kind there is a tendency to regard the perpetrators as psychologically abnormal and deviant. Terrorist acts are often abhorrent, and attempts to understand them is often framed in terms of the abnormality of the individuals responsible. To attempt comprehension in any other terms can, in many eyes, be seen to imply a level of sympathy and acceptance of what has been done and of who has done it. For example, consider the caustic assessment of the Northern Ireland's Chief Constable, Ronnie Flanagan, who – when commenting on efforts to better understand terrorist activity in Ulster – said that '*For me, understanding [such activity] comes dangerously close to authorising, sanctioning and approving*'.[32]

Arguments against the search for objective insight are especially common in the aftermath of attacks which result in large numbers of casualties. Suffering and loss of life on a large scale, especially when it involves innocent women and children, raises serious and understandable questions about the motivations and morality of the individuals responsible. Terrorism is a topic which provokes extreme perceptions; perceptions which spill easily into interpretations of the actors behind the violence. Yet, misconceptions and prejudices born in the wake of the callousness of terrorist acts can influence the policies used to combat terrorism and leave a lasting impression on official attitudes on how to deal with terrorists.

In the wake of attacks involving mass casualty in particular, it is often supremely difficult to engage in objective analysis of the causes and processes leading to the event. Instead, governments, analysts and the wider public can become obsessed simply with response and punishment. The terrorists are demonized, stripped of their humanity and correctly or mistakenly assumed to be callous fanatics delighting in the carnage they have created, against whom extreme measures are not simply appropriate and justified but obligatory. Those who suggest otherwise are dismissed as sympathisers or appeasers. Yet three decades of study on terrorism has taught one lesson with certainty: and that is that terrorism is not a simple phenomenon with easy explanations and direct solutions. On the contrary, it is a highly complex subject. Worse, it is a highly complex subject whose understanding is undermined and corrupted by a cabal of virulent myths and half-truths whose reach extends even to the most learned and experienced.

Secret group

Military strategists of the past recognized that it was the duty of a responsible leader to always aim to gain an accurate understanding and appreciation of the foe before him. Yet the effort devoted to gaining an objective understanding of terrorists has often been extremely deficient. Such deficiency may not have often led to the collapse of the system combating the terrorists, but it has certainly prolonged and exacerbated conflicts which could have been resolved with greater speed and at less cost and suffering.

The issue of the psychology of terrorists is a case in point here. Research on the mental state of terrorists has found that they are rarely mad. Very few suffer from personality disorders.[33] Yet the long existence of research confirming this state of affairs has not prevented a steady stream of 'experts', security personnel and politicians from freely espousing and endorsing views to the contrary. For example, writing shortly after the events of 11 September, Walter Lacquer wrote that:

> Madness, especially paranoia, plays a role in contemporary terrorism. Not all paranoiacs are terrorists, but all terrorists believe in conspiracies by the powerful, hostile forces and suffer from some form of delusion and persecution mania … The element of … madness plays an important role [in terrorism], even if many are reluctant to acknowledge it.[34]

One of the more worrying consequences of attempting to locate the terrorist within the ranks of the psychologically deviant are the assumptions this then creates about terrorist motivations. Terrorist behaviour is thus placed outside the realms of both the normal rules of behaviour and the normal process of law, a consequence which leads inevitably to faulty assessments and incognizant policies.

Problems caused by ill-judged assumptions and myths guiding policies for dealing with deviant behaviour are not new. Criminology, for example, has recorded the same predicaments in how criminal justice systems have sought to deal with a range of offenders. The long-cherished belief that crime was essentially always a result of the maliciousness and vice of the individual perpetrator has fostered cruel and grossly ineffective systems of control and punishment.[35] Only in more recent decades has there been recognition that such views (and the policies derived from them) are ineffective and overlook the true causes and complexity of crime.

It is especially easy to forget the context surrounding a terrorist incident when that attack results in large numbers of victims. It is easier to interpret the extreme consequences of the act in terms of the callousness and brutality of the perpetrators rather than in a more inclusive and complex framework. Any given act of terrorist violence will defy simple explanation; but while the temptation to view it wholly as a manifestation of evil is understandable, it is nonetheless ill-judged. Such a view provides no practical insight, no understanding of the circumstances and processes which produced the act, and no true insight into the perpetrators and their supporters. Thus one is no better prepared to prevent similar acts of violence in the future.

Every terrorist attack has important lessons to teach. However, it is often extremely difficult to find these out. In too many minds the only acceptable response to terrorism is revulsion and condemnation.[36] Those who appear to respond differently – such as arguing for a balanced understanding of the causal forces and actors – can all too easily be labelled as sympathisers, apologists and appeasers. Yet understanding is not about any of these things and never is. Understanding is simply about perceiving the nature of reality. Effective perception lays the groundwork for effective response.

Embracing the caricatures which often pass as explanations for the causes of terrorist violence only facilitates embracing the caricatures which pass for competent responses. Military strategists throughout history have recognized from bitter insight that an open and cool understanding must always be part of the responsible and professional mindset in confronting an adversary. Too often in the fight against terrorism, we see little acceptance and practice of this basic tenet of military *mental keenness*

acumen. Amid the carnage and rubble of atrocity we must not allow or encourage the luxury of a simple and demonized foe. Terrorism is not an elementary struggle to be so easily dismissed: rather it is complex conflict, one that evolves and often possesses terrible resilience. Ultimately, lasting solutions and lasting safety will not be found until wider understanding matches more closely the wider horror.

9/11: A RESEARCH FAILURE

The events of 11 September 2001 are often seen as a profound failure of the intelligence communities, but they are also certainly a damning result of failure in the research world. The research literature in the decade prior to the attacks provided no coherent sense of the looming disaster or of the perpetrators. In those ten years, the terrorist group responsible, al-Qa'eda, did not even manage to make the top 20 list of terrorist groups which received the most research attention. Indeed, in the 1990s only one article appeared in the core specialist journals which focused on al-Qa'eda (and even then, half of that paper was devoted to also considering the Japanese cult Aum Shinrikyo).[37] What on earth happened? How had such a dangerous movement been allowed to slip through the cracks?

After all, it was not as if al-Qa'eda had been dormant prior to 9/11 or restricted to only one or two Third-World countries. During this period, operating at a transnational level, al-Qa'eda carried out several high-profile terrorist attacks. The USA, which for two decades had almost never retaliated openly against terrorism, launched high- profile missile attacks against al-Qa'eda in 1998. The research community certainly knew al-Qa'eda was there. Going back to 1992, the group was believed to have been behind three bombings that targeted US troops in Yemen. It was also believed to have been involved in the 1996 attack against the Khobar Towers facility in Saudi Arabia, a bombing that killed 19 American citizens and wounded another 500. In August 1998, al-Qa'eda killed some 301 people and injured over 5,000 in attacks against US embassies in Kenya and Tanzania. Then, in October 2000, there was another high profile attack, this time against the USS *Cole* off the coast of Yemen. A suicide assault on the ship killed 17 US Navy personnel and injured 39 more. The group was also involved in plans to simultaneously bomb the US and Israeli Embassies in Manila and other Asian capitals in 1994. In 1995 it planned to use bombs to destroy a dozen US trans-Pacific flights and also aimed to kill

President Clinton during a visit to the Philippines. Behind the scenes, al-Qa'eda was known to be funding, supporting and training militants from a wide range of Islamist groups. It had links to the fighting in Bosnia, Chechnya and Kashmir, and was building a network of extremists that reached across Africa, Europe, the Middle East, Central Asia and South East Asia and even stretched into North America. The organization's profound hostility to the USA was never a secret. In August 1996, Osama bin Laden issued a declaration of jihad against the USA from his base in Afghanistan. This was followed by similarly aggressive fatahs in following years which explicitly encouraged Muslims to kill Americans – *any* Americans – anywhere in the world where they could be found. Throughout the 1990s, al-Qa'eda grew dramatically in strength and influence and the threat it posed increased alarmingly.

Yet the terrorism research world appeared to show little awareness or interest. Instead, the terrorist group which *did* attract most research interest in the decade prior to 9/11 was not one rising in threat and importance, but was instead an organization which was in self-imposed decline and which was becoming steadily less active and less violent with every year: the Provisional Irish Republican Army (PIRA). As Chapter Ten in this volume highlights, far more articles focused on the activities and structure of this organization than on any other terrorist group.

While al-Qa'eda certainly seemed to slip through the cracks, the research community was closer to the mark in other respects. There was a widespread recognition that acts of international or transnational terrorism were growing increasing lethal. Several articles and books on this disturbing trend were published in the years prior to 9/11 and some commentators, notably Bruce Hoffman, were arguing that this increasing lethality was linked with the growing role of religious fundamentalism in terrorism. Indeed, while little attention was given to al-Qa'eda itself, the research community did show an increasing concern with the growing threat posed by extremist Islamic groups. Studies on these groups more than doubled as the 1990s progressed (as shown in Chapter 10). The research community then was detecting and acting on some warning signs of serious trouble ahead.

Good science is fundamentally all about prediction. Good science *allows* reliable prediction. Terrorism research has generally been very poor when it comes to predicting future trends; but, again, there were signs of improvement here as well. For many years, Walter Enders and Todd Sandler have been studying long-term trends in terrorism. Their work has identified that terrorist attacks tend to run in cycles, peaking at roughly two-year intervals. This work had identified that the latter half of 2001 was an especially high risk period for international terrorist attacks.[38] It was a prediction which proved remarkably accurate. The problem, however, was that the research was unable to identify the groups likely to be involved, the regions where the attacks could occur or the methods the terrorists might use. These are gaping holes, but the work of Enders and Sandler at least indicated that research on terrorism was beginning, finally, to provide reliable insight into the future.

The research community was also beginning to show increased interest in the tactic of suicide terrorism used to such devastating effect on 9/11. Early in 2001, the ICT published a book called *Countering Suicide Terrorism*. One of the contributors to this warned that:

> The greatest potential risk suicide terrorism may pose in future is if terrorists carry out operations combined with other spectacular tactics such as blowing up aeroplanes or the use of weapons of mass destruction. Such a combination will increase immensely the death toll of a single terror attack and will have a shocking psychological effect on public morale. At this level, suicide terrorism would constitute a genuine strategic threat, and would probably be confronted as such.[39]

Within months this warning was borne out as al-Qa'eda hijackers slammed passenger jets into buildings in New York and Washington. Yet, it would be unfair to suggest that the field as a whole was astutely focused on such fears. Suicide terrorism was rarely explored in the core journals and while the book above talked at length about Palestinian, Lebanese and Tamil suicide terrorists, al-Qa'eda was hardly mentioned.

Elsewhere, the terrorism research world seemed transfixed with the threat of terrorists using weapons of mass destruction (WMD) rather than how conventional tactics could be used to inflict massive casualties. The Real IRA accidentally murdered more people in a botched car bombing in 1998 than have been killed in *every* terrorist attack using biological, chemical or radioactive weapons before or since *combined*. Yet, the perspective such a fact presented was lost and ignored amid public and media hype; there was also the not inconsiderable fact that WMD-related research was one of the very few areas where government funding was available to terrorism researchers. If the failure to mark out the importance of al-Qa'eda was the biggest oversight in research prior to 9/11, the obsession with work on WMD threats – as opposed to more mundane tactics – will likely be judged as the second most significant failing.

THE IMPACT OF 9/11

Where will terrorism research go now in the years after 9/11? For some, the future – perhaps strangely – appears bright, as 11 September and the subsequent USA-led 'War on Terrorism' has raised dramatically the profile of the subject. There has been a reportedly heavy increase in demand for university courses on subjects related to terrorism and terrorists. Lecturers confirm that classes which previously attracted modest student interest were inundated after 9/11, with students prepared to sit in the aisles in their search to understand the new world which seemed to be developing. Marking this heightened interest, the very first taught Masters course on terrorism began enrolling students in 2002. Funding, a rare commodity for so long, finally became available for large-scale projects.

Within academia, interest in the long-running (and largely uncelebrated) terrorism journals increased massively. The number of indices which include a particular journal that provides a rough measure of how interesting and prestigious that journal is to the academic world. Since 9/11 there has been a 50 per cent increase in the number of indices which include the two key journals in the area, reflecting a considerable growth in the exposure and potential readership of the journals.

The published output on terrorism has also exploded. Yonah Alexander recently commented that more than 150 books on terrorism were published in the first 12 months after the attacks on New York and Washington. This works out as roughly three new books each week, a level which looks to have been largely sustained since then. He questioned – rightly – whether the quality of this flood of print would stand the test of time.[40]

The attacks in New York and Washington on 11 September were the most destructive terrorist events of the modern age. It is fair to say though that in most countries the response from the social sciences has been relatively muted and largely uncoordinated. Even in the UK, which boasts (by international standards) a large, high quality and productive social science community, there has been no comprehensive campaign to harness the knowledge and skills of this circle in a systematic and serious manner.

Individual university departments and professional organizations, such as the British Psychological Society, have sponsored conferences and seminars; while funding bodies such as the ESRC have been quick to allocate and approve funding for terrorism-related projects (some

£600,000 in the case of the ESRC).[41] But the efforts of these various organizations have been relatively low-key and are essentially stand-alone affairs. There has been no push to develop a comprehensive national effort which could be strongly linked with government agencies and activities.

In contrast, the USA has been much more ambitious in its efforts to fully harness what social science has to offer in the fight against terrorism. The USA was spending enormous sums on terrorism research even before 11 September. In 2000, the US government spent some $727 million on terrorism-related research (though the vast majority of this was focused on WMD research in biological and medical areas). Post-11 September there has been a substantial increase to this figure, with at least another $2.4 billion earmarked for relevant research and development programmes. These figures exclude the considerable additional funding now coming from scientific organizations, charities and private industry.

Apart from the obvious motivating factor of proximity, the response of the social science community in the USA has been aided by a number of other factors. Notably, the social science community in the USA is very large in size. However, it also benefits from the existence of a number of multidisciplinary bridging organizations and a clear government willingness to listen and assist efforts.

The increased attention, interest, money and activity are taken by many as an indication that the terrorism research world is on the threshold of becoming an academic discipline in its own right. For them, we are at the dawn of a new discipline of 'Terrorism Studies', a development which will soon see the creation of the first departments of terrorism studies in universities (as yet there are none); a huge increase in the number of taught courses (at the time of writing, Aberswyneth's MSc remains the only taught postgraduate course *primarily* focused on terrorism); and a flood of funding to pay for the growth of a large and sustainable research community (outside of the USA, however, funding has been rather sparse and even within the USA, that available to the social sciences has been relatively limited).

Suffice to say, the signs are not hugely encouraging that a new dawn is unfolding for terrorism research. Certainly there is increased interest and increased resources and this will – and has – fuelled more activity and output. But will it last? In the end, the current heavy focus must fade with time – and will probably fade quicker than many expect. At a more philosophical level, many experienced commentators are doubtful that the study of terrorism can (or should) emerge as a distinct discipline. Paul Wilkinson, for example, has long stressed that terrorism is a subject matter which attracts interest across a range of academic disciplines and is not a discipline in its own right. In his opinion, it frankly never will be. Others – such as Avishag Gordon – who makes the case in her chapter in this volume, see 'Terrorism Studies' as a viable and growing discipline. Time will tell which view is correct.

Ultimately, the study of terrorism is probably much akin to the study of organized crime. There is no academic discipline of organized crime studies (and no push for the creation of such either). Instead, much like terrorism, there are a small number of centres and institutes spread across the world which specialize in the study of organized crime. Usually these are embedded in larger departments and schools of criminology, criminal justice or law (much as the few terrorism centres and institutes have found their homes within departments of politics, international relations or military studies). Yet, at a fundamental level, organized crime is probably a more serious threat to the world than terrorism, in terms not only of its massive economic impact, but also in the role it plays in destabilizing states, and the raw human suffering it causes. If organized crime has not yet fomented an academic discipline for its study and understanding, the ability of terrorism to do so is far from certain.

In the end, the hopes many harbour of an emerging era of 'Terrorism Studies' will probably not be realized, and we may find that surprisingly little changes over the long term. It would be deeply disappointing if the old state of affairs reasserted itself entirely. While the case arguing for the emergence of a new discipline may not be entirely convincing, there is unquestionably a deep and pertinent need for new researchers to start work in this area, and for older investigators to be able to more easily acquire the funding needed to consistently produce high quality research. If that can be achieved beyond the current period and the proximate motivation of 9/11, there is much to be hopeful about.

Ultimately, terrorism *can* be avoided or prevented, and ameliorated when it does occur. To do all this, however, requires the right knowledge, the right understanding and a willingness to act on the lessons already learned. Currently, we are lacking on all three of these fronts. Recognizing these deficiencies is a first step. The next, is to accept the responsibility to do something about them.

I seek the truth, which never yet hurt anybody.
It is only persistence in self-delusion and ignorance which does harm.

Marcus Aurelius (121-80)

NOTES

1. Brian Jenkins, 'The Organization Men: Anatomy of a terrorist attack', in James Hoge and Gideon Rose (eds), *How Did This Happen? Terrorism and the New War* (Oxford: PublicAffairs, 2001) pp. 1-14.
2. Alex Schmid and Albert Jongman, *Political Terrorism*, 2nd edn (Oxford: North-Holland Publishing Company, 1988).
3. James Poland, *Understanding Terrorism: Groups, Strategies, and Responses* (Upper Saddle River, NJ: Prentice-Hall, 1988).
4. J. Shafritz, E. Gibbons and G. Scott, *Almanac of Modern Terrorism* (Oxford: Facts on File, 1991).
5. As quoted in Adams Roberts, 'Can We Define Terrorism?', *Oxford Today*; see http://www.oxfordtoday.ox.ac.uk/archive/0102/14_2/04.shtml, 7 April 2003.
6. Ariel Merari, 'Academic Research and Government Policy on Terrorism', *Terrorism and Political Violence*, 3/1 (1991), pp. 88–102.
7. Conor Gearty, *Terror* (London: Faber and Faber, 1991), p. 6.
8. See Alex Schmid, 'The Response Problem as a Definition Problem', in Alex Schmid and Ron Crelinsten (eds), *Western Responses to Terrorism* (London: Frank Cass, 1993).
9. Ibid., p. 12.
10. Ibid., p. 12–13.
11. Martha Crenshaw, 'How Terrorists Think: What Psychology Can Contribute to Understanding Terrorism', in L. Howard (ed), *Terrorism: Roots, Impact, Responses* (London: Praeger, 1992), pp. 71-80.
12. N. Friedland, 'Becoming a Terrorist: Social and Individual Antecedents', in Howard, *Terrorism: Roots, Impact, Responses*, pp. 81–93.
13. See, for example, Ed Cairns and Ronnie Wilson, 'Stress, coping, and political violence in Northern Ireland', in J. Wilson and B. Raphael (eds), *International Handbook of Traumatic Stress Syndromes* (New York: Plenum Press, 1992); and, Ginny Sprang, 'The Psychological Impact of Isolated Acts of Terrorism', in Andrew Silke (ed.), *Terrorists, Victims and Society: Psychological Perspectives on Terrorism and its Consequences* (Chichester: Wiley, 2003) pp. 133–60.
14. For example, see P. Curran, P. Bell, A. Murray *et al.*, 'Psychological Consequences of the Enniskillen Bombing', *British Journal of Psychiatry*, 153/5 (1990), pp. 479–82.
15. Alaster Smith, 'Behavioural Variation in Terrorist Kidnapping', unpublished doctoral dissertation, Liverpool, University of Liverpool, 1998.
16. Schmid and Jongman, *Politcal Terrorism*.
17. Martha Crenshaw, 'The Logic of Terrorism: Terrorist Behavior as a Product of Strategic Choice', in Walter Reich (ed.), *Origins of Terrorism* (Cambridge, MA: Woodrow Wilson Center, 1990), p. 24.
18. Edward Mickolus, 'How Do We Know We're Winning the War against Terrorists? Issues in Measurement'. Paper presented at the Terrorism: Today and Tomorrow Conference, Oklahoma City, 17–19 April 2000.
19. K. Rudestam and R. Newton, *Surviving Your Dissertation* (London: Sage, 1992).
20. There are many potential examples here but for brevity consider Steve Bruce's well-known analysis of loyalist paramilitaries in Northern Ireland: Steve Bruce, *The Red Hand: Protestant Paramilitaries in Northern Ireland* (Oxford: Oxford University Press, 1992).
21. Again, there are many potential examples, but Drake's study on terrorist target-selection is a good representative: Charles Drake, 'The Factors Which Influence the Selection of Physical Targets by Terrorist Groups', unpublished doctoral dissertation, St Andrews, University of St Andrews, 1996.
22. Crenshaw, 'How Terrorists Think'.
23. R. Lee, *Dangerous Fieldwork* (London: Sage, 1995).
24. J. Brewer, 'Sensitivity as a Problem in Field Research: A Study of Routine Policing in Northern Ireland', in C. Renzetti and R. Lee (eds), *Researching Sensitive Topics* (Newbury Park, CA: Sage, 1993).
25. See G. Ellison, 'Professionalism in the RUC', unpublished doctoral dissertation, Coleraine, University of Ulster, 1996.
26. N. Howell, *Surviving Fieldwork: A Report of the Advisory Panel on Health and Safety in Fieldwork*

(Washington, DC: American Anthropological Association, 1990).

27. See Renzetti and Lee, *Researching Sensitive Topics*.
28. Edward Herman and Gerry O'Sullivan, *The Terrorism Industry: The Experts and Institutions that Shape our View of Terror* (New York: Pantheon, 1990).
29. Don Radlauer, 'An Engineered Tragedy: Statistical Analysis of Casualties in the Palestinian-Israeli Conflict September 2000–June 2002': http://www.ict.org.il/articles/articledet.cfm?articleid=439
30. See Amnesty International, 'Israel and the Occupied Territories and the Palestinian Authority Killing the Future: Children in the Line of Fire': http://web.amnesty.org/ai.nsf/Index/MDE151472002?OpenDocument&of=COUNTRIES\ISRAEL/OCCUPIED+TERRITO-RIES
31. Jenkins, 'The Organization Men', p. 2.
32. As quoted in a BBC interview. Sections of this interview were printed in Toby Harnden and George Jones, 'Early Release of Terrorists under Attack', *The Daily Telegraph*, 4 February 1999.
33. For a review of the relevant research, see Andrew Silke, 'Cheshire-Cat Logic: The Recurring Theme of Terrorist Abnormality in Psychological Research', *Psychology, Crime and Law*, 4/1 (1998), pp. 51–69.
34. Walter Lacqueur, 'Left, Right and Beyond: The Changing Face of Terror', in James Hoge and Gideon Rose (eds), *How Did This Happen? Terrorism and the New War* (Oxford: PublicAffairs, 2001), pp. 71–82.
35. The interested reader will find a useful introduction to this subject in Mike Maguire, Rod Morgan and Robert Reiner, *The Oxford Handbook of Criminology*, 2nd edn (Oxford: Oxford University Press, 1997).
36. A point reflected in the comments of the RUC Chief Constable Ronnie Flanagan quoted earlier (see Harnden and Jones, 'Early Release of Terrorists under Attack').
37. Gavin Cameron, 'Multi-Track Micro-Proliferation: Lessons from Aum Shinrikyo and al Qaida', *Studies in Conflict and Terrorism*, 22/4 (1999), pp. 277–309.
38. See Chapter Seven in this volume for more on this.
39. Yoram Schweitzer, 'Suicide Terrorism: Development and Main Characteristics', in Yoram Schweitzer (ed.), *Countering Suicide Terrorism* (Herzliya: International Policy Institute for Counterterrorism, 2001) pp.75–85.
40. Yonah Alexander, 'September 11: US Reactions and Responses'. Paper presented at the ESRC Conference of the St Andrews/Southampton Research Project on the Domestic Management of Terrorist Attacks, 19–20 September 2002, Southampton, UK.
41. See, for example, http://www.esrc.ac.uk/esrccontent/news/features2.asp

The Case for Firsthand Research

JOHN HORGAN

'If we are to achieve results never before accomplished, we must
employ methods never before attempted.'
Francis Bacon

INTRODUCTION

DESPITE THE interdisciplinary label attributed to terrorism
research, conceptual development within its research efforts
remain gravely limited. Psychological approaches to terrorism remain
especially fraught, theoretically underdeveloped and, from the perspective of contemporary psychological research, even naïve.[1] A basic lack of
researchers plays a part in this,[2] but a more obvious problem that
plagues existing efforts results from an almost total reliance on
secondary and tertiary source material to inform theoretical development. Martha Crenshaw recently reminded us that terrorism research
efforts still lack an empirical foundation of 'primary data based on interviews and life histories' of those engaged in terrorism.[3]

However, and despite it being easy to criticise the progress of
terrorism research on paper, to say that terrorism does not 'easily lend
itself' to reliable, valid, and above all, systematic, research from any
discipline is a considerable understatement.[4] It is in such light that one
common issue emerges from discussions on terrorism research – a
reluctance for researchers to enter the violent field.[5] Terrorism may be
a social and political process, but it is essentially psychological factors
that drive individual motivation, action, and decisional processes:
consequently, it remains inevitable that if one is to effectively study

terrorism and terrorists from criminological and psychological perspectives, one *must* meet with and speak to individuals who are, or who have been, directly involved with a terrorist organization.[6] Many may argue with the perceived tone of this assertion, but it remains pivotal to progression and is certainly one of the most valuable options open to researchers disillusioned with a tiring reliance on secondary sources and increasing specialization within terrorism research which continues in particular to shy away from interviewing those involved in terrorism.

The primary purpose of this chapter, then, is to contribute to the argument that firsthand research involving direct contact with terrorists is, despite its difficulties, quite possible. Furthermore, once we collectively acknowledge the benefits of exploiting such approaches for informing our theoretical and conceptual development, this may open the possibility of comparative analysis of researchers' experiences. That this can only lead to fresh perspectives in answering perennial questions can only represent a positive step.

PROCURING INTERVIEWS

A small number of scholars have personified efforts at firsthand research on terrorism – that is, involving direct contact with either active and/or former terrorists. These include, but are not exclusive to: J. Bowyer-Bell,[7] Steve Bruce,[8] Tim Pat Coogan,[9] Donnatella della Porta,[10] John Horgan,[11] Alison Jamieson,[12] Max Taylor[13] and Robert White.[14] However, no consensus exists regarding the procedures to procure and undertake interviews, with perceptions of researchers differing considerably regarding its assumed practical difficulty[15] – the current consensus is that interviews are sparse and it seems that more often than not, it may be some more 'unconventional' elements such as personal contacts that may facilitate access to such interviews. Brief perusal of 'Acknowledgements' pages quickly reveals the quantity and quality of the contacts of an author.[16] Before the research process adopted by the present author for Irish–based research is described, it is first necessary to introduce some of the issues relating to terrorism research from this 'hands-on' perspective.

From the outset, it would be wise to reassert what might seem obvious – communication is central to terrorist campaigns. In going some way towards explaining his own success in accessing PIRA members, J. Bowyer-Bell writes:

Everyone likes to talk about him or herself, none more than the
saved. And talking is much easier when your arrival somehow
validates the seriousness of the local armed struggle ... Such
investigation based on access – achieved after an endless vigil in
some largely uninhabited hotel at the back of the beyond – often
assures that the orthodox assume sympathy with the rebel.[17]

Once researchers seriously consider access options, routes become
clearer. An obvious avenue is to contact imprisoned terrorists: many
terrorist groups have support structures within prisons and it is sometimes useful to direct an interview request through a designated political representative outside. In Northern Ireland, where there has traditionally been a great deal of contempt for the prison authorities by prisoners, it would have been perhaps futile for a researcher to attempt to
arrange an interview through the prison authorities. However, in the
case of a single terrorist who may be isolated in a foreign country (such
as Islamic extremists imprisoned in British jails) then the full co-operation between the researcher and prison authorities may be essential in
facilitating access. In the latter case, the isolated terrorist prisoner is
effectively without a broader support network that for other imprisoned
terrorists, as is the case of Northern Ireland's paramilitaries, continued
to exist inside prison walls. Therefore, effort spent producing carefully
drafted letters, fully stating the researcher's intentions, background and
motive, can be well worth the time when communicating with either or
both prisoner or prison official, depending on the context.

If, on the other hand, meetings are arranged by a higher 'legitimate'
source within the terrorist group itself, perhaps for example via the
movement's political wing, then there is more often than not a set course
of procedures to be followed.[18] Organizations such as Sinn Fein continuously receive such requests, mostly from journalists seeking private
interviews. It may be required that detailed lists of questions to be asked
be handed over in advance of the proposed interview. Of course, this
approach assumes some familiarity with the potential interviewee, even
if through media exposure – that is, the researcher has identified one
particular individual whom the researcher feels important to the work.
This is not a prerequisite for those researchers who, rather than attempt
to approach known individuals, simply 'seek an interview or comment'
per se. It is similarly possible to approach the political wing of a terrorist
group and ask to speak with, for example, 'Republicans', in order to
ascertain answers to a particular research question, which might include
why people joined the Republican movement (as Bowyer-Bell's work

has done), attitudes to crime, drugs, or other social problems, etc. This will be returned to in more detail, but let us acknowledge that there *are* several easily identifiable avenues of approach.

These aside, valuable open sources exist – websites, newspapers, newsletters – in which one may identify at least potential 'gatekeepers'. Details of public meetings can be useful as researchers may attend: introductions can be made to potential interviewees in such non-threatening environments and, if successful, researchers have much to potentially gain in establishing first steps on the interview ladder, given the numbers of individuals present at such meetings and their familiarity with each other.

Approaching former terrorists informally represents another avenue, assuming perhaps some familiarity, if only at an intermediary level through a third party.[19] Broad types of potential interviewee that emerge at this point might include the retired terrorist who has renounced his/her involvement; and the retired terrorist who has not renounced involvement. An important element of such research can relate to the 'location' of the researcher, and how that *might* relate to ease of access: a researcher in Ireland would have much more access to local knowledge than a researcher who comes to Ireland without *at least* some local contacts to facilitate access to knowledge. This *knowledge* refers to an aspect of large terrorist organizations that may appear surprising to many: terrorism is not as clandestine as may be assumed. Certainly in Northern Ireland, if one has local knowledge, it is not difficult to discover who the local IRA personnel are and how/where an interview request may be directed. 'Outsiders' may encounter difficulties, naturally, but if one is sensible and does some basic research, it is not difficult to know where well-known figures may, at the very least, be contacted. And, importantly, researcher nationality does not appear to be a problem.[20] Indeed it appears that 'outsiders' are greeted with less suspicion than local researchers.

Naturally, however, we ought to consider perceptions of the terrorists: Bowyer-Bell was granted permission by the IRA leadership to write his book on the history of the movement.[21] The leadership appears to have facilitated his access given that an account of the movement's history should (from their own perspective) portray them in as best a light as possible. From the present author's experiences in Ireland, terrorist figures assume a level of naïvety in outsiders to be firmly exploited for international audiences.

The *discipline* of the researcher may bring its own baggage and affect how the researcher may be perceived. For example, as Martha

Crenshaw pointed out, a psychologist's request for interviews may indeed be perceived as an attempt at clinical diagnosis.[22] But, more specifically, one needs to consider how the nature of any research ought to be communicated to the terrorist movement: obviously, it is wise not to attempt to engage in discussion on what might be seen as sensitive or dangerous issues. These could be matters which, from the perspective of the terrorist group, might have potential intelligence use to the security forces. It is best for a researcher to avoid placing him or herself in a potentially compromising position in the first place rather than mulling over ethical or moral dilemmas subsequently. Moreover, if a particular discussion occasionally drifts into revelations of sensitive material, what is always implied by the paramilitaries, of course, is the threat of violence: a threat which few interviewers who value their safety will be unaware of.[23] That is not to say that researchers should ever exceed their ethical and legal boundaries. Robert White describes J Bowyer-Bell as having been present while IRA bombs were being prepared, which raises a separate set of concerns altogether.[24]

On another level, terrorist organizations are fully appreciative of how academic research may be exploited for their own purposes. The present author interviewed a former Director of Intelligence of the Official IRA in 1999, who mentioned that it was common practice to have his own intelligence officers read scholarly work on terrorism and counterterrorism. Equally, on page 21 of the IRA's *Green Book* (its training manual), Bowyer-Bell's (1979) *The Secret Army* is listed as recommended reading for the recruit's 'frame of reference' in appreciating Republican history!

Following a necessary discussion of some of the factors influencing *how* researchers study terrorism, the present author has chosen briefly to illustrate the complexity of some of the methodological research issues in the study of terrorism, primarily by reference to the Provisional IRA. This is because this organization is the one with which the author is most familiar when using firsthand methodologies. Obviously, as with cautions on generalizations about terrorist behaviour, there can be no sweeping statements about 'doing' terrorism research, and the issues raised in this chapter cannot possibly be exhaustive. Time will tell if there are any patterns to be found in researchers' experiences of the kinds of 'issues' raised here. This section outlines, in narrative form, some practical issues around the research process that the author adopted for researching terrorism in Ireland.

A CASE STUDY: INTERVIEWS WITH THE IRA

Between late-1995 and 2000, I studied the activities of the Provisional IRA, the largest of all Irish paramilitary groups, through a number of research avenues. These included more than one type of participant-observation, also library and case study research, and above all, extensive structured and unstructured interviews with 301 individuals lasting a total of 948 hours. Those interviewed included alleged members of four Republican terrorist groups and their political affiliates, though primarily members of the main Republican terrorist grouping and its political wing: Sinn Fein and the IRA. The accounts presented in the doctoral thesis of the author[25] also derived from interviews and communication with security forces and police personnel from various countries, as well as a number of experienced journalists and others closely connected to Irish terrorism affairs (including academic researchers and a small number of non-Republican politicians).

The principal focus of the thesis was a conceptual and theoretical critique of the literature on the psychology of terrorist behaviour, incorporating two extensive case studies conducted by the author – namely, on the Provisional IRA's command and functional structure, as well as their elaborate fundraising activities – in order to illustrate the nature and importance of incorporating organizational themes within a comprehensive psychology of terrorist behaviour.

When I began to formulate research questions specific to the doctoral thesis that emerged as the end product of the research, it became clear very quickly that, even if I were granted access to members of the security forces, I would probably achieve, as Bowyer-Bell and White recognised,[26] a rather synoptic view of the IRA. On the other hand, if I was to rely solely on what research efforts I could produce through attempted fieldwork, I could potentially (as with Bowyer-Bell and White) achieve a great deal of information about certain matters and maybe little or none about other, even more valuable, matters. From speaking to IRA members, I could probably gather a great deal of information on how personal relationships worked and, with luck, I might be able to arrive at a picture of how the IRA's command and functional structure is constructed (and with even greater luck understand how it operates in practice, as well as the factors that direct, control, and hinder this). On fundraising activities in particular, at most I expected to simply gain a glimpse of how the IRA themselves placed their involvement in crime into some organizational context. Conversely, if I were eventually successful (both formally, and informally, I hoped) in gaining similar access to members of the security forces, it would be likely that I might, even if only briefly, have access to a potential goldmine of data on individuals or perhaps some aspect of their organization. Either way, I would not feel comfortable with what would surely amount to a skewed focus resulting from reliance on one type of source.

I also became quickly concerned that, even if I were to produce an empirical piece of work – certainly as assessed within a social science context – then, despite the clear need to go to the 'source', in contrast to most other research efforts, there was a possibility that much doubt could be cast upon my use of sources and the reliability of the information they imparted to me during the research process. I was in no doubt that if I were to speak to both police and terrorists, I would probably be given some private information, which – even at that point, regardless of its reliability and validity – I could only use in a very restricted way (for ethical reasons, even if only to prevent the possible identification of individuals). Such issues need acknowledgement at the planning stages of the research, and given that some terrorism research does not easily lend itself to criticism from peers anyway, I was extremely careful to safeguard against simply producing a few hundred pages of journalistic conjecture. Also, when attempting to provide alternative descriptions and accounts of terrorist behaviour to redress the nature and direction of existing behavioural approaches to terrorism it would not be useful to try to disguise the almost overwhelmingly real and practical research issues. With these concerns in mind, the interview attempts began.

FINDING AND 'COLLECTING' PARTICIPANTS

The research proper began in late 1995, when I made a formal approach to the Sinn Fein National Headquarters, in 44 Parnell Square, Dublin. I had sent a letter, which followed several telephone calls, to the head of the Prisoner of War (POW) Department, explaining that I was a student of psychology who wanted to meet with and speak to people who had been involved in political violence. I identified this person through the Republican newspaper, *An Phoblacht*. As the weeks went by, however, I received no reply and my calls were not being returned. Having received no answer to my letter, I decided to telephone again to ask for a meeting. I asked to speak to the Head of the POW Department and she informed me that she had been too busy to ring me back. However, she said that if I came to Dublin to meet with her, she would be there and would listen to what I was looking for, and the purposes of my research.

I travelled to Dublin a few days later and met with this person. After explaining to her that I wanted to speak to people in Sinn Fein and the IRA about 'people involved in the armed struggle', I was told that there were two men I should speak to. She gave me the details of both of these men: one based in Dublin and the other in Belfast, both described to me as members of Sinn Fein. Through them, I was told, I would at the very least find means of approaching other potential participants.

After leaving the Sinn Fein National Headquarters, I visited the Dublin man who asked me to go into great detail concerning my research. I did so, and told him that there were some sensitive questions I wanted to ask (relating to fundraising – the subject of a then recent publication), at which point he told me that I would not get 'much help on that'. On hearing this, I decided to focus on the issues posed by involvement in the Republican movement, and kept the focus of the discussion (as far as my research was concerned) strictly on examining the experiences of members: specifically, 'Why people joined the Republican movement?' and 'What life is like as a member of the Republican movement?'. This was not a deception, but was an expression of my general interest before more specific questions were asked of individual interviewees. I emphasized my concerns about wanting to gain direct access to people who had been, or were, directly involved in paramilitary activity. When I asked this man about being able to speak to Republican prisoners, I was told that prison visits to interview Republican inmates would be extremely difficult. In a telephone call a week later to this man, I was told it would be completely out of the question. Apparently, my timing had not been fortunate. I was referred to a case in which, during the weeks before I had made my request for interviewees, a journalist had interviewed one particular Republican prisoner. The journalist, according to this man, had deliberately misinterpreted comments made by the prisoner. Upon the 'misquoted' comments being published, there was uproar in Republican circles. 'Everyone knew', according to my contact, that 'she had been deliberately misquoted' about the treatment of prisoners in the Republic. There were now some immediate measures to ensure that such 'misquoting' would not happen again: that is, there was an informal embargo on outsiders being allowed to interview Republican inmates. My request clearly did not figure in this process. The contact recommended, however, that I attend meetings at which recently released prisoners would be present to discuss various matters. These meetings, he told me, would not be in the public forum but he told me that he did not see any problem in me attending them if I 'wanted to':

> ... It's a good place to go up and introduce yourself, to say that you were talking to me, and you're going to have to explain what you're doing, and ah ... chances are that they're probably going to talk to you. I can't say for definite you know, it all ... ah ... depends on the day, y'know, but I know that ... [name of a then recently released prisoner] is going to be there on Tuesday, and she would, I'm sure, talk to you about what you're asking.

These meetings would take place in anterooms of the Sinn Fein Headquarters in Parnell Street, Dublin. He then recommended that I speak to one woman in particular, who in 1997–98 had become a senior Sinn Fein delegate at multi-party negotiations in Hillsborough. This was the first clear indicator that I was going to be 'given' to someone. As White notes, with every research method there is the possibility that respondents will tailor what they say, for a number of reasons, including making themselves and/or their political movement look good.[27] For this reason, and as White has advocated, *prolonged* interaction in the field, carefully constructed questions, and carefully selected respondents provide more valuable insights, and potentially more valid data.

This contact continued responding to all subsequent telephone calls I made to him, and he appeared very co-operative and facilitative, in so far as he knew what 'kinds of questions' I was going to be asking, and to whom they were going to be addressed. He told me over the telephone that he could personally arrange 'three or four' Republicans to meet me and speak about their involvement and experiences as IRA members. These interviews would take place both in Northern Ireland and in the Republic. He asked me to send him lists of *all* of the questions and topics I wanted to discuss with them. I did this and phrased several general questions relating to the following broad themes, the final three of which I planned to concentrate on:

1. Why people joined the Republican movement.
2. How people join the Republican movement.
3. What kinds of backgrounds members have.
4. What life was like within the movement.
5. What life was like specifically as an activist (that is, a member of the IRA) and how operations impinged on their person.
6. How they viewed accusations that the IRA are 'criminals', involved

in elaborate fundraising activities to raise money for the organization.

7. What their views were on 'criminal activity' (for example, localized robbery and other illegal activities against which the IRA has been known to take action in several urban areas in which the movement is based in Northern Ireland).

These, I had planned, were to be the very 'general' issues that would be discussed, which with luck would allow me to instigate more detailed discussion with respect to the main themes that I wished to be explored.

Following this initial meeting, and upon leaving Dublin, I realized very quickly from speaking to this man that any respondents met through this channel were going to be selectively chosen, articulate individuals, and probably those with experience in discussing 'sensitive' issues as well as more general ones. I had made it clear from the outset that I was a student of psychology and that I wanted to discuss issues of motivation and 'various aspects' of Republicanism, later including what Republicans describe as 'black propaganda' (that is, fundraising). During these early stages of the research, and before I fully understood how 'selected' people were going to be 'given to me', I was generally surprised at the level of co-operation and welcome I received from Sinn Fein and the IRA.

I also asked the Dublin man by telephone, about one week after our meeting, if there was a possibility of being able to speak with someone who was *actively* involved in the IRA. He hesitated for a short time, and replied that it would 'probably take a long time, and it would probably be very difficult.' I did not resume contact with this man later as my initial perception that he was reluctant to address any questions relating to fundraising was confirmed in a conversation with other Republicans and a subsequent telephone conversation between us. It emerged in late 1999 that this man had actually made final efforts to block any interviews with Republicans which he felt I might procure without his knowledge or assistance, but the exact details remain unclear.

During this initial phase, however, and while making efforts to establish a grounding in speaking to Republicans about issues relating to their activities, I became aware that a good technique to broaden my participant base (and therefore, in accordance with White's comments,[28] to become more selective as regards potential respondents) would be through the use of 'snowballing' or 'snowball sampling'. This research method is useful in 'dangerous' field research, or where there are important issues of trust and apprehension, as in the present context, and can be vital for establishing contacts and building on previous efforts.[29] Essentially, the procedure involves asking interviewees to recommend other potential interviewees, and so on.

At this time, I began to simultaneously initiate contact with members of the Irish security forces. With the assistance of a friend who had been working as a Gardai in Cork (whom I had never approached formally in such a context before), and subsequent assistance of those Gardai I met through this man, I soon built up what was to be a surprisingly good (and relatively large) informal network of Gardai who worked or had worked across several levels of the organization, including in the anti-terrorism branches of An Garda Síochána. These individuals came from many parts of Ireland, and some of them described themselves as having worked in 'anti-subversive' work since the IRA's rebirth in the early 1970s. Informal co-operation from the Gardai in participating in interviews was exceptionally good, as was the very high level of assistance from individual members in helping me gain access to 'other members'.

It is possible to characterize individuals in both terrorist groups and security services (and also perhaps even some of the academics interviewed informally during consultation), according to how easy it was to elicit information from them. Participant types can be epitomized by the following 'categories' of general interviewee types (as initially described by Swanson, Chamelin and Territo): honest and co-operative; 'Hear nothing, say nothing'; reluctant/suspicious interviewees; hostile/deceitful interviewees; timid interviewees; boastful interviewees; and the slightly common 'under the influence' interviewees.[30] This last category aptly describes many Republican sympathisers who – when not interviewed in participant–observation contexts such as Republican fundraiser parties, which I began to attend as my research progressed – attempted to become 'friendly' with me and also became anxious that I could relate the finer points of Republican history correctly (as they would have it). It is important to state, however, that such categorization of interviewees and potential participants applied equally to members of the security forces that I interviewed. The similarity in the dynamics of creating and building a network of likely participants from the IRA and Irish security forces was remarkable. The power of the snowball sampling method was quickly realized, and my overall conclusion was that informal enquiries and informal attempts at access proved much more fruitful than official attempts at accessing individuals (given the bureaucratic nature of both the security services and the terrorists and their political wings).

I quickly discovered that my approach to interviewing would have to be flexible enough to vary with each of the 'types' of interviewees I would encounter, some of whom were reluctant to discuss, or impart any comment relating to, fundraising. Although I had planned to ask questions in a systematic, semi-formal fashion, this initially proved difficult in practice and quite a lot of flexibility had to be employed with most interviewees. It was only when details about two specific case studies on fundraising came to light that I was able to begin to purposefully target chosen individuals, and to pose organized and relevant questions about those case studies.

Following my initial experiences with Sinn Fein members in Dublin, I realized that I should begin to initiate two other research outlets, and to explore the possibility of exploiting them as best as possible in order to procure a sufficient level of access to members of IRA and Sinn Fein. It was also clear that this would have to be done as quickly as possible, in case my initial attempts at making contacts failed due to my Dublin contact dismissing my requests (either indirectly through avoiding answering my questions, or through simply giving me an outright 'no'). Through local knowledge, media reports and assistance from a number of helpful journalists, together with informal interviews of both Gardai and Sinn Fein sources, I soon began to build a picture of localized Sinn Fein and IRA membership in various locations around Ireland. An example of one interview will be presented to help illustrate how such localized knowledge (as I described earlier) can materialize into a more fruitful outcome, and consequently lead to the establishment of an 'IRA participant base'.

A CASE STUDY: INTERVIEWING A TERRORIST

In early 1996, I contacted a person (to be referred to as 'Peter') whom I had known about through the Irish media (in connection with a paramilitary crime for which Peter had been charged). I knew roughly where Peter lived, and also knew from media reports that he worked in a certain pub in a certain town. I telephoned the pub asking to speak with Peter but instead spoke to a man who described himself as 'a friend of Peter's'. I asked him to deliver a message to Peter – simply stating my name, that I was a student from University College, Cork (UCC), and that I would call back. A few days later I called back and spoke to Peter himself. I introduced myself to him as a student of psychology from UCC, and requested that Peter help me get in touch with one of his colleagues, a well-known IRA man who had frequently appeared both on television and in the print media as a result of several allegations of IRA membership and paramilitary offences. Peter told me that if I wrote a letter to this man (whom I shall refer to as 'Michael'), addressing it to Peter, describing my background and intentions regarding the 'interview', that he would pass the letter on to my targeted participant. The participant was well-known to the Gardai as an IRA activist whom they alleged was then a member of the IRA's Army Council; this had been alleged in several television and print media sources. I thanked Peter for his help and told him that he would receive the letter within a few days. I wrote the letter to 'Michael', and sent it care of Peter at his address.

About five weeks later, I received a telephone call from a man identifying himself as a colleague of Peter's saying that 'a meeting' could be arranged – 'no problem'. It was specified that I would meet Michael. I was told that he had received the letter and that 'he'll talk to you alright'. Peter's colleague said that he would arrange the interview and would communicate again when a time and place could be confirmed with Michael.

A few days after this, this 'second' intermediary, Peter's contact, called me and told me that the interview with Michael was 'definitely on', and that I was to come to a specific location for an interview with him. Peter's colleague told me that Michael would arrive to meet me two days later, early in the morning, to discuss a 'few things' in the letter I wrote to him. Peter's colleague told me that he himself would pick me up at the train station and that I would stay in his house for the night before travelling on to the town in which Peter's pub was located. His closing remark was, 'y'know this man, now, wouldn't have time for people who call him a terrorist'. I said that I understood. I knew that I did not have a lot of time. I had been told on Thursday evening that Michael would meet me in Peter's pub on the following Saturday morning. On Friday morning, I travelled by train to a town where after waiting about ten minutes, I was picked up in a car by Peter's friend.

I stayed in Peter's friend's house on that Friday night and he called Peter on the telephone (in my presence) to check that Michael was still coming. Their conversation was very short, lasting less than a minute. The man then told me: 'Yeah, it's on, tomorrow morning, at 10 o'clock'. The next morning, the man drove me for about 35 minutes to the interview location, Peter's pub, where the interviewee would meet me. A barman (himself a convicted IRA gunman) waved from inside a window, gesturing us around to the side of the building. He greeted us both as he let us enter through a back door, the pub not having yet opened for business. Michael had not arrived and the barman said that he would 'be along in a few minutes', following which he and my 'chauffeur' engaged in conversation about business in the pub. After about five minutes, a tall, middle-aged slightly greying man walked in with a newspaper under his arm. I recognized Michael immediately from pictures I had seen of him in books and on television, and introduced myself to him. I was surprised to find a quiet, very soft-spoken man. With a sense of urgency, Michael asked me where did I want to go to hold the interview. The barman intervened, saying there was an unused room upstairs in the pub and that we could use it. We ascended a long flight of stairs and entered a small, stuffy and dusty room, which was a lounge section of the bar under renovation. There were four or five tables in the room, and I suggested that we sit down at the middle one.

I sat with my back to a wall and Michael sat directly opposite me across a narrow table. I placed my briefcase on the table and took out a notepad, reiterating some points made in the letter about confidentiality as I began to describe my background and intentions for research. I had said that I had just begun to speak with Republicans previous to our meeting and that I had also just begun to seek and gain interviews and meetings with members of the security forces. I emphasized that there was no co-operation or collusion with them, and that for all of the interviews I had conducted and would in the future be seeking to conduct, identifiable features of interview materials and discussions were not and would not be retained or communicated in any way to any other participant or outsider. Michael nodded his head as I emphasized these points, but said nothing. I thought to myself that he would have doubtless known about me anyway through the meeting organizers and they would have ensured that no collaboration did exist, or at the very least, that I was indeed just a student who posed no threat whatsoever to Michael.

I then asked Michael if he would mind that I used a tape recorder as this would facilitate the 'quality of the research'. I also gave him my guarantee that the tapes would be transcribed and destroyed 'within 24 hours'. Michael nodded and said, 'yeah, that's all right ... I'll take your word for it'.

The tape recorder was switched on and the interview began. A number of themes were addressed, but I began the interview by asking Michael very general questions about his involvement in the Republican movement. I asked him about his reasons for joining the movement as well as his involvement in the actions for which he had been convicted. I did not ask about activities for which Michael had not been charged. As the interview progressed, I began to attempt to guide the discussion onto more specific issues relating to the IRA's organizational structure and its

involvement in criminal activities for the purpose of fundraising. As
noted already, the practice of asking general questions of interviewees
before more specific ones is one practised by the few researchers who
speak to terrorists first hand.[31] This practice also applied to how questions were asked of security sources and other participants: security
sources were asked general questions (such as, 'Is the IRA involved in
criminal activities to raise funds?'), before more specific ones were posed
(for example, 'Does the IRA make use of professional expertise in the
private business sector to facilitate money laundering?').

Michael responded to all of my questions without hesitation, even
with respect to the 'sensitive' questions when I began to ask him about
the IRA's involvement in criminal activities. He was very forthright and
direct at all times in response to each question I asked him. I got the
feeling that I could have asked him *anything* about the IRA and at least I
would have been answered directly. This contributed to the compelling
nature of what he had to say, and how he was saying it. This was very
far removed from the more traditional republican 'rhetoric' on nationalism which is so evident when terrorists talk about themselves (and
from the rhetoric repeated *ad nauseam* at Republican meetings, which I
frequently attended in both Northern and Southern Ireland in order to
reach other participants). As he began to describe his activities he made
no excuses for what he had done as a member of the IRA, nor did he
try to excuse the present IRA for any atrocious acts committed since.

The interview with Michael lasted about 50 minutes, and at the time
I felt that I had some 'good' material – a solid starting point for building
my picture of the IRA's command structure, as well as some valuable
commentary (from a significant source) on what the IRA thinks of criminal activities. I switched off the tape recorder and thanked him for
coming to meet me and for speaking so openly to me. He said it was 'no
problem' and said, 'I wish you luck with whatever it is you're doing'. I
then realized that this was probably one of hundreds of such interviews
Michael had conducted, none necessarily of great consequence other
than it gave him the chance to create a sense of co-operation with the
'outsiders', the non-Republican observers, including the media,
academics and others. We left the room while talking about some local
issues – an attempt by me to make some informal conversation. I then
asked him: 'Do you know of some other members that would be willing
to talk to me?' He said that there would be many people who would be
willing to talk to me and that: 'If ever you want to be put in touch with
someone, give me a ring. I'm usually fairly busy, but leave a message and
I'll get back to you if I'm not there'. This I did, and Michael proved to

be very useful in acquiring the participation of several further Republicans.

We were once again in the bar area, which had since opened for late morning business, with five to six people sitting on stools or at tables. The barman asked Michael if he would have a drink, but he promptly refused, saying that he had to attend to some business. We shook hands and I thanked him once more as he left. The barman spoke a few words to me and to the man who had driven me to the interview: 'He's a very nice man ... a lovely fella ... I'll tell you something else ... There's not a lot of people he'd come and do that for now ... Especially on his day off y'know.'

About ten minutes later, my 'chauffeur' and I left the bar. The driver immediately asked 'Well, did you get what you wanted?' I replied that the meeting had gone very well and I thanked him once more for his own role in facilitating the meeting. He said, 'Yeah, he's a very nice fella, very intelligent, and would go out of his way to help you'. The same driver took me back to the train station from which I had arrived and wished me 'Good luck'.

Following the interview, I listened to the tape recording through an earpiece on the train journey back to Cork. I also began taking notes of what had happened in the interview, as much of my perceptions as of what Michael had told me when answering my questions. Upon reaching Cork, I transcribed the tape and destroyed it after about six to seven hours of laborious transcriptions. I have since destroyed all the tapes and transcripts involving all the interviews in which participants granted me permission to use the tape recorder, after choosing the select pieces to be included in the material presented here, or used to support general points.

I then began 'processing' the transcript of the interview, making sure that it did not contain any recognizable names, dates, places etc. – a wise step to avoid accidentally compromising the identity of any individual. I subsequently began to examine the transcript to ascertain its 'value', with respect to those research questions I wanted to attempt to answer. It was only about a week after my interview with Michael, and after I had read and re-read the transcript, that I began to realize just how irrelevant most of the material was that I had gained from what I initially thought was a very fruitful interview. I later learned, however, that the initial experiences in interviewing people such as Michael would help provide a solid foundation upon which later experiences and interview efforts could subsequently be improved. I certainly had felt nervous in interviewing him, and was probably more so given that he is alleged to be an IRA Army Council member, and also because he was a well-known Sinn Fein member in his local area (in the vicinity of the pub). I thus had some prior perceptions of him, and although my concerns about him being an aggressive character were quickly allayed by his behaviour toward me, my initial nervousness was reflected in the way in which I probably failed to guide the interview more effectively from the outset.

I chose this interview example for a number of reasons. It was one of the very first interviews I had conducted with an actual 'terrorist', and is thus memorable in a personal sense in the first year of my studies. However, I feel that it also illustrates the wide variety of issues that can arise for a would-be researcher. It is also particularly memorable for me in that it demonstrated how writing a simple letter could lead to an interview with a significant IRA figure.

Many dozens of such interviews were conducted, the result of which helped form the descriptions of both the IRA's command and functional structure, and selective aspects of the movement's fundraising operations.[32] Most of the interviewees were met in person at least once, the exceptions being a large proportion of the security sources, who were interviewed by telephone instead. Many of those who were interviewed on more than one occasion were interviewed over the telephone on subsequent occasions, including a small proportion of the IRA members.

In contrast to the interview with Michael, the substantial majority of the respondents did not wish their voices to be recorded. One individual in particular, whom I interviewed in 1999 in a remote region of one of the border counties, asked me to place the recorder on the table so that he could see that it was switched off. Just on a purely practical level, this issue poses even more difficulties, especially when good note-taking skills are not an inherent characteristic of the researcher. Relying on one's own memory is a quick and easy way to conduct an interview, but there is the possibility of limited assimilation and recall of information, not to mention subjective interpretation.[33] And, of course, most information is lost shortly afterwards, so there is a need for immediate recall if such a situation presents itself – that is, assuming that the emergent details from the interview are to be described in any proper, meaningful and coherent fashion. Forced to regard the taking of short notes in the interview as sufficient in most cases, I managed to capture the most important details, and certainly in many cases this prevented the need to re-interview the same person.

INTERVIEW CONSIDERATIONS

Meeting with and talking to people involved in terrorist activities requires patience and the knowledge that what is expected throughout the course of any such meeting may not actually happen. Interviews can be cancelled at the last minute for various reasons, such as security considerations or perhaps just plain old cold feet, and a wasted journey, sometimes of considerable length, is not an uncommon feature in these investigations. Regardless of erudition, there are a number of lessons that a researcher can only learn through experience by talking to any individuals involved in violence, and this has been the case for the present researcher.

An important (and not always obvious, even in academic circles) lesson to be learned by the student who intends to speak to either a retired or currently active terrorist for the first time, is that the caricatured images of fanatics are not confirmed in the meetings when they are finally established. A striking feature of many of the terrorists interviewed for the research presented in the research is their 'normality'. The terrorists interviewed during the course of this research (and their supporters) were no different in appearance and public behaviours than the researcher. Indeed, on one level, this can be more disturbing than if an overtly 'fanatical' person were sitting across from the interviewer. This theme certainly pervades even some of the early psychologically based literature from various researchers whose findings, as we have seen, were not based on any contact with terrorists whatsoever. Bruce Hoffman relates similar personal experiences, one of which is worth including:

> I have been studying terrorists and terrorism for more than 20 years. Yet I am still always struck by how disturbingly 'normal' most terrorists seem when one actually sits down and talks to them. Rather than the wild-eyed fanatics or crazed killers that we have been conditioned to expect, many are in fact highly articulate and extremely thoughtful individuals for whom terrorism is (or was) an entirely rational choice, often reluctantly embraced and then only after considerable reflection and debate.[34]

The process of gaining interviews with police and intelligence personnel operated more or less along the same lines as I employed for the Republican respondents, although the snowballing procedure seemed to operate much faster, as did the mechanism for being granted or denied interviews.

Across both camps there were some refusals to participate, but encouragingly, not as many as I had initially expected. I received approximately double the number of refusals from the IRA and Sinn Fein as I did from security forces. Many IRA members to whom I had sent letters never replied through any channel at all, while others simply sent me a short and polite message of refusal. Several Sinn Fein members referred me to Sinn Fein 'publicity' officers, whom they said would take responsibility for arranging such interviews. Many Gardai in the Republic of Ireland also refused to grant me an interview with them, but this was (in formal cases) responded to with a letter of declination, often stating that due to time constrictions, or operational reasons, interviews could not be granted at that time. When I formally approached (that is, without relying on the informal nature of the snowballing technique) specialized divisions (including the anti-terrorism branch) of An Garda Síochána with letters, telephone calls, and 'references' from other Gardai, I received very little help. The snowballing sample method and informal 'vetting' from important figures was, I believe, responsible for the extent of my success in accessing participants.

Perhaps surprisingly (especially now with hindsight and more experience) I received very little intimidation from IRA members; indeed the most disconcerting incident arose when I was overtly chastized by some members of the Gardai. As far as intimidation from the IRA was concerned, presumably this was not forthcoming because I did not represent a realistic threat or nuisance to either the security or well-being of those participants I succeeded in interviewing, or to the organization to which they belong. On one occasion, I did start to question the degree of risk I was prepared to live with in order to conduct the research. One former IRA prisoner, whom I had interviewed in the very early stages of my research, actually followed me and a friend into a public restaurant one evening. To our amazement, he sat at our table and then proceeded to explain what would happen to me if he discovered that I had given the police information about him that might in any way incriminate him. It later emerged that the Gardai had raided his house on suspicion that he was in possession of a weapon. This raid, unfortunately for me, had taken place about two to three days after I had interviewed him. He was quick to let me know what the situation was: 'It's like this. You asked me to talk to you about my involvement in the Republican movement and the next thing, the cops are breaking down my door. The bastards only found the Proclamation hanging on the wall. So now where does that leave us?' I assured him that I did not disclose any information to the police, but he continuously interrupted my attempts to placate him. He referred to his being 'fed up' with people like me, and that 'y'know, something will have to be done if you're trying to screw me'. I was obviously becoming extremely uncomfortable with his comments, not to mention my friend, who suggested that she should leave. The IRA man stopped her, apologizing for his interruption, and left just as quickly as he had appeared at our table. The next day, I attempted to contact him again to explain that I had not done what he thought. He then apologized and said that he had behaved out of character, and that he had realized once he had cooled down that there was nothing to suggest that I had been in collusion with the police. I was obviously relieved at this, but was not too enthusiastic about interviewing for a few weeks to come.

There are similar accounts by others who have conducted research in Northern Ireland[35] but the consensus by and large appears to be that their experiences have been danger-free. Obviously, however, it only takes one serious incident to change the common view for a considerable time. For example, Anderson, an American journalist and researcher, first came to Belfast in 1986 and returned several times. He was also researching fundraising, and encountered explicit threats.[36] He described how he met a senior IRA member in Belfast, by whom he appears to have been 'accepted':

> With each new secret I shared, I was being held that much more accountable by the hard men. This became bluntly clear to me on a spring night in 1998, when I was taken to a heavily fortified row house just off the Falls Road to meet a man whom I will call Martin, a senior commander in the Provisional IRA. 'Do you know what the most dangerous thing to possess in Northern Ireland is?', Martin asked me. 'Knowledge. People run into trouble here for knowing things they're not supposed to … What you are looking into, the money aspects, no one in Belfast talks about – it's a death sentence. If you ever identify me in any way, I will be destroyed. If that happens, you will be destroyed. This is not a threat; it's simply a new fact in your life.

Adams described IRA financing as 'extremely difficult to research on the ground' due to the sensitive, and particularly secretive nature of this element of terrorist activity.[37] He adds that: 'various British journalists have attempted to write about the subject, and all have been threatened by different terrorist groups'. Adams notes that he received warnings not to travel to specific cities while researching for his book on terrorist finances and again highlights the particular sensitivities in researching this topic.[38] In many ways, then, it appears that I have been quite fortunate. Although not all those Republicans I approached agreed to meet me, on the basis that I was asking 'sensitive questions' with 'questionable motivation' (according to one Sinn Fein publicity officer), not only was it possible for me to describe detailed examples of IRA fundraising operations but also to construct a detailed description of the IRA's command and functional structure. Although nothing dramatic happened to me during my research, I did receive a telephone call from an interviewee during the writing of my thesis (August 1999), who commented that:

> No one's doing what you're doing. They've all been doing the other stuff to death, hundreds of times over, but no one's looked at the money side of things. And the reason is because they're afraid of being killed. No one's done anything detailed since [the mid-1980s] … and you can be sure that if you pose a threat in any way you're going to be executed.

Fortunately for me, I received no direct threat or injury, but this call, and other examples like it, serve as a reminder to always be careful when making approaches.

Another approach I took in obtaining information relevant to my research questions was a brief period of what might be considered a form of participant-observation carried out in a number of pubs (hosting Republican fundraisers) and graveyards (hosting Republican commemorations). Graveyards provided me with the perfect opportunity to not only observe one of the most important and sacred traditions of Republicans – honouring their dead – but also to introduce myself, either to graveside orators (in the hope of using the snowballing technique) or to Sinn Fein/IRA members in the 'congregation' whom I recognized from media sources. This technique proved particularly valuable during the Republicans' Easter Commemorations (to honour the dead leaders of the 1916 IRA Easter Rising in Dublin) in one county in the Republic, and represented a valuable first step in procuring several subsequent interviews.[39]

The information gained across all interviews and all respondents included some extremely detailed and highly technical information (particularly, for example, from former IRA members and security force personnel when detailing the IRA's command structures and its related terminology), in interviews lasting from literally *five minutes* to *five and a half hours*. The shortest interview happened when a Sinn Fein member left after I began to ask questions relating to IRA fundraising (questions which he had earlier been briefed on via a telephone call). The longest interview, which incorporated several breaks, took place in the Republic when a senior member of the Irish anti-terrorist police agreed, at the end of 1998, to meet and discuss the veracity of my description of the IRA's command structure. I had already interviewed this valuable participant twice before.

Detailed accounts of the information presented in my research papers range from what could be seen as single points, sentences or *assertions*, to accounts and descriptions of the command structure, as summarised in one paper.[40] While many participants agreed to have their comments quoted verbatim, many others did not, insisting that their comments be paraphrased or used simply to help build a level of knowledge about the IRA. It must be said that no interview was a waste of time – apart from the 16 interview meetings for which my respondents did not show up (four of these were journalists, five were Gardai, and seven were alleged IRA members) after having made commitments to be present. They did not make any subsequent attempt to contact me or to explain why they had not come.

Three interviews in particular were of very special value: in one, a member of the security forces provided me with a copy of the IRA's *Green Book*; in another, an IRA interviewee provided me with a copy of a short 'mini-manual' (perhaps more a collection of personal notes by an IRA member shot dead in 1988); and in the third case, a different man again provided me with a copy of the OIRA intelligence manual (the 'Reporter's Guide to Ireland'). All of these were given to me in similar circumstances, in what seems to have been gestures of 'good will'. The security force detective in the first case above asked me, after I interviewed him for his views on IRA fundraising, 'Do you have the *Green Book*?' When I said 'No', he left the room (the interview was taking place in an empty debriefing room of a police station) for about 20 minutes and came back to say that he had photocopied his 'version' for me.

Although I have highlighted the reasons why no participant in such research is without value, I began to realize early on that some of the interviewees clearly seemed more valuable than others, particularly as regards to my attempts to narrow the 'gaps' in the then emerging accounts of fundraising and command structure, but also as regards their length of experience and the value of their long-term views of the topics under examination. In particular, I interviewed three men who had each been an IRA leader at very different stages of the conflict: one during the 1950s until the split in 1969 (who was later to become the Official IRA's Director of Intelligence and a prominent Army Council member); another during the post-split period in the turbulent 1970s and early 1980s; while the last (a member of the IRA's Army Council) is presently considered to be one of the most important figures behind the Republican movement's shift towards peace.

ISSUES OF VALIDITY AND RELIABILITY

Despite the relative novelty of firsthand research with terrorists, we must not ignore its limitations. Robert White outlined several important issues that may proceed to hamper the validity of those accounts gained through intensive interviewing in such circumstances.[41] Such 'biases', according to him, include interviewer/respondent interaction and recall and memory distortion.

The present author checked factual details from respondents – particularly in relation to fundraising operations – with 11 journalists (out of the 24 interviewed in total) who had intimate knowledge and extensive experience of the Northern Ireland problem. Other details (especially those relating to the IRA's command structure and some issues relating to fundraising) were checked and verified with some terrorist sources and sources from the above-mentioned media agencies with expertise and long experience in covering Northern Ireland terrorism. However, I did not go beyond this and adopt the same practice that Steve Bruce, for example, employed while researching his book. Bruce actually gave drafts of his book, *The Red Hand*, to 'a number of well–informed loyalists', and reports them having made 'helpful suggestions'.[42] Given the sensitive nature of the particular subjects being discussed in my thesis, I felt from the outset that this would be ill advised in my case. The nearest I came to this method is detailed at the end of the description of the command structure of the IRA: I discussed the 'final product' of this description with a small number of select Republicans whom I felt had the necessary experience and level of knowledge to be able to comment on the strengths and weaknesses of my account. Two of these individuals were of a high standing in the movement. It is important to realize therefore, in accordance with White's further important assertion, that the conclusions reached in the dissertation were 'not solely based' on the accounts given by participants in the interviews.[43] As per White's recommendation, I also searched the data for 'patterns and for accounts that negated respondents' – and my own – interpretations', not least from seasoned and very experienced and respected terrorism analysts from well-established academic contexts, and also from several of the most experienced journalists who had covered Northern Irish terrorism for many years. As with White's research, this practice not only reinforced the veracity of the final accounts, but also 'allowed the discovery'[44] of influential factors in the accounts of the fundraising activities and the command structure that were 'not necessarily apparent' to any or all of the participants in this study – particularly given that I relied on results that were produced ultimately by the snowball sampling methodology.

White's model discusses the problem of memory error in such research and it is also an issue deserving of inclusion here. Memory error in interviewing contexts is a potential problem that does not sit easily within the rigorous demands of academic investigation, and fuels the kinds of issues raised by Ariel Merari about how psychologists and others – perhaps through their own fault – often do not contribute worthy pieces of work.[45] However – and given that, where appropriate, my note-taking was at the very least effective in capturing major details – White says, 'instead of rejecting all recall data as invalid, reconstructive accounts may be treated as working hypotheses', which can then be verified.[46]

The fact that I did not describe sources by name must leave the strength of my emergent research open to trenchant criticism. Where possible, however, a researcher would do well to adopt the same practice as Adams, in his 1986 study of the financing of terrorism, by supporting relevant points or assertions with verifiable references from newspaper reports and other sources. I adopted this approach to make my accounts of the IRA command structure and initial discussion of IRA fundraising as valid as possible in the context of some (although few in number and variable in quality) existing attempts to describe the same areas of study.

A final point to assert here is that despite the constrictions which prevent research efforts in the study of terrorism from using traditional psychological methodologies,[47] case studies offer several distinct advantages over experimental methodologies and other methods of investigation. Case studies, put simply, represent an 'intensive investigation of a single case of some sort'.[48] Given the nature and direction of the literature in this area, detailed case studies appear to offer a welcome respite from the generalized and increasingly ill-informed accounts that plague terrorism research. On the whole, the generalizability of principles from case studies is fraught with difficulty, but case studies are extremely important because they allow necessary avenues of exploration 'when one desires simply to gain some idea as to the breadth and range of the problem of interest'.[49] Thus, while case studies may not appear to have universal appeal within mainstream psychology (given their essentially *descriptive* nature), it is clear that they offer substantial contributions to particular areas. Having reviewed the terrorism literature, this might seem particularly applicable to terrorism research.

CONCLUSIONS

Whatever the future of terrorism brings, there is a need to encourage primary research involving access to terrorists. Furthermore, there needs to be a systematic discussion and dissection of issues that emerge for a terrorism researcher, perhaps via comparative analyses. Only two specific commentaries on interview issues have emerged in recent times,[50] but these represent an encouraging step in the right direction; and an important meta-analysis of research methods in terrorism studies has, more recently, highlighted a continuing dearth of interviews being used to gather data.[51]

The author of this chapter chose to highlight a variety of personal experiences in an attempt to support greater transparency in what many assume to be a necessarily secretive approach whenever firsthand research is even contemplated. As researchers, we ought to know better: that terrorism research findings often do not lend themselves easily to criticism from peers should not discourage us from discussing methodological issues more openly and rigorously, in line with mainstream disciplines.

Finally, the points raised here may well justify *sui generis* claims. It is difficult to form conclusions or falsify hypotheses in the literature which might emerge from some of the methodological approaches described here, if only for the simple reason that no attempt has yet been made to identify common themes or experiences between those who have studied terrorism at first hand. This reflects a large gap in serious analyses and, consequently, any form of firsthand research on terrorist behaviour perhaps needs no justification. However, it is hoped that other researchers will be encouraged to discuss experiences in their firsthand research so that we may progress on this front.

NOTES

1. See John Horgan and Max Taylor, 'The Making of a Terrorist', *Jane's Intelligence Review*, 13/12 (2001), pp. 16–18.
2. See Chapters Three and Ten in this volume.
3. Quoted on p. 416 of Martha Crenshaw, 'The Psychology of Terrorism: An Agenda for the Twenty-First Century', *Political Psychology*, 21/2 (2001), pp. 405–20.
4. See Ariel Merari, 'Academic Research and Government Policy on Terrorism', *Terrorism and Political Violence*, 3/1 (1991), pp. 88–102; and Ariel Merari and Nehemia Friedland, 'Social Psychological Aspects of Political Terrorism', in S. Oskamp (ed.), *Applied Social Psychology Annual*, Vol.6, *International Conflict and National Public Policy Issues* (London: Sage, 1985), pp. 185–205.
5. See John Horgan, 'Issues in Terrorism Research', *The Police Journal*, 50/3 (1997), pp. 193–202; John Horgan, 'Psychology and Terrorism Research'. Paper presented at the Psychological Society of Ireland 30th Annual Conference, Cork, 11–14 November 1999; and Robert White, 'Issues in the Study of Political Violence: Understanding the Motives of Participants in Small Group Political Violence', *Terrorism and Political Violence*, 12/1 (2000), pp. 95–108.
6. See Max Taylor and Ethyl Quayle, *Terrorist Lives* (London: Brassey's, 1994).
7. See J. Bowyer-Bell, *The IRA 1968–2000: An Analysis of a Secret Army* (London: Frank Cass, 2000); and J. Bowyer-Bell, *The Dynamics of the Armed Struggle* (London: Frank Cass, 1998).
8. Steve Bruce, *The Red Hand: Protestant Paramilitaries in Northern Ireland* (Oxford: Oxford University Press, 1992).
9. See, for example, Tim Pat Coogan, *The IRA* (London: HarperCollins, 1995); and Tim Pat Coogan, *The Troubles: Ireland's Ordeal 1966–1995 and the Search for Peace* (London: Hutchinson, 1995).
10. Donnatella della Porta, *Social Movements, Political Violence and the State* (Cambridge: Cambridge University Press, 1995).
11. John Horgan, 'Terrorism and Political Violence: A Psychological Perspective', unpublished PhD dissertation, Cork, University College Cork, 2000.
12. Alison Jamieson, *The Heart Attacked: Terrorism and Conflict in the Italian State* (London: Marian Boyers, 1989).
13. See Max Taylor, *The Terrorist* (London: Brassey's, 1988) and Max Taylor, *The Fanatics: A Behavioural Approach to Political Violence* (London: Brassey's, 1991).
14. Robert White, *Provisional Irish Republicans: An Oral and Interpretive History* (Westport, CT: Greenwood Press, 1993). See also White, 'Issues in the Study of Political Violence'.
15. Bowyer-Bell, *The Dynamics of the Armed Struggle*; Horgan, 'Issues in Terrorism Research'; Taylor and Quayle, *Terrorist Lives*.
16. For example, see Coogan, *The IRA*, pp. ix–x; and Coogan, *The Troubles*, p. xi.
17. Bowyer-Bell, *The Dynamics of the Armed Struggle*, p. xv.
18. As proposed more fully in Horgan, 'Issues in Terrorism Research'.
19. See ibid., for more on this.
20. Ibid.
21. See J. Bowyer-Bell, *The Secret Army: The IRA 1916–1979* (Dublin: Academy Press, 1979); and Bowyer-Bell, *The Dynamics of the Armed Struggle*.
22. As quoted on p. 248 in Martha Crenshaw, 'Questions to be Answered, Research to be Done, Knowledge to be Applied', in Walter Reich (ed.), *Origins of Terrorism: Psychologies, Ideologies, Theologies, States of Mind* (New York: Cambridge University Press, 1990), pp. 247–60.
23. See, for example, Jeffrey Sluka, *Hearts and Minds, Water and Fish: Support for the IRA and INLA in a Northern Irish Ghetto* (Greenwich, CT: JAI Press, 1989), p. 22.
24. White, 'Issues in the Study of Political Violence', p. 102.
25. Horgan, *Terrorism and Political Violence*.
26. Bowyer-Bell, *The Dynamics of the Armed Struggle*; and White, *Provisional Irish Republicans*.
27. Ibid.; White, 'Issues in the Study of Political Violence'.
28. Ibid.
29. For good examples in similar contexts, see Bowyer-Bell, *The Dynamics of the Armed Struggle*; G. Knowles, 'Dealing Crack Cocaine: A View from the Streets of Honolulu', *FBI Law Enforcement Bulletin*, July 1996, retrieved on 22 January 1997 from http://www.fbi.gov/library/leb/july961.txt; and White, *Provisional Irish Republicans*.

30. C. Swanson, N. Chamelin and L. Territo, *Criminal Investigation*, 4th edn (New York: McGraw Hill, 1988).
31. Again, see White, 'Issues in the Study of Political Violence'; and White, *Provisional Irish Republicans*.
32. For initial but brief summaries, see John Horgan and Max Taylor, 'The Provisional Irish Republican Army: Command and Functional Structure', *Terrorism and Political Violence*, 9/3 (1997), pp. 1–32; and John Horgan and Max Taylor, 'Playing the Green Card: Financing the Provisional IRA – part 1', *Terrorism and Political Violence*, 11/2 (1999), pp. 1–38.
33. See Swanson, Chamelin and Territo, *Criminal Investigation*.
34. Bruce Hoffman, *Inside Terrorism* (London: Victor Gollancz, 1998), p. 7.
35. For examples, see F. Burton, *The Politics of Legitimacy: Struggles in a Belfast Community* (London: Routledge and Kegan Paul, 1978); R. Elliot and J. Hickie, *Ulster: A Case Study of Conflict Theory* (London: Longman, 1971); Sluka, *Hearts and Minds*; Taylor, *The Terrorist*; Taylor and Quayle, *Terrorist Lives*; White, 'Issues in the Study of Political Violence'; White, *Provisional Irish Republicans*.
36. Simon Anderson, 'Making a Killing', *Harper's Magazine*, 288 (1 February 1996), retrieved on 8 July 1996 from http://www.elibrary.com.
37. James Adams, *The Financing of Terrorism* (London: New English Library, 1986), p. 275.
38. Ibid., p. x.
39. See Horgan 'Issues in Terrorism Research'.
40. See Horgan and Taylor, 'The Provisional Irish Republican Army'; and also Horgan and Taylor, 'Playing the Green Card'.
41. White, *Provisional Irish Republicans*.
42. Bruce, *The Red Hand*, p. vii.
43. White, *Provisional Irish Republicans*, p. 186.
44. Ibid.
45. Merari, 'Academic Research and Government Policy on Terrorism'.
46. White, *Provisional Irish Republicans*, p. 187. Also see Swanson, Chamelin and Territo, *Criminal Investigation*, pp. 136–8.
47. Horgan, 'Issues in Terrorism Research'; Merari, 'Academic Research and Government Policy on Terrorism'.
48. D. Elmes, B. Kantowitz and H. Roediger, *Research Methods in Psychology*, 4th edn (St Paul, MN: West Publishing Company, 1992), p. 57.
49. Ibid., p. 59.
50. Horgan, 'Issues in Terrorism Research'; White, 'Issues in the Study of Political Violence'.
51. See Chapter Three in this volume for more on this.

The Devil You Know:
Continuing Problems with Research
on Terrorism*

ANDREW SILKE

WHAT IS the function of research? Ultimately, all research is concerned with the creation of new knowledge. But the level of this knowledge varies as do the methods which are used to reach it. Psychologist Colin Robson noted that research was generally concerned with producing knowledge which could meet one of three purposes. The first was *exploratory*, the second *descriptive* and the third *explanatory*.[1] At the initial levels, researchers are generally concerned with very basic issues. The subject at hand is like a blank sheet of paper and the researcher wants to sketch in an outline. There is an emphasis on qualitative research methods in particular (for example, case studies). The methods commonly used are not overly concerned with issues of reliability and validity, as the primary importance is to set the scene and identify what may be the main forces at work. Descriptive research aims to build on this earlier work, while explanatory research aims to provide reliable insight into the subject, to explain what has happened and is happening and, importantly, to also provide the ability to predict what will happen in the future. At this final level, the research methods used are more rigorous and more intensive than in the previous stages, partly because the researcher must address greater concerns that the findings be clearly reliable and valid.

* This paper was originally published in the journal, *Terrorism and Political Violence*, 13/4 (2001), pp. 1–14. It is reproduced here with permission.

The ultimate aim for any research field is to progress from one level of understanding to the next, until a significant number of studies can be conducted at the explanatory level. Subject areas which fail to make this final transition are left with constant gaps in their knowledge base and a fatal uncertainty over the causes of events and what the truly significant factors at work are. Most troubling of all, there is an obvious inability to make accurate predictions of future events. Such areas are characterized by a marked absence of conceptual agreement and a wide diversity of views on even basic issues. Yet, even while bogged down in conceptual mire, a troubled field may appear relatively active, especially if the area is in applied research. Research which has a real world focus will nearly always have outlets for some form of exploratory or descriptive research.

Thus, it is possible for a research community to remain active indefinitely without ever producing meaningful explanatory results (while tolerating very high levels of conceptual confusion and disagreement). It seems relatively clear that terrorism research exists in such a state and that after over 30 years of enquiry, the field shows little evidence that it is capable of making the leap to consistently producing research of genuinely explanatory and predictive value. Why is this the case?

The first problem is that terrorism quite simply is not a topic which is easily researched. Or at least, it gives that impression on first inspection.[2] The central actors involved in the phenomenon are difficult to access – and extremely difficult to access in a systematic manner. As Ariel Merari notes, 'The clandestine nature of terrorist organizations and the ways and means by which intelligence can be obtained will extremely rarely enable data collection which meets commonly accepted academic standards.'[3] Terrorism itself is an emotive subject and researchers have traditionally not been overly concerned with remaining objective and neutral in how they view the activity and its perpetrators. It has been noted that many researchers seem confused by their roles. As Schmid and Jongman have pointed out, the researcher's 'role is not to "fight" the terrorist fire; rather than a "firefighter", [the researcher] should be a "student of combustion".'[4] But such objectivity is relatively rare in the field (not especially surprising when most of the research is paid for by one side in the terrorism equation). Most researchers do seem to believe they are fulfilling – or are meant to fulfil – a firefighting role. The result is that research is largely driven by policy concerns and the area has fallen into a trap where it is largely limited to government agendas. This is unfortunate as government agendas rarely if ever stretch beyond the next election, and the result is

that research tends to be driven by similarly short-term tactical considerations. The other problem with the impact of policy is that it tends to
lead to research fads which can divert an excessive amount of scarce
resources down unnecessary and unproductive paths (for example, the
massive amount of energy channelled into WMD research). Other
problems emerge from the tenacious conceptual confusion which
mires the area. What *is* terrorism? What makes an act a *terrorist* act? What
makes a group a *terrorist* group? These are such basic questions; and yet
satisfactory answers continue to elude the field.

Such issues as these are not, however, the principle concern of this
paper. Instead, this paper is concerned with the research activity itself –
the practical nature of research on terrorism. As stated earlier, research
ultimately is aimed at arriving at a level of knowledge and understanding where one can explain why certain events have happened and where
one can accurately predict the emergence and outcome of similar events
in the future. Terrorism research has failed to arrive at that level of
knowledge. This paper will examine what measure of responsibility for
this failure rests with the activities of the research community itself,
particularly in how it gathers data and in the level of analysis it submits
harvested data to.

THE METHODOLOGY OF TERRORISM RESEARCH

Already referred to, the most important review of research and
researchers into terrorism to date is that carried out by Alex Schmid and
Albert Jongman, and reported in their seminal book, *Political Terrorism*.[5]
Schmid and Jongman, surveyed the opinions, views and experiences of
terrorism researchers and analysts. While their book is of massive interest and importance in general, of particular relevance to this paper was
the fact that one of the questions posed to the surveyed researchers was
where did they obtain information on terrorism?[6] The responses to this
important question are outlined in Table 3.1 below.

The replies given to the queries on data-gathering methods were
worrying for a number of reasons. First, it was clear that there was a very
heavy reliance on open source documents. Most of the researchers were
not producing substantively new data or knowledge. Primarily they were
reworking old material which already existed. This impression was
confirmed by Schmid and Jongman who found that only 46 per cent of
the researchers said that they had managed to generate data of their own
on the subject of terrorism.[7] For the majority of researchers, all of their

Table 3.1. Sources of Research Data on Terrorism⋆

Rank	Method	Researchers
1	Scholarly books and articles	100%
2	Media and news services	92%
3	Open government documents	92%
4	Documents originating from terrorists/sympathizers	58%
5	Interviews with government officials	46%
6	Classified government documents	26%
7	Interviews with terrorists	24%
8	Other	20%

⋆ *Source*: Adapted from Schmid and Jongman, p. 138.

writings and analyses were based entirely on data produced by others. This 'lack of individual data generation and research' was a profound concern. Schmid and Jongman believed that the respondents represented a good cross section of the research community and it included many of the leading figures in the field. The respondents' own views of the state of the research work being done also tended to be quite pessimistic. One respondent noted that there were really only about five researchers who actually 'knew what they were talking about' and that the rest were simply 'integrators of literature'. Table 3.1 suggests that there was a least some truth to that harsh assessment.

Schmid and Jongman themselves were fairly bleak in their assessment of the state of research on terrorism. They concluded that 'there are probably few areas in the social science literature in which so much is written on the basis of so little research. Perhaps as much as 80 per cent of the literature is not research-based in any rigorous sense ...'[8] However, this unhappy state of affairs was the predicable result of the methodologies which were dominating the field. As Table 3.1 indicates, the surveyed researchers were very heavily dependent on just two methodologies: the main one being analysis of documents (or secondary data analysis); and the second form being interviewing. There are some real benefits to both methodologies but there are also some serious limitations. Normally, such limitations are not profoundly felt in any given research field simply because most long-running research communities will use a relatively balanced range of methods which – when combined – provide complimentary forms of knowledge. However, that was not the case in 1988 with regard to work on terrorism and the predictable result was that the field was unable to make progress on a wide number of key issues and there was no evidence whatsoever of a theoretical framework emerging. The question to answer now is, has this situation improved at all in the intervening years?

TERRORISM RESEARCH TODAY: A HEALTH CHECK

In attempting to assess the nature and quality of a body of research, two questions dominate. The first is, how was the raw data gathered? The second is, how was this raw data analysed? Schmid and Jongman tried to assess the state of the art by sending a questionnaire survey to active researchers. Arguably an even clearer way to identify trends and patterns in research efforts is to examine the published literature produced by researchers. The presence today of two well-established journals, which exist as the primary publishing outlet for research on terrorism, makes this a feasible and relatively straightforward possibility. The two journals are, of course, *Terrorism and Political Violence* (*TPV*) and *Studies in Conflict and Terrorism* (*SICAT*). Taken together – and bearing in mind their different publishers, separate editorial teams and largely separate editorial boards (though there is some overlap on this last) – the two journals can be regarded as providing a reasonably balanced impression of research activity in the field.

Recognising this – and motivated by a desire to understand the current trends in research activity in the field in recent years – this paper presents the results of a review of the published output of the primary journals in the area for the years 1995–1999. Each article and research note published in the two journals for this period were reviewed. A record was made of the methodology/ies used to gather data and the level of analysis such data was then subjected to.

Figure 3.1 below provides a breakdown of the methodologies currently being used by published active researchers.

SECONDARY DATA ANALYSIS

Figure 3.1 clearly shows that – as in 1988 – a very small range of methodologies continue to dominate research on terrorism. Again, most research is based on secondary data analysis and more specifically on analysis based on archival records. Figure 3.1 shows that over 80 per cent of all research on terrorism is based either solely or primarily on data gathered from books, journals, the media (or media-derived databases), or other published documents. This figure seems to indicate that little has changed since the 1988 comment that the field was overly dominated by 'integrators of literature'.[9] Most of the documents involved in these studies are open access and are not classified. While a few are – and others can be – extremely difficult to access and require

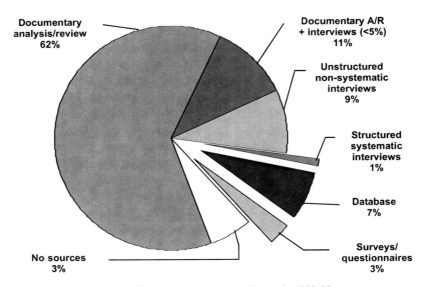

Figure 3.1. Methods in Terrorism Research, 1995–99

considerable effort to obtain on the part of the researcher, most of the source material does not fall into such categories.

There are a number of advantages to secondary data analysis and it is worth outlining these briefly. The first and foremost benefit is that the method involves considerably less effort and expense to obtain than if the researcher sets out to collect primary data. As a result, it is often used for research on topics for which it is particularly difficult to gather raw data. Its popularity among researchers of terrorism is therefore not completely surprising. Such research is also useful in establishing the wider context in which a phenomenon is occurring and in illustrating the potential complexity of the various factors which may be involved. There are disadvantages, however. As an illustration of some of these, let us consider the case of information gathered through media sources (an especially common source in terrorism research).

There are three main concerns with research which draws heavily on media sources. The first issue concerns accuracy. The researcher is depending on the media account to be accurate – yet it is well established that even very reputable media outlets frequently make factual errors in their reports, not to mention unintentional technical errors.[10]

The second issue is bias. Media reports rarely aim to be entirely neutral on any subject. As a result, an element of distortion enters the coverage of any event or phenomenon. This distortion may reflect the preferences of the proprietor, the editor or the journalist producing the copy. It can also arise from the source – as when a politician is giving his or her account of events or when the journalist relies on the press release of some public body or organization. Distortion can also arise because of the need to compress a story into the available space or to meet an editor's requirements for a punchy headline. Distortion can be more machiavellian as well. This was a point recognized by Keith Macdonald and Colin Tipton, two sociologists who noted that 'the most fundamental form of distortion is ... that of propaganda, where the source of the news is engaged in wholesale creation of a particular view of events, which in the case of war,* for example, is undertaken in what is perceived to be the national interest or with the object of systematically deceiving an enemy'.[11]

A third concern with media reports is that of audience context. Quite simply, any form of communication is undertaken with an audience in mind. So, for example, cultural norms, jokes, deliberate mistakes, irony and so on all depend on the writer and the reader sharing a common frame of reference. If the researcher is out of this loop, then serious misinterpretations and misapprehensions can be made.

These are just some of the concerns with a reliance on media reports; but they are also problems inherent in academic books and journals, in government publications (both classified and open), and in documents from terrorist groups and their supporters. As a result, there are concerns over the reliability of research which depends heavily on such sources.

INTERVIEWING

As Figure 3.1 indicates, interviews account for the next most common source of data in terrorism research. In total, for 22 per cent of articles, the researchers conducted some interviewing in an effort to gather information. In roughly half of these cases the interviews represent a very minor feature of the overall effort and contributed to no more than four per cent of information contained in the article. For these articles, the vast majority of the information has again come via secondary data analysis (as outlined above). However, in nearly 13 per cent of cases, interviews do play a much more substantial role. Here extensive interviewing accounts for a substantial source of the information reported.

---

* For war, read 'terrorism' in this context.

Yet, even here, there are problems. In only one per cent of reports are the interviews conducted in a systematic and structured manner. For all the rest the interviews are carried out on an *ad-hoc*, opportunistic basis, generally using only a semi-structured approach at best. This means that again there are concerns with the reliability of the data.

There are a number of advantages to using personal interviews as a way of gathering data. First, it is a very flexible method (especially in the unstructured form which dominates terrorism interviews). This allows interviewers to probe for additional information when interesting or unexpected avenues open up. Interviews also give the researcher a good measure of control. They can ensure that full answers are provided to specific questions (and if answers are not forthcoming, the researchers will at least know that this is a deliberate decision on the part of the respondent rather than an oversight). Interviews also tend to have good response rates and can produce a great deal of extra information. Indeed, supplementary information gathered in interviews can be of great value in establishing the wider context.

Again, however, there are disadvantages. First, interviewing is an expensive method both in terms of finance and time and researchers are usually severely limited in the number of interviews they can conduct (a problem exacerbated by the difficult target populations terrorism researchers must contend with). There is also a risk of interviewer bias entering the data, a factor exacerbated by flexibility of interviews. For example, how a particular question is phrased can influence the type of answer the respondent gives. The result is that the same individual when interviewed by two different researchers about the same topic, could provide noticeably different answers. The use of a standardized and structured interview can help reduce such bias but, as Figure 3.1 points out, 97 per cent of interviews in terrorism research are *not* standardized or structured. Related to this problem with bias is the issue of lack of anonymity in the interview situation. The presence of the interviewer may make the respondent reluctant to talk about sensitive issues and may also encourage respondents into giving socially acceptable replies or responses which they think the interviewer wishes to hear.

A further problem with interviews in terrorism research is that, again, 97 per cent are carried out primarily through opportunity sampling. This means that the interviews are carried out with conveniently available groups or individuals and little effort is made to sample systematically. This is not entirely unexpected. Opportunity sampling is a common method when dealing with groups or individuals who are difficult to access (so its use in terrorism research is understandable), but the lack of proper sampling does mean that there are serious limits to the generalizability of any findings to wider populations.[12] The researcher has no real way of knowing if he or she is dealing with a biased sample that is noticeably different from the population of interest. The sample may be representative; but then again it may not. With opportunity sampling there is no way to tell whether it is or not. As a result of this uncertainty, opportunity sampling tends to be only used in exploratory research in the social sciences. The dominance of the method in terrorism research, however, adds a question mark over the reliability of the information being generated.

A further cause for concern from Figure 3.1 involves the finding that six per cent of articles published in the journals give no indication of the source of their information. Most of these articles have been written by individuals who work in government or in the security services, and the assumption is that the paper is based on their own personal experience. However, such articles are impossible to assess in terms of reliability and validity, and as a result their value in research terms is contentious.

Overall, Figure 3.1 shows that the concerns expressed by Schmid and Jongman in 1988 about the quality of terrorism research remain as valid as they were then. Indeed, the situation does not appear to have improved noticeably in any respect. Researchers remain very heavily dependent on easily accessible sources of data and only about 20 per cent of articles provide substantially new knowledge which was previously unavailable to the field. The field thus is top-heavy with what are referred to as pre-experimental research designs. Unfortunately, these are:

> ... the weakest designs since the sources of internal and external validity are not controlled for. The risk of error in drawing causal inferences from pre-experimental designs is extremely high and they are primarily useful as a basis ... for exploratory research.[13]

Even when serious concerns exist with the manner in which data is collected, a researcher can still take steps to address this when they progress to analysing the gathered data and it is to this issue that the focus of this paper now turns.

MORE BAD NEWS ...

Since the 1950s, all of the social science disciplines have experienced a rapid increase in the use of statistics. People are extremely complex, and their behaviour and thoughts are the result of a confusing interaction of emotions, motivations, learned behaviours and genetically determined traits. Consequently, social science researchers typically have to work with very 'noisy' data where there are potentially a vast number of factors exerting an influence on any one behaviour, event or trend. Statistical analysis has emerged as a way for researchers to determine which factors are genuinely important and which are not. Descriptive statistics enable the researcher to summarize and organize data in an effective and meaningful way. Inferential statistics allow the researcher to make decisions or inferences by interpreting data patterns. Inferential statistics are regarded as particularly valuable as they introduce an element of control into research which can help to compensate if relatively weak data collection methods were used. In experimental designs, control is normally achieved by randomly assigning research subjects to experimental and control groups. However, this can often be very difficult to achieve in real world research and consequently the lack of control throws doubt on any association between variables which the research claims to find. Inferential statistics, though, can help to introduce a recognised element of control, so that there is less doubt and more confidence over the veracity of any findings.[14]

Figure 3.2, however, shows that even though terrorism researchers tend to rely heavily on the 'weaker' uncontrolled data gathering methods, in recent years very little effort has been made to balance this by the use of statistical analysis.

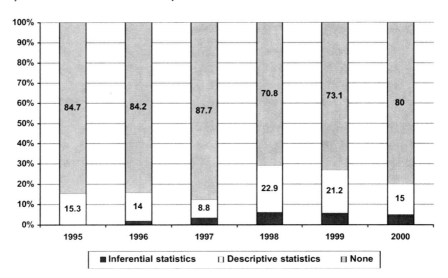

Figure 3.2. Statistical Analysis in Terrorism Research, 1995–99

Figure 3.3 puts the trend seen above in Figure 3.2 in an especially sobering light. It shows that from 1995–1999, just over three per cent of research papers in the major terrorism journals involved the use of inferential analysis. For comparison purposes, journal publications in two other areas of research were also reviewed. The first was forensic psychology and the second was criminology.[15] The reason for choosing these particular areas is that the research backgrounds of both these disciplines have a number of similarities with research conducted on terrorism. The subject matter published in journals in these areas focus on the various actors and activities involved in the criminal justice system and in the commissioning of crime. As a result, the subject matter often shares comparable similarities with terrorism in terms of difficult research populations, real world relevance as well as considerable concerns with human suffering and injustice. Thus when compared to other areas within the social sciences, such journals do seem to offer some legitimate comparison with the terrorism journals.

However, despite the similarities, the manner in which researchers in these two areas treat data is very different to how it is treated by terrorism researchers. Eighty-six per cent of research papers in forensic

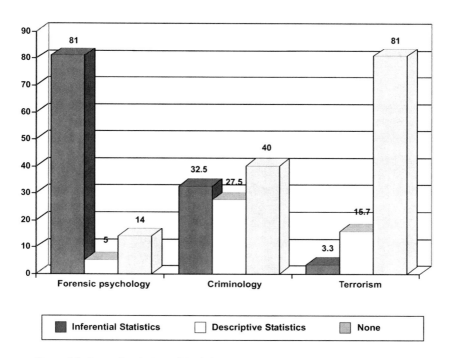

Figure 3.3. Comparing the Use of Statistical Analysis in Social Science Research, 1995–99

psychology and 60 per cent of papers in criminology contain at least some form of statistical analysis. In both cases, inferential statistics account for the majority of this analysis. In both disciplines, the use of statistics is seen as an important and accepted way in which to ensure that the claims made by researchers meet recognised quality controls. In stark contrast, terrorism articles rarely incorporate statistics and when they do, they are nearly five times more likely to be just descriptive statistics.[16] Barely one article in 30 published in the last five years incorporated inferential analysis.[17]

It is important to stress here that this paper is not arguing that statistical analysis should be a feature of *every* research study on terrorism. On the contrary, much valuable research can be conducted which does not involve the use of statistics. However, terrorism research clearly suffers from a serious imbalance and the argument here is that more effort should be made to address this imbalance. Statistics alone are not the way forward, but neither is avoiding their use to the degree that the terrorism research community currently does.

Why is statistical analysis so uncommon in terrorism research? At least part of the answer probably has to do with effort. Engaging in statistical analysis requires effort and also requires at least some degree of expertise. Unlike research in forensic psychology or criminology, most research papers on terrorism are the work of a lone individual. A previous review found that in the 1990s, only 9.4 per cent of published research on terrorism was the result of collaborative efforts. Over 90 per cent of the published work in the field was done by a researcher working independently and alone.[18] In contrast, small teams of researchers account for a much higher proportion of papers in the other two areas. At one very basic level, this means that the workload on any one individual in these fields is less onerous and they are better able to take on the additional tasks of statistical analysis. Further, these disciplines tend to use a much wider range of data gathering methods than that seen in terrorism research, some of which are much more amenable to statistical analysis. In contrast, terrorism research – with its very heavy dependence on reviewing published documents coupled occasionally by opportunistic interviewing – fails to provide the same degree of raw material to work with.

CONCLUSIONS

Ultimately, terrorism research is not in a healthy state. It exists on a diet of fast-food research: quick, cheap, ready-to-hand and nutritionally dubious. The result of a reluctance to move away from the limited methodologies and levels of analysis of the past is that while the field may appear to be relatively active and energetic, growth in key areas remains stunted and halting. What then can be done to improve matters?

Part of the problem is that there are simply too few researchers. As already stated, over 90 per cent of research studies are planned, conducted, analysed and then written-up by just one person working alone. This places a relatively heavy burden on the researcher. Individuals face very real limits in resources, time and energy, and academic researchers face considerable pressure to publish regularly and often. The result is an understandable preference for methodologies and levels of analysis which are perceived as less time-consuming. The fact that terrorism is not an easy subject to research in the first place makes the situation even worse.[19] A further problem – and a related one – is that a great proportion of the material produced in the area is the work of transients: researchers out for a one-off publication and who have no real interest in making a substantial contribution to the field. Over 80 per cent of research articles published in the 1990s were from one-timers (that is, writers who wrote only one article in the mainstream terrorism journals during the entire ten-year period).[20] Ariel Merari has been particularly caustic in his assessment of the research contribution of these myriad transients. He commented that:

> The result has been, sometimes, an unexpected fresh look at the issue, which carried a promise of generating a new line of research, but more often it has been a superficial treatment of a singular aspect of the problem, ignorant of the complex and heterogeneous nature of terrorism, at times suffering from factual errors. Usually, a contribution of this kind is well-grounded in the empirical and theoretical findings of the writer's particular area of expertise, but lacking in knowledge on terrorism ... it seems that the majority of the academic contributions in this area have been done by people whose main research interests lie elsewhere, who felt that they had something to say on this juicy and timely subject.[21]

The difficult solution to such a state of affairs is to attempt to create more researchers and, equally important, to try to hold on to those that do come along. The slippage from the field appears to be enormous. Research by Avishag Gordon has shown that a slowly growing number of postgraduate researchers are doing dissertations on terrorism. In the past ten years, Gordon found that at least 160 research dissertations have been carried out in the area.[22] However, there is no sign that anything but a small handful of these graduates are following up this initial effort with further research.

Ultimately, people are more likely to remain active in research in at least to a limited degree – as long as there are rewarding outlets for their work and interests. The presence of two dedicated journals is an important asset, but other things could be done, particularly for new and emerging researchers. The creation of a research association offers some potential (particularly in the internet age). Regular conferences – and especially ones such as the *Conference on Contemporary Research on Terrorism* in St Andrews[23] – can also help immensely.

Undeniably, considerable responsibility lies in the hands of the editors and editorial boards of the two major journals. Editorial policies should encourage and help research which attempts to use more rigorous research methods. Of course, this may already be the case! It needs to be remembered that the editors' hands are very much tied by the quality and quantity of material that they receive from potential contributors. If most of the articles they receive use the same two or three methodologies, the editors have little scope in promoting alternative methods. The situation, though, could possibly be helped by the commissioning of special journal issues based on the grounds of methodology (as opposed to the current norm of subject focus).[24]

Ultimately, however, the onus for progress rests on the whole academic community. In Schmid and Jongman's 1988 review of researchers, most respondents were rightly pessimistic about the potential for developing a stronger theoretical understanding of terrorism. While individual reasons for such pessimism may be phrased differently, inevitably one cannot build a structure if the correct raw materials are not available. A limited range of methodologies in data gathering, combined with a reluctance to use more rigorous analysis, has left the field with serious deficiencies in many respects. Ultimately, the methods used by terrorism researchers are essentially exploratory. As a result, the field struggles in its efforts to explain terrorism or to provide findings of genuine predictive value. It has been argued that 'the ability to make correct predictions [is] ... the outstanding characteristic of science. If knowledge is deficient, prediction is impossible'.[25] Our knowledge of terrorism most certainly is deficient but the field shows no clear ability to improve this situation. After 30 years of study, we simply should know more about terrorism than we currently do. That we continue to languish at this level of ignorance on such a serious subject is a cause of grave concern.

NOTES

1. Colin Robson, *Real World Research* (Oxford: Blackwell, 1993), pp.41–2.
2. Some researchers, however, have argued that terrorism is not as difficult to research as many tend to believe. John Horgan, for example, has made a good case that there are a large number of ways in which useful and worthwhile research on the subject can be carried out with little or no more difficulty than that faced by other researchers in the social sciences. He also points out that often even the most difficult research obstacles in the area can be overcome with patience and forethought. See John Horgan, 'Issues in Terrorism Research', *The Police Journal*, 70 (1997), pp. 193–202.
3. Ariel Merari, 'Academic Research and Government Policy on Terrorism', *Terrorism and Political Violence*, 3/1 (Spring 1991), pp. 88–102.
4. Alex Schmid and Albert Jongman, *Political Terrorism: A New Guide to Actors, Authors, Concepts, Databases, Theories and Literature* (Oxford: North Holland, 1988), p. 1 79.
5. Ibid.
6. Ibid., p. 138.
7. Ibid., p. 137.
8. Ibid., p. 179.
9. Ibid., p. 180.
10. Keith Macdonald and Colin Tipton, 'Using Documents', in Nigel Gilbert (ed.), *Researching Social Life* (London: Sage, 1993), p. 191.
11. Ibid.
12. Robert Burns, *Introduction to Research Methods* (London: Sage, 2000), p. 93.
13. Chava Frankfort-Nachmias and David Nachmias, *Research Methods in the Social Sciences*, 5th edn (London: Arnold, 1996), p. 147.
14. Ibid., pp. 427–8.
15. Two journals from both disciplines were reviewed. In all the cases the review period stretched from 1995 to 1999 and a random selection of eight issues from each journal title were reviewed.
16. Even this is a generous figure. In a substantial proportion of cases, the statistics were not generated by the researcher(s) – instead they were copied from other sources (for example, government reports). In contrast, such practices were very rare in the forensic psychology and criminology journals. If they did occur they were nearly always also accompanied by statistics which were generated by the researcher(s).
17. This, of course, just refers to the two main journals in the area. A number of other research articles on terrorism which do incorporate inferential analysis have been published elsewhere in this time period. Indeed, it is possible that many of the more methodologically rigorous studies are never sent to the two mainstream journals. For example, very little has been published in the two journals on victims' and communities' experience of terrorism. Yet considerable research has been carried out on these topics. The authors, however, have then tended to report away from the primary terrorism research outlets and publish instead in more mainstream social science outlets. Why? These articles are essentially describing empirical positivist research and the authors are prioritizing. Journals which operate preferential policies of publishing only papers reporting such research (with accompanying inferential analysis) tend to be perceived as having a higher prestige in certain areas compared to journals which are less concerned about statistics and other questions of methodological rigour.
18. Andrew Silke, 'The Road Less Travelled: Trends in Terrorism Research 1990–1999', in Terrorism Prevention Branch (ed.), *Global Terrorism Survey* (Vienna: United Nations, 1999).
19. This also means that even 'easy' research can be incredibly time-consuming and difficult when compared to equivalent studies in other areas of the social sciences.
20. Silke, 'The Road Less Travelled'.
21. Merari, 'Academic Research and Government Policy on Terrorism'.
22. Avishag Gordon, 'Terrorism Dissertations and the Evolution of a Speciality: An Analysis of Meta-Information', *Terrorism and Political Violence*, 11/2 (Summer 1999), pp.141–50.
23. This conference is singled out here for its particular emphasis on encouraging postgraduate researchers to attend and present papers together with more established researchers.
24. The special issues tend to be either dedicated to particular forms of terrorism (either in terms of tactics or targets) or else they are dedicated to specific regions (for example, South Africa, Northern Ireland). A special issue with a focus on research methodology could be very valuable.
27. Frankfort-Nachmias and Nachimas, *Research Methods in Social Sciences*, p.10.

4

Weapons of Mass Destruction Terrorism Research: Past and Future

GAVIN CAMERON

INTRODUCTION

The terrorist use of weapons of mass destruction (WMD) has been a concern throughout the modern era of terrorism, which is usually regarded as beginning in 1968.[1] This chapter will assess the literature dealing with terrorism and WMD from that period, will analyse past trends within this subject, identify some of the key issues, and suggest some future directions within the field. For the purposes of this study, WMD will be assumed to mean only chemical, biological, radiological and nuclear weapons (CBRN).[2] Massive conventional weapons, although obviously capable of mass destruction, will not be considered here because space precludes such a broad discussion. For the same reason, this article will not examine the literature on responses to terrorism with WMD, as this is in itself an increasingly vast and complex subject.

PAST RESEARCH

The earliest key book that considered terrorist use of WMD was Willrich and Taylor's *Nuclear Theft*.[3] This predominantly considered the threat posed to nuclear facilities by terrorist organizations, arguing that building nuclear weapons was relatively straightforward, provided that terrorists could acquire the necessary fissile material. Willrich and

Taylor concentrated on the opportunities for theft of such material from the US programme and urged that greater precautions be taken to safeguard it. This tendency to focus on nuclear, rather than chemical or biological, weapons was a feature of most of the WMD terrorism literature as a whole until after the end of the Cold War. The next major book was Norton and Greenberg's *Studies In Nuclear Terrorism*, an edited collection of articles and conference papers. There was no overarching hypothesis that linked these essays; instead, it reflected the best survey of the arguments to that date on the likelihood of nuclear terrorism. It included work by authors who believed that nuclear terrorism posed a real threat that had to be addressed immediately (Beres); and that state sponsorship, leading to a heightened danger, was plausible (Krieger); along with others who believed that terrorists would be unwilling to 'go' nuclear (Jenkins); that nuclear terrorism was unlikely (Mullins); and that proliferation by states was not only more likely but also more dangerous (Schelling). The book considered the threat to nuclear facilities (Flood), and how to combat the threat (Kupperman), as well as the possibility of theft of nuclear materials and the means to prevent it.[4] Two similar collections of essays on different aspects of nuclear terrorism were published in the mid-1980s. Both books were edited by Paul Leventhal and Yonah Alexander, and contained: first, a report on the proceedings of a conference; and second, in the later book, a report on the findings of the International Task Force on the Prevention of Nuclear Terrorism which was established as a result of the earlier meeting. These reports were combined with essays that assessed various aspects of the problem. In the earlier book, *Nuclear Terrorism: Defining the Threat*, these included a discussion of the plausibility of nuclear terrorism (Jenkins), and of the means and targets that terrorists might use (Davies). The book also contained articles on preventing the threat (O'Keefe), and possible responses by government and industry to the issue (Giuffrida).[5] The later book, *Preventing Nuclear Terrorism*, included analysis of the means that terrorists could use to employ nuclear weapons; the factors that might make them want to do so; and responses to, and strategies for dealing with, a threat – including safeguards, international actions and threat minimization.[6]

The 1970s and 1980s also saw a series of important studies by the RAND Corporation which added significantly to the existing literature. These reports considered, in various forms, several central aspects of the subject of nuclear terrorism, including the likelihood of terrorists resorting to such weapons and the key attributes of potential adversaries, including hostile employees, within the context of the overall threat. Among the most important of these studies were: Bass, Jenkins, Kellen *et al.*, *Motivations and Possible Actions of Potential Criminal Adversaries of US Nuclear Programs*;[7] Reinstedt and Westbury, *Major Crimes as Analogs to Potential Threats to Nuclear Facilities and Programs*;[8] Bass and Jenkins, *A Review of Recent Trends in International Terrorism and Nuclear Incidents Abroad*;[9] and deLeon, Hoffman, Kellen *et al.*, *The Threat of Nuclear Terrorism: A Reexamination*.[10]

The early literature on terrorism with chemical or biological weapons was much less extensive than that for nuclear terrorism. As late as the mid-1990s, Ron Purver, in his survey of the literature on terrorism with chemical and biological (CB) weapons, was able to write: 'For the most part, speculation about "CB terrorism" has been dealt with perfunctorily within broader discussions of "high technology terrorism"…"mass destruction terrorism", "superviolence" … and the like'.[11] Moreover, the literature that did deal specifically with chemical or biological terrorism was generally less influential than that relating to nuclear weapons. Although the threat of terrorism with chemical or biological weapons was not entirely overlooked, either in the academic[12] or policy communities,[13] the focus on nuclear weapons reflected an extension of the Cold War and concerns of the use by states of such devices. In the immediate aftermath of the Cold War, concerns over the insecurity of the Soviet nuclear stockpile and lack of protection for Soviet nuclear material made nuclear terrorism seem not only the most catastrophic form of mass destructive terrorism, but also the most plausible. Such fears were at their height in the early- to mid-1990s, but as clearcut examples of such substate proliferation failed to emerge the focus of study altered, particularly in the wake of Aum Shinrikyo's attacks.

Purver's assessment was written before Aum Shinrikyo's use of sarin in March 1995, and in the aftermath of those attacks the literature on WMD terrorism increasingly dealt with chemical, biological and nuclear weapons as separate entities, certainly for the acquisition of strategic materials, but also for the willingness and ability of terrorist organizations to use such devices. This trend has been accompanied by a growth in the literature that deals exclusively with terrorism using chemical or biological weapons.[14]

However, the critical aspect of WMD terrorism, and one that remains much debated, is terrorists' willingness to use such weapons. Here, the seminal early study was Brian Jenkins' 1975 article, 'Will Terrorists Go Nuclear?'[15] In this, Jenkins made the argument that 'Terrorists want a lot of people watching and a lot of people listening and not a lot of people dead'.[16] The maxim and the wider paper were important on two related levels: it made terrorists' motivations and intentions as important as a group's ability to use WMD when analysing the threat posed by WMD terrorism. However, Jenkins' convincing argument that terrorists did not want to use such weapons continued to be uncritically accepted even after it ceased to be analytically safe to do so, ensuring that too often the WMD terrorism literature focused on capability rather than intent. In spite of encouraging this flaw in analysis, Jenkins' assessment was largely supported by terrorist activities, arguably until Aum Shinrikyo's attack on the Tokyo subway in March 1995. Certainly, Jenkins' judgment was no less germane when he reiterated it in 1985, suggesting that: 'Simply killing a lot of people has seldom been one terrorist objective ... terrorists operate on the principle of the minimum force necessary. They find it unnecessary to kill many, as long as killing a few suffices for their purposes'.[17] With a few caveats, such as the objectives of apocalyptic groups such as Aum Shinrikyo or groups that faced an existential threat, many scholars would have continued to argue that Jenkins' concept of instrumental proportionality was a key rationale for most terrorism right up until 2001. The end of a presumption of minimum force is just one of the ways that the events of 11 September 2001 have altered our perceptions of terrorism. However, it is interesting to note that this presumption uncomfortably co-existed with growing concerns about WMD terrorism, particularly after Aum Shinrikyo's attacks in 1995. In the wake of these attacks, the literature on terrorism could be split into pessimistic and optimistic perspectives. Pessimists argued that terrorism was becoming increasingly lethal and that this coincided with the increased opportunities for acquiring and using WMD, stemming in part from the collapse of the Soviet Union.[18] Two examples of such pessimism from this period are Walter Laqueur, 'Postmodern Terrorism' and Carter, Deutch and Zelikow, 'Catastrophic Terrorism'.[19] Optimists included Ehud Sprinzak and David Rapoport. Sprinzak argued that the threat of WMD terrorism had been greatly exaggerated and that although

> There is, in fact, a growing interest in chemical and biological weapons among terrorist and insurgent organizations worldwide for small-scale tactical attacks ... the flourishing mystique of chemical and biological weapons suggests that angry and alienated groups are likely to manipulate them for conventional political purposes.[20]

Rapoport argued that much of the concern about the increasing likelihood of WMD terrorism stemmed from a series of assumptions: that the level of terrorist violence was increasing largely because the proportion of religiously motivated groups was increasing compared to secularly motivated terrorist organizations; and that religion is less likely to inhibit extreme or indiscriminate violence. Rapoport cited Bruce Hoffman as a major exponent of this argument in, for example, 'Holy Terror', an influential article published in 1995.[21] Rapoport suggested that such assumptions were flawed, not least because the historical evidence for religion as a motivation for extreme violence was at best equivocal.[22]

As well as a large number of articles on the subject, there have been also a number of books that dealt exclusively with WMD terrorism. The best of these have been Falkenrath, Newman and Thayer, *America's Achilles Heel*[23] and Stern, *The Ultimate Terrorists*.[24] Both books contained systematic assessments of the possibilities for terrorist acquisition of chemical, biological and nuclear weapons, either through state assistance or other means; of the willingness of groups to use such weapons; and of the means by which governments might counter the danger.

In order to address the dispute over terrorist motivations, and thus the willingness of such groups to use WMD, Jonathan Tucker edited a series of primary source case studies of groups that either actively sought or acquired chemical or biological weapons. The 12 cases, dating from 1945 to 1998, reflected those that were most often cited in the academic literature as examples of groups pursuing such weapons and included organizations with a range of motivational bases. The study, *Toxic Terror*, showed that several of the most frequently cited cases were, in all likelihood, apocryphal. Although studying 12 historical cases might have only limited efficacy for predictions of future terrorist activities, the book did provide an important empirical basis for subsequent assessments of the threat of WMD terrorism. However, in his conclusion, Tucker reiterated many of the points that remain mainstream opinion on the subject. The groups most likely to use chemical or biological weapons were unlikely to have a secular audience to constrain their actions and were more likely to exist as an underground movement led by a charismatic individual. Such weapons may be acquired not to cause mass casualties, but for tactical attacks instead; terrorists are often technologically conservative, favouring weapons that will work predictably. However, many groups also have grandiose aspirations, are inclined to escalate the level of violence they employ, and are innovative in their use of violence, so may be willing to try new techniques if the organization's campaign appears to be failing.[25]

Although the Tucker book is by far the most ambitious example of a case-study approach to the issue of WMD terrorism, it is not the first. Several studies of Aum Shinrikyo appeared shortly after the cult's attacks. Among those were Kaplan and Marshall's excellent study, *The Cult At The End of the World*[26] and Brackett's book, *Holy Terror.*[27] Many of the assessments in these books were drawn from US Senate committee hearings in the autumn of 1995.[28] Both the committee hearings and Kaplan and Marshall's work have been extensively relied upon and quoted since each was published. This has led to, as Milton Leitenberg has described it, a serial propagation of misinformation.[29] Leitenberg focused on the cult's biological weapons programme and questioned some of the analysis in the earlier work, based on subsequent research. However, Leitenberg's more significant point was that the Senate Committee report and Kaplan and Marshall's book remained unchallenged and unquestioned by scholars for several years after the attacks in 1995, even after contradictory evidence became available. This is a trend that is supported by Tucker's book: several of the case studies were apocryphal, despite being widely cited in the literature on WMD terrorism. As much of the evidence for WMD terrorism is, by definition, difficult to acquire (often in retrospect and always beforehand), many of the assessments in the literature are made on the basis of scant hard evidence and are often therefore incorrect in detail and sometimes even in substance. It is an important point.

Although several excellent books have appeared on Osama bin Laden and al-Qa'eda[30] and any number of articles, particularly after the attacks of 11 September, most have focused on the organization generally, rather than on the effort of its members to acquire WMD. Other articles have dealt with al-Qa'eda only in the context of the broader threat, or have assessed the organization only as one of several.[31] A definitive examination of al-Qa'eda's proliferation attempts therefore remains to be written.[32]

One effort to provide further empirical information on WMD terrorism has been the development of databases on the topic. The RAND-St Andrews Database of International Terrorism provided important information both on terrorism generally and WMD terrorism more specifically.[33] The first open-source database devoted entirely to WMD terrorism is at the Center for Nonproliferation Studies. Annual summaries of the database have been published in *The Nonproliferation Review*[34] and the contents of the Database have informed a series of articles, notably by Jonathan Tucker and Amy Sands.[35]

ISSUES

Two main issues continue to dominate the literature on WMD terrorism: would terrorists want to use such weapons?; and, if so, how easy would it be for these groups to acquire the weapons? Even now, motivation remains secondary to opportunity and fixes in too much of the current literature.[36] Concepts of terrorism are changing and need to change further: such 'traditional' types of terrorist as that motivated by nationalist-separatism or left-wing ideologies are less prevalent than when many of the key early works on WMD terrorism were originally written. Recent attacks show a growing range of motivations that call into question whether today's terrorists are all as rational as once appeared the case. The argument that terrorists want publicity is clearly no longer the sole motivation for many groups and the concept that such organizations do not want a lot of people dead is also questionable in the case of apocalyptic groups and those seeking to inflict punishment attacks. Not only has there been a growth in alternative motivations, but also in structures. Terrorist organizations arranged as networks may affect the dynamics of groups in ways that we do not fully understand. It may also affect the control exerted from the centre of the organization, resulting in fewer restrictions for hardliners within a group. As motivations alter, so too do the traditional constraints on terrorist activity: the idea of a constituency as a restraining influence on activities now clearly applies only to some groups but not to others.

The likelihood of terrorist use of WMD in the wake of 11 September remains extremely unclear. The scale of the attacks suggest that mass destructive terrorism is now a fact and it thus seems unlikely that, given the option, al-Qa'eda would avoid using WMD to cause mass casualties. However, although discoveries in Afghanistan and the disruption of plots in Europe continue to show that al-Qa'eda and its associated groups are interested in WMD, these discoveries do not indicate that the organization has successfully acquired such weapons. Moreover, the evidence clearly shows that al-Qa'eda has simply been trying to develop any type of weapon that might help its cause. The suggestion, therefore, would be that WMD are being pursued simply as part of a range of options, for instrumental purposes, rather than as an end in itself. The attacks of 11 September show that WMD are not necessary to cause mass casualties. Given the difficulty and expense of acquiring and effectively using such weapons, al-Qa'eda may continue to seek WMD, but probably not rely on doing so successfully. The attacks of 11 September, and the subsequent discoveries, suggest a group that is pragmatic and has an instrumental approach to WMD acquisition.

Al-Qa'eda appears to have actively pursued an all-options strategy for its attempts to acquire CBRN, simultaneously seeking chemical, biological, radiological, and nuclear weapons. Moreover, groups associated with al-Qa'eda have continued to plot to use such weapons in Europe and in the USA.[37]

This, then, was the situation on 10 September last year: despite the attempts to acquire WMD by groups such as Aum Shinrikyo and al-Qa'eda, and the use of such weapons by several groups, including Aum Shinrikyo, no terrorist organization had perpetrated a high casualty incident using WMD. When terrorist groups had sought to cause high levels of casualties, they did so using conventional weapons, such as explosives. The overwhelming majority of incidents involving nuclear, chemical or biological materials were hoaxes or threats, particularly in the USA since 1998, and the instances of use of an agent tended to be examples of 'low-end' or household products.[38] It was questionable whether such uses had anything significant to do with terrorist use of WMD for high casualty events, except maintaining the issue of WMD terrorism in the forefront of public, media, academic and governmental awareness. The threat from 'high-end' nuclear, biological or chemical terrorism arose because groups, such as al-Qa'eda, continued to seek such weapons; and that these weapons remained, at the very least, theoretically available to a well financed and connected organization, one that would probably be willing to use such weapons to cause high levels of casualties.

The 11 September attacks certainly revealed al-Qa'eda's organizational ability and the willingness of the group to commit attacks that resulted in thousands of casualties. In that respect, the attacks of 11 September were unprecedented, causing numbers of casualties that exceeded any previous terrorist attack by several orders of magnitude. However, al-Qa'eda committed these attacks using conventional weapons, albeit in an unusual and highly innovative way, and the political and social effect of the attacks could scarcely have been greater if the group had used a WMD. On the other hand, however, the group's attacks raises the issue of whether other like-minded organizations could create the same effect without resorting to WMD. However, terrorism and attacks by terrorist organizations cannot be viewed as a linear process. The most obvious example of this is the aftermath of Aum Shinrikyo's sarin attack in Tokyo in 1995. Although not the first use of a chemical or biological weapon by a terrorist group, Aum's attack seemed different, using a high-end agent to cause indiscriminate casualties. Most analysts and those charged with countering terrorism assumed that Aum's attack represented a harbinger of the future and that other, increasingly lethal, attacks with WMD would follow and that terrorism was on an escalatory spiral. Such assessments were not supported by the experience of the following years: there was not a wave of similar attempts. This in spite of the increased knowledge of WMD and availability of weapons-usable technologies from a range of sources including the former Soviet Union.[39] Al-Qa'eda's attacks of 11 September, far from relying on WMD, used a technologically conservative weapon and were based on variants of familiar tactics, such as hijacking and vehicle-bombing, to cause carnage. Although al-Qa'eda was undoubtedly interested in a range of WMD, and clearly investigated each for their potential value in committing an attack, ultimately the organization chose a different route from the one implied by Aum's 1995 attack. The precise reason for this tactical choice is not currently certain, but it seems likely that al-Qa'eda decided to use methods that its leaders believed had the best chances of success. Although WMD have supposedly grown increasingly accessible in the past ten years, there remain substantial technical difficulties in acquiring, weaponizing and delivering an effective WMD. Although the wealth, resources and contacts of an organization such as al-Qa'eda would undoubtedly have helped to reduce this risk, the example of Aum Shinrikyo, also wealthy and well connected yet unable to deliver a successful attack with chemical or biological weapons, shows that such problems still exist. Al-Qa'eda, therefore, appears to have chosen a method that, as well as being cheaper and technologically less sophisticated, also had a better probability of causing mass casualties than an attack using WMD.[40]

Aum Shinrikyo were far from the first group to seek chemical or biological weapons. For example, DIN ('Avenging Israel's Blood'), in 1946, contemplated killing nearly two million Germans by poisoning the water supplies of four major cities in revenge for the Holocaust. DIN did not carry out this attack, but rather a much smaller one against Stalag 13 near Nuremberg.[41] Other significant incidents involving chemical or biological agents include the Rajneeshees, a religious cult that used salmonella to contaminate salad bars in The Dalles, Oregon, in 1984, with the intention of influencing a local election. In the process, the group poisoned 751 people.[42] 'The Covenant, the Sword, and the Arm of the Lord' (known as the CSA), a US group influenced by 'Christian Identity' beliefs in the mid-1980s, acquired a barrel of potassium cyanide, a toxin with widespread industrial uses, with the intention of poisoning US urban water supplies to further the group's ideological and religious objectives. However, the CSA compound was surrounded and the group's members detained by the FBI before such an attack could occur.[43] Both the PKK and Liberation Tigers of Tamil Eelam (LTTE) are alleged to have used chemical weapons on at least one occasion. It is important to note, however, that, in each case, the use of non-conventional weapons was for a small-scale tactical attack, not to attempt an act of mass-destructive terrorism. On 28 March 1992, the PKK poisoned three water tanks of a Turkish air force base outside Istanbul. The water was foamy, and, when tested, was found to be contaminated with cyanide. The tanks contained 50 mg of cyanide per litre, a lethal dose.[44] LTTE have also resorted to non-conventional weapons. On 18 June 1990, the Sri Lankan Army reported that the group had attacked a Sri Lankan Army encampment with canisters filled with an unidentified poison gas, later identified as chlorine.[45] The LTTE and PKK attacks are significant because they clearly disprove the idea that all 'traditional' terrorist groups would avoid using nuclear, chemical or biological weapons under any circumstances.[46]

There remains no consensus on how easy it would be for terrorists to acquire such weapons. The difficulty of acquisition remains a key area of dispute within the literature. The variety of agents and techniques available for such low-level proliferation permit both pessimists and optimists to make a plausible case. Pessimists continue to point to the easy access to key materials, the ability in many cases to exploit dual-use technologies and equipment and that, for most conventional terrorist purposes, a partially successful attack using WMD would be sufficient. Optimists cite the difficulties in acquiring and effectively using nuclear, biological or chemical materials and use Aum Shinrikyo as the key example of this. The cult, in spite of its membership, assets, organization and contacts across the world, failed to acquire a nuclear capability, failed in every one of its experiments with biological weapons and was only partially successful in its use of chemical weapons. Aum had difficulties developing virulent batches of the pathogens and then in effectively delivering the agents. The sarin used in the 20 March attacks was contained in plastic bags that were placed on the floor of the subway car and then pierced with the sharpened point of an umbrella. The impurity of the sarin and the crude delivery method were both crucial in undermining the efficacy of Aum's attack.

One of the central challenges to effective deployment of either chemical or biological weapons is the weaponization and delivery. Chemical weapons would be relatively easy to deliver in an enclosed space, but much harder to disperse in a way so as to cause high levels of casualties in an open space. Effective delivery of biological agents is more problematic. To be effective, biological agents would need to be dispersed in an aerosol cloud consisting of particles small enough (one to five microns, or 5 thousandths of a millimetre across) to be easily inhaled and retained in the lungs. This requirement poses significant hurdles on the terrorist attempting to use such pathogens to cause high casualties.[47] The efficacy of a biological agent would depend on several factors: the agent itself, the delivery system, the quantity of agent used, the efficacy of the aerosolization of the agent and the weather conditions at the time of release. For example, strong winds may affect the dispersal of the agent, and bright light, significant heat or dryness may all adversely affect the time the pathogen remains infectious after release. However, the degree to which a biological agent is affected by these factors varies: anthrax, for example, is relatively hardy; a significant advantage for a terrorist.

The acquisition of chemical and biological agents varies enormously in difficulty. For example, while smallpox is supposedly held in just two sites in the world, some other biological pathogens are easier to acquire: notably ricin, for which the main ingredient is beans from the castor plant, and for which a plethora of publications, many originating with the radical right in the USA, provide instructions on production.[48] Both the plague and anthrax are naturally available in some areas of the world in which they are endemic. However, a terrorist group would have to ensure that it held a virulent strain of the pathogen: if it acquired anthrax from soil samples, for example. Moreover, although the raw materials and production methods for making ricin are straightforward, and ricin is a highly lethal pathogen, this does not mean that producing a weapon capable of causing mass casualties is equally easy: there remains the issue of effective delivery. Several of the groups, such as the Minnesota Patriots' Council, which have produced ricin in this way have also produced only a very impure version of the pathogen.[49]

Both chemical and biological agents can be produced using dual-use technology, methods and equipment that have legitimate as well as illegitimate purposes. Fermenters can be used to grow pathogens but are also widely available for production in a range of legitimate industries from brewing and pharmaceuticals to biotechnology. Freeze-drying and milling machines, extremely helpful in the conversion of agents into a dry finely ground powder, ideal for dispersion, are widely used in the pharmaceutical industry. Such usage makes it difficult to impose meaningful restrictions on access to weapons-usable equipment, particularly if the terrorist organization operates behind a front company to make its purchases.

Chemical agents, being compounds, may be acquired as a series of precursors, rather than as an entire agent. For obvious reasons, acquiring precursors is an easier route, although tight controls exist on some of these as well, through the Chemical Weapons Convention and Australia Group. In spite of this, groups seeking such precursors can use front companies and other evasive measures to circumvent such restrictions, particularly if a complicit supplier can be found. In other cases though, constituent chemicals are used so widely in industry that controlling them is all but impossible. Such chemicals can then be used to produce the chemical precursors or, ultimately, the chemical agent. Here, the problem for the terrorist lies not so much in acquiring most of the key ingredients, but in the process of manufacturing an effective agent from those ingredients. Although many 'recipes' are readily available, either in the open literature or on the Internet, the reliability of these recipes is often limited.[50]

A radiological device is likely to be the easiest type of WMD for terrorists to acquire. At its simplest, it requires no more than conventional explosives and a radioactive source, such as cesium-137 from a hospital X-ray machine. Such radioactive sources remain widespread and poorly protected, certainly compared to other types of nuclear materials. In spite of this, the disruptive potential of a radioactive weapon or 'dirty bomb' is considerable.

A nuclear-yield weapon is likely to be the hardest type of device for terrorists to acquire. Terrorists intent on acquiring a nuclear-yield device have three options: steal or purchase an intact weapon; steal or purchase a sufficient quantity of weapons-usable materials to build a crude nuclear-yield device; or enrich enough weapons-grade material to build a device. In reality, the second option is widely regarded as the most credible of the three.

Most terrorist groups seem unlikely to follow the example of Aum Shinrikyo in attempting to enrich material to a weapons-usable state. The process is lengthy, costly and, for many of the cruder forms of enrichment, potentially easily discovered. Success is also far from assured: many state programmes spend millions and take years trying to enrich enough material for a viable nuclear weapons programme.

A group unwilling or unable to enrich its own weapons-usable nuclear material would have to rely on buying or stealing it. Another pathway to nuclear terrorism is to acquire nuclear material to construct a device. However, acquiring sufficient nuclear material is likely to prove difficult and, in spite of reports of nuclear 'leakage' in the FSU, only a handful of cases are known, notably in the early 1990s. Never was the quantity involved sufficient to build a weapon. In late 2001, the International Atomic Energy Agency (IAEA) stated it knew of 175 incidents involving 'weapons-significant' material, but of those, only 18 involved highly enriched uranium or plutonium. Such a figure is not conclusive as it reflects only the incidents that are discovered; however, it is indicative. Moreover, the need to acquire a considerable quantity of fissile material would seem to preclude all but the most affluent or state-sponsored groups.

Whether through enrichment or acquisition of enough fissile material for a nuclear-yield weapon, terrorists seeking to build a nuclear weapon then have a number of design options: constructing a gun-type weapon using highly enriched uranium (HEU), or developing an implosion device using plutonium. In terms of design, the crude gun-type device is significantly the easier of the two, requiring between 50 and 60 kilograms of HEU. An implosion device would require around eight kilograms of plutonium. The difficulties of such a device arise in two areas: the sphere of plutonium needs to be minutely engineered, and the shock wave has to be calibrated to the millionth of a second. If either condition is not met, there is a substantial risk of an unpredictable nuclear yield or, more likely, a failure to reach supercriticality. A gun-type assembly would have a high probability of achieving some nuclear yield without requiring the testing of components and using literature in the public domain. An implosion device is likely to be more sophisticated, requiring a higher degree of technical competence. However, in each case, the crucial barrier is the acquisition of enough nuclear material for the device.[51]

The final method for terrorists to acquire a nuclear-yield device is to steal or purchase an intact weapon. Concerns over nuclear-yield terrorism heightened significantly after the Soviet Union's collapse, due largely to the fear over 'loose nukes' and the opportunities for nuclear materials and nuclear expertise to leave the country and be exploited by rogue states or terrorists. That terrorists could acquire an intact nuclear weapon seems far-fetched: states obviously have a considerable stake in protecting their mass-destructive weapons generally.

CONCLUSION: FUTURE RESEARCH

Future study of WMD terrorism needs to focus on the two broad areas: how would a group acquire such weapons?; and why would they want them? However, beyond these traditional and very obvious aspects of opportunity and intent are a series of less straightforward issues. Although the necessity for such understanding is clear, the reasons why groups seek WMD are not so transparent that any degree of predictability is presently possible. Based on the motivations of members, it is now possible to suggest which groups are unlikely to seek WMD and to suggest types of group that are more likely to do so. However, extending such assessments so that they are less broad, and thus more useful, will be a continuous but vital priority for study. The work of Tucker and others has demonstrated that previous groups seeking such weapons did have some characteristics in common, but it is not certain that future groups would necessarily share those same features. The need for assessments, on a case-by-case basis, is on-going. Such work will be occurring already for al-Qa'eda, as the most pressing example of a group seeking such weapons, but there are likely to be other equally important but less prominent organizations that require analysis.

Tactical decision-making is a related aspect of terrorists' activities that requires more work, although it is clearly related to motivation and opportunity. Why, for example, do groups choose certain types of weapons over another, and what would lead groups to alter those choices, particularly between conventional and mass destructive weapons? Again, such decisions occur on a group-by-group basis and therefore subsequent study is likely also to require such an approach.

The substate or terrorist acquisition of WMD is closely related to non-proliferation at a state level. There has to be more rigorous assessments of state-sponsorship for WMD terrorism: has it occurred already?; and how valid are previous assumptions that it was not in states' interests to allow client groups access to such weapons? Assessments of the WMD terrorism threat need also to take account of the opportunities for groups to exploit vulnerabilities in states' protection of key facilities and strategic materials. However, a terrorist programme of acquisition and weaponization requires a much lower threshold than for state-level proliferation of WMD. Addressing once and for all just how easy it would be for groups to develop a workable capability would be an extremely useful contribution to the literature. It is also essential in any meaningful threat assessment and thus in considering how best to counter the danger.

More specifically, there remains much work to be done on radiological terrorism: in terms of study, still the poor relation of terrorism using nuclear, chemical or biological weapons.[52] Although less catastrophic, the relatively easy access to the required material and scope for disruption makes radiological terrorism a plausible threat. The topic needs to be considered in the same way that terrorism using chemical or biological weapons have been, assessing the possibilities for acquisition, weaponization and consequences of each of the main radiological agents. In doing so, a better gauge of the extent of the problem could be made.

Finally, study of WMD terrorism needs to consider related issues, but above all, not lose sight of the context in which such terrorism occurs. Related issues include the possible use of nuclear, chemical or biological agents against strategic targets rather than people. One possible such target might be agriculture;[53] another might be communication or cyber-targets.[54] The context of WMD terrorism is terrorism, more broadly, and the political, religious and social milieu in which it occurs. Although WMD terrorism can form a specialist subset of terrorism studies, it makes no sense to treat it in isolation from the broader examination of terrorism, particularly when considering the motivational aspects of the topic. Likewise, assessments of capability need to take account of the literature on proliferation , as it relates to small but weaponizable quantities of chemical, biological or nuclear materials. The best studies of WMD terrorism recognize that it is a phenomenon that occurs at the nexus of several other fields and therefore take account of that.

The implications of 11 September for groups seeking WMD remain to be seen. There are a number of critical areas that are imperfectly understood by analysts. Given the importance of the topic, this should remain an area of terrorism studies that will continue to receive attention. However, too often in the past, such work has tended towards an alarmist perspective. Future studies will hopefully be firmly grounded in the motives and context of such threats, as well as simply the opportunities for WMD terrorism. It is only by examining the issue in its full complexity that a meaningful assessment can be made, and a credible response formulated to this most pressing of dangers.

NOTES

1. Bruce Hoffman, *Inside Terrorism* (New York, Columbia University Press, 1998), p. 67.
2. For a discussion of why such a limited definition of WMD is problematic, see Gavin Cameron, 'WMD Terrorism in the United States: The Threat and Possible Countermeasures', *The Nonproliferation Review*, 7/1 (Spring 2000), pp. 162–3
3. Mason Willrich and Theodore B. Taylor, *Nuclear Theft: Risks and Safeguards* (Cambridge, MA: Ballinger Publishing, 1974).
4. Augustus Norton and Michael Greenberg, *Studies In Nuclear Terrorism* (Boston: G.K Hull, 1979).
5. Paul Leventhal and Yonah Alexander, *Nuclear Terrorism: Defining the Threat* (Washington, DC: Pergammon, 1985).
6. Paul Leventhal and Yonah Alexander, *Preventing Nuclear Terrorism* (Lexington, MA: Lexington Book, 1987).

7. Gail Bass, Brian Jenkins, Konrad Kellen *et al.*, *Motivations and Possible Actions of Potential Criminal Adversaries of US Nuclear Programs* (Santa Monica, CA: RAND, 1980).
8. Robert Reinstedt and J. Westbury, *Major Crimes as Analogs to Potential Threats to Nuclear Facilities and Programs* (Santa Monica, CA: RAND, 1980).
9. Gail Bass and Brian Jenkins, *A Review of Recent Trends in International Terrorism and Nuclear Incidents Abroad* (Santa Monica, CA: RAND, 1983).
10. Peter deLeon and Bruce Hoffman, with Konrad Kellen and Brian Jenkins, *The Threat of Nuclear Terrorism: A Reexamination*, No.2706 (Santa Monica, CA: RAND, 1988).
11. Ron Purver, *Chemical and Biological Terrorism: The Threat According to the Open Literature* (Ottawa: Canadian Security Intelligence Service, 1995), p. 2.
12. Examples of this literature include: Elliott Hurwitz, 'Terrorists and Chemical/Biological Weapons', *Naval War College Review*, 35/3 (May–June 1982), pp. 36–40; Charles A. Watkins, 'Terrorist Use of Biological Warfare Agents: A Threat to US Security', in Yonah Alexander (ed.), *The 1986 Annual on Terrorism* (Dordrecht: Martinus Nijhoff Publishers, 1987), pp. 191–9; Joseph D. Douglas Jr and Neil C. Livingstone, *America The Vulnerable: The Threat of Chemical and Biological Warfare* (Lexington, MA: D.C. Heath, 1987); Jeffrey D. Smith, *Terrorists and the Potential Use of Biological Weapons: A Discussion*, No.R-3771 (Santa Monica, CA: RAND, 1989); Robert H. Kupperman and David M. Smith, 'Coping with Biological Terrorism', in Brad Roberts (ed.) *Biological Weapons: Weapons of the Future?* (Washington, DC: Center for Strategic and International Studies, 1993), pp. 35–46.
13. A key piece of US legislation relating to biological terrorism was the Biological Weapons Anti-Terrorism Act of 1989. See, for example, US Senate, Committee on the Judiciary, *The Biological Weapons Anti-Terrorism Act of 1989*, Hearing, 26 July 1989, Serial No. J-101-32 (Washington DC: US Government Printing Office, 1990).
14. See, for example, the series of articles in the September/October edition of *Politics and the Life Sciences*: Jonathan B. Tucker, 'Chemical/Biological Terrorism: Coping with a New Threat', *Politics and the Life Sciences*, 15/2 (September/October 1996), pp. 167–83; Richard Falkenrath, 'Chemical/Biological Terrorism: Coping With Uncertain Threats and Certain Vulnerabilities', *Politics and the Life Sciences*, 15/2 (September/October 1996), pp. 201–3; Graham S. Pearson, 'Chemical/Biological Terrorism: How Serious A Risk?', *Politics and the Life Sciences*, 15/2 (September/October 1996), pp. 210–13. Other examples of studies of chemical and biological terrorism include: Ron Purver, 'The Threat of Chemical/Biological Terrorism', *Commentary*, No. 60 (Ottawa: Canadian Security Intelligence Service, August 1995); Brad Roberts (ed.), *Terrorism with Chemical and Biological Weapons: Calibrating Risks and Responses* (Alexandria, VA: The Chemical and Biological Arms Control Institute, 1997); W. Seth Carus, *Bioterrorism and Biocrimes: The Illicit Use of Biological Agents in the Twentieth Century* (Washington, DC: Center for Counterproliferation Research, National Defense University, 1998); Amy Smithson, *Ataxia: The Chemical and Biological Terrorism Threat and the US Response* (Washington, DC: The Stimson Center, 2000).
15. Brian Jenkins, *Will Terrorists Go Nuclear?*, No. P-5541 (Santa Monica, CA: RAND Corp, 1975).
16. Ibid.
17. Brian Jenkins, *The Likelihood of Nuclear Terrorism*, No. P-7119 (Santa Monica, CA: RAND, 1985).
18. John F. Sopko, 'The Changing Proliferation Threat', *Foreign Policy*, 105 (Winter 1996/7), pp. 3–20.
19. Walter Laqueur, 'Postmodern Terrorism', *Foreign Affairs*, 75/5 (September/October 1996), pp. 24–36; Ashton Carter, John Deutch and Philip Zelikow, 'Catastrophic Terrorism: Tackling the New Danger', *Foreign Affairs*, 77/6 (November/December 1998), pp. 80–94.
20. Ehud Sprinzak, 'The Great Superterrorism Scare', *Foreign Policy*, 112 (Fall 1998), p. 118.
21. Bruce Hoffman, 'Holy Terror: The Implications of Terrorism Motivated By Religious Imperatives', *Studies in Conflict and Terrorism*, 18 (1995), pp. 271–84. See also Bruce Hoffman, 'Terrorism and WMD: Some Preliminary Hypotheses', *The Nonproliferation Review*, 4/3 (Spring/Summer 1997), pp. 45–53.
22. David C. Rapoport, 'Terrorists and Weapons of the Apocalypse', *Nonproliferation Policy Education Center Essays*, http://www.wizard.net/~npec/papers/rapoport.html.
23. Richard A. Falkenrath, Robert D. Newman and Bradley A. Thayer, *America's Achilles Heel: Nuclear, Biological, and Chemical Terrorism and Covert Attack* (Cambridge, MA: MIT Press, 1998). Falkenrath summarized this work in: Richard A. Falkenrath, 'Confronting Nuclear, Biological, and Chemical Terrorism', *Survival*, 40/3 (Autumn 1998), pp. 43–65. This, in turn,

sparked debate on the extent of the problem and possible solutions between Falkenrath, Jessica Stern, Joseph F. Pilat and Karl-Heinz Kamp, published as 'WMD Terrorism: An Exchange', *Survival*, 40/4 (Winter 1998/99), pp. 168–83.

24. Jessica Stern, *The Ultimate Terrorists* (Cambridge, MA: Harvard University Press, 1999).
25. Jonathan B. Tucker (ed.), *Toxic Terror: Assessing Terrorist Use of Chemical and Biological Weapons* (Cambridge, MA: MIT Press, 2000), pp. 266–7.
26. David E. Kaplan and Andrew Marshall, *The Cult at the End of the World* (London: Random House, 1996).
27. D.W. Brackett, *Holy Terror: Armageddon in Tokyo* (New York: Weatherhill, 1996).
28. US Congress, Senate, Committee of Governmental Affairs, Permanent Subcommittee on Investigations (Minority Staff), 'Staff Statement, Hearings on Global Proliferation of Weapons of Mass Destruction: A Case Study on the Aum Shinrikyo', 31 October 1995.
29. Milton Leitenberg, 'Aum Shinrikyo's Efforts to Produce Biological Weapons: A Case Study in Serial Propagation of Misinformation', *Terrorism and Political Violence*, 11/4 (Winter 1999), pp. 149–58.
30. See, for example, Peter L. Bergen, *Holy War, Inc.: Inside the Secret World of Osama bin Laden*, (London: Weidenfeld & Nicolson, 2001); Rohan Gunaratna, *Inside al Qaeda: Global Network of Terror* (London: Hurst, 2002).
31. See, for example, Gavin Cameron, 'Multi-Track MicroProliferation: Lessons from Aum Shinrikyo and Al Qaida', *Studies In Conflict and Terrorism*, 22/4 (September–December 1999), pp. 277–309.
32. The Center for Nonproliferation Studies' website includes assessments of much of the open literature relating to al-Qa'eda's proliferation activities. Center for Nonproliferation Studies, *WMD Terrorism and Usama bin Laden*, available at: http://cns.miis.edu/pubs/reports/binladen.htm
33. Bruce Hoffman and Donna Kim Hoffman, 'The RAND-St Andrews Chronology of International Terrorism, 1994', *Terrorism and Political Violence*, 7 (Winter 1995), pp. 178–229; Bruce Hoffman and Donna Kim Hoffman, 'The RAND-St Andrews Chronology of International Terrorist Incidents, 1995', *Terrorism and Political Violence*, 8 (Autumn 1996), pp. 87–127; Bruce Hoffman and David Claridge, 'The RAND-St Andrews Chronology of International Terrorism and Noteworthy Domestic Incidents, 1996', *Terrorism and Political Violence*, 10 (Summer 1998), pp. 135–80; Bruce Hoffman, 'The Debate Over Future Terrorist Use of Chemical, Biological, Nuclear and Radiological Weapons', in Brad Roberts (ed.), *Hype or Reality: The 'New Terrorism' and Mass Casualty Attacks* (Alexandria, VA: The Chemical and Biological Arms Control Institute, 2000).
34. Gavin Cameron, Jason Pate, Diana McCauley *et al.*, 'A Chronology of Substate Incidents Involving CBRN Materials, 1999', *The Nonproliferation Review*, 7/2 (Summer 2000), pp. 157–74. Jason Pate, Gary Ackerman and Kimberley McCloud, '2000 WMD Terrorism Chronology: Incidents Involving Sub-National Actors and Chemical, Biological, Radiological, or Nuclear Materials', accessed on: http://cns.miis.edu/pubs/reports/nuclear, biological or chemical2k.htm, 12 March 2002.
35. See, for example, Jonathan B. Tucker and Amy Sands, 'Chemical and Biological Terrorism: An Unlikely Threat?', *Bulletin of the Atomic Scientists*, 55 (July–August 1999), pp. 46–52.
36. Hoffman, 'The Debate Over Future Terrorist Use of Chemical, Biological, Nuclear and Radiological Weapons'.
37. Daniel McGrory, 'Al-Qaeda's $1 million hunt for atomic weapons', *The Times*, 15 November 2001, accessed on: http://www.thetimes.co.uk/article/0,,2001390014-2001395984,00.html, 29 November 2001. Bob Woodward, Robert G. Kaiser and David Ottaway, 'US Fears Bin Laden Made Nuclear Strides: Concern Over "Dirty Bomb" Affects Security', *Washington Post*, 4 December 2001, p. A1. Stephen Farrell, 'Bin Laden Makes Nuclear Threat' *The Times*, 10 November 2001, accessed on: http://www.thetimes.co.uk/article/0,,2001380020-2001391616,00.html, 29 November 2001. Tom Walker, Stephen Grey, Nick Fielding, 'Al-Qaeda's Secrets: Bin Laden's Camp Reveal Chemical Weapon Ambition', *The Sunday Times*, 25 November 2001, accessed on: http://www.Sunday-times.co.uk/article/0,,9002-2001540887,00.html, 29 November 2001. Zahid Hussain, 'Bin Laden Met Nuclear Scientists from Pakistan', *The Times*, 12 November 2001 accessed on: http://www.thetimes.co.uk/article/0,,2001390003-2001392244,00.html, 29 November 2001. 'Bush: Bin Laden Seeking Nuclear Bomb', CNN, 6 November 2001, accessed on: http://www.cnn.com/2001/WORLD/europe/11/06/gen.europe.conf/index.html, 9 November 2001. Anthony Lloyd, 'Bin Laden's

Nuclear Secrets Found', *The Times*, 15 November 2001, accessed on http://www.thetimes.co.
uk/article/0,,2001390014-2001395995,00.html, 29 November 2001. Philip Webster and
Roland Watson, 'Bin Laden's Nuclear Threat', *The Times*, 26 October 2001, p. 1. Adam Nathan
and David Leppard, 'Al-Qaeda's Men Held Secret Meetings to Build "dirty bomb"', *Sunday
Times*, 14 October 2001, p. A5. Nick Fielding, Joe Laurier, Gareth Walsh, 'Bin Laden "almost
had uranium bomb"', *Sunday Times*, 3 March 2002, Section 1, p. 13. Khalid Sharaf-al-Din,
'Bin-Ladin Men Reportedly Possess Biological Weapons', *Al-Sharaq al-Awsat*, 6 March 1999,
(FBIS Document ID: FTS19990306000273). *Agence France Presse*, 'Egypte: le Jihad affirme
détenir des armes chemiques', 19 April 1999, accessed on: http://web.lexis-nexis.com. *Deutsche
Presse-Agentur*, 'Egyptian Militant Says Bin Laden's Group Possess Deadly Weapons', 19 April
1999, accessed on: http://web.lexis-nexis.com. *Agence France Presse*, 'Le Jihad a obtenu des
armes chimiques et biologiques d'Europe de l'est', 20 April 1999, accessed on: http://web.lexis-
nexis.com. Buccianti Alexandre, 'Des extrémistes musulmans détiendraient des armes
chimiques et bactériologiques, selon un dirigeant islamiste', *Agence France Presse*, 21 April 1999,
accessed on: http://web.lexis-nexis.com. 'Suspect Chemical War Camp Found', CNN, 16
December 2001, accessed at: http://www.cnn.com/2001/WORLD/europe/12/16/ret.rumsfeld.
afghan/index.html, 17 December 2001. 'In the House of Anthrax: Chilling Evidence in the
Ruins of Kabul', *The Economist*, 24 November 2001, accessed on: http://www.economist.com/
world/asia/PrinterFriendly.cfm?Story_ID=876941, 23 November 2001. Anthony Lloyd and
Martin Fletcher, 'Bin Laden's Poison Manual', *The Times*, 16 November 2001, accessed on:
http://www.thetimes.co.uk/aticle/0,,2001390015-2001397104,00.html, 29 November 2001.
'Evidence Suggests al Qaeda Pursuit of Biological and Chemical Weapons', CNN, 14
November 2001, accessed on: http://www.cnn.com/2001/WORLD/asiapcf/central/11/14/
chemical.bio/ index.html, 15 November 2001.

38. The 'Database of Incidents Involving Chemical, Biological, Radiological, or Nuclear (CBRN)
Materials, 1900–Present', at the Center for Nonproliferation Studies, Monterey Institute of
International Studies, lists around 680 incidents perpetrated between 1900 and 2002. Of these,
only around half were classified as having been perpetrated by groups or individuals with
political or ideological motivations (ideological being taken to include religious motivations),
and which could thus be considered sub-state terrorism. The rest consist of criminally-
motivated acts for economic gain, or were judged to be false (apocryphal) cases. However, of
these, the overwhelming majority of incidents are important not because they represent a
significant threat, but rather because they show a growing interest in non-conventional
weaponry amongst such groups and individuals. Of the incidents listed between 1995 and
2000, a third were hoaxes and pranks and many others involved the attempted acquisition of
such weapons, so the number of incidents that genuinely involve CBRN weapons is significantly smaller than it might initially appear to be. In 1999, 65 incidents involved the use or
possession of an agent, and 113 incidents in 2000 involved the use or possession of an agent.
Of these, most incidents resulted in zero or very few fatalities and were intended to achieve
such results. This is in large part due to the agents involved, the majority of which were non-
warfare 'household' agents. In 1999 and 2000, these included agents such as acid, pepper spray,
chlorine, insecticide or pesticides, and rat poison. A few incidents did involve military-grade
agents such as ricin, capable of causing an extensive number of casualties. However, where an
agent was used, it was likely to be a low-end or household agent. In 1999, for example, over
half of the incidents of agent-use involved tear gas. Although this cannot be considered a
household agent, it is unlikely to cause fatalities and is certainly at the low end of the scale,
compared to anthrax, ricin or sarin, for example. Other uses of agents involved non-specific
'poisons' or cyanide, for example, neither of which should be regarded as 'high end'.
Cameron, Pate, McCauley *et al.*, 'A Chronology of Substate Incidents Involving CBRN
Materials, 1999'. Pate, Ackerman and McCloud, '2000 WMD Terrorism Chronology:
Incidents Involving Sub-National Actors and Chemical, Biological, Radiological, or Nuclear
Materials', accessed on: http://cns.miis.edu/pubs/reports/nuclear, biological or chemical2k.
htm, 12 March 2002.

39. Peter Chalk, 'Re-Thinking US Counter-Terrorism Efforts', *RAND Op-Eds*, accessed on:
http://www.rand.org/hot/op-eds/092101SDUT.html, 26 September 2001.

40. Ibid.

41. Michael Bar-Zohar, *The Avengers* (New York: Hawthorne Books, 1967), pp. 40–52.

42. W. Seth Carus, 'The Rajneeshees', in Jonathan B. Tucker (ed.), *Toxic Terror: Assessing Terrorist
Use of Chemical and Biological Weapons* (Cambridge, MA: MIT Press, 2000), pp. 115–38.

43. Jessica Eve Stern, 'The Covenant, the Sword, and the Arm of the Lord', in Tucker, *Toxic Terror*, pp. 139–58.

44. Reuters, 'Turks Report Attempt to Poison Air Force Unit', 28 March 1992; Alexander Chelyshev, 'Terrorists Poison Water in Turkish Army Cantonment', TASS, 29 March 1992.

45. Hoffman, 'The Debate Over Future Terrorist Use of Chemical, Biological, Nuclear and Radiological Weapons'; James Pringle, 'Tamil Rebels Face All-Out War Launched by Colombo', *The Times*, 19 June 1990; Xinhua News Agency, 'Sri Lankan Tamil Tigers Use Poison Gas Against Government Troops, Says Senior Officer', 18 June 1990.

46. Xinhua News Agency, 'PKK Rebels Kill 16 People in Southeastern Turkey', 22 January 1994; Nedret Ersanel, 'PKK's Chemical Arms Depots', *Nokta* (Istanbul), 30 January 1994, pp. 8–9, accessed on: FBIS-WEU-94-023. This may be the same incident as that cited by Purver, in which a chemical attack on a village in eastern Turkey, in January 1994, killed 21: Purver, *Chemical and Biological Terrorism*, pp. 88–9. See also 'Sri Lanka Charges Rebels Use Gas', *Washington Post*, 26 November 1995, p. A31.

47. Jonathan B. Tucker, 'The Proliferation of Chemical and Biological Weapons Materials and Technologies to State and Sub-State Actors', testimony before the Subcommittee on International Security, Proliferation and Federal Services of the US Senate Committee on Governmental Affairs, 7 November 2001.

48. Tucker, ibid.

49. See, Tucker and Pate, 'The Minnesota Patriots Council', pp. 159–84.

50. Tucker, 'The Proliferation of Chemical and Biological Weapons Materials and Technologies to State and Sub-State Actors'.

51. Gavin Cameron, *Nuclear Terrorism: A Threat Assessment for the Twenty-First Century* (Basingstoke: Macmillan Press, 1999), pp. 131–2.

52. One rare example, within the terrorism literature, of an article devoted entirely to radiological terrorism is James L. Ford, 'Radiological Dispersal Devices: Assessing the Transnational Threat, Strategic Forum, No.136' (Washington, DC: Institute for National Strategic Studies, National Defense University, 1998).

53. See, for example, Floyd Horn, 'Agricultural Bioterrorism', in Roberts (ed.), *Hype or Reality*; Paul Rogers, Simon Whitby and Malcolm Dando, 'Biological Warfare Against Crops', *Scientific American*, 72 (June 1999), pp. 70–5; Corrie Brown, 'Agricultural Terrorism: A Cause for Concern', *The Monitor*, 5/1-2 (1990), pp. 6–8; Peter Chalk, 'The Political Terrorist Threat to US Agriculture and Livestock', in Gavin Cameron, Jason Pate and Kathleen Vogel (eds), *Agro-Terrorism: Assessing the Threat* (Livermore, CA: Center for Global Security Research, Nonproliferation, Lawrence Livermore National Laboratory, forthcoming).

54. See, for example, John Arquilla, David Ronfeldt and Michele Zanini, 'Networks, Netwar and Information-Age Terrorism', in Ian Lessor (ed.), *Countering the New Terrorism* (Santa Monica, CA: RAND, 1999), pp.39–84; Frank Cilluffo and Curt Gergely, 'Information Warfare and Strategic Terrorism', *Terrorism and Political Violence*, 9/1 (1997), pp. 84–94; Matthew Devost, Brian Houghton and Neal Pollard, 'Information Terrorism: Political Violence in the Information Age', *Terrorism and Political Violence*, 9/1 (1997), pp. 72–83; and Kevin Soo Hoo, Seymour Goodman and Lawrence Greenberg, 'Information Technology and the Terrorist Threat', *Survival*, 39/3 (1997), pp. 135–55.

5

Everything that Descends Must Converge: Terrorism, Globalism and Democracy

LEONARD WEINBERG AND WILLIAM EUBANK[1]

IF ONE were to conduct a poll among journalists, social scientists, policy analysts (and public intellectuals, more generally) asking them to identify the most widely discussed issues over the last few decades, the likelihood is that three topics – democratization, globalization(s) and now, after the World Trade Center attacks, terrorism – would be mentioned most frequently. The volume of books, professional and popular journals, newspapers, television programmes and academic conferences devoted to these subjects has become enormous.[2] What we intend to do in this paper is: (1) define each of these three terms; then (2) investigate what, if anything, they have to do with one another; and (3) seek an explanation of the dynamics of their interaction: what causes what to occur, and why?

Providing readers with definitions of terrorism, democratization and globalization likely to satisfy all concerned is a virtually impossible task. All three concepts have been and continue to be the subject of 'wars of the words'; their meanings have been contested by a variety of groups and individuals based on their own social and political agendas. So, let us begin with a recognition of the fact that a search for 'essential' definitions is an inherently fruitless task, because words have no essential meanings, and confine ourselves to the simply useful.[3] In short, let *us* define *our* terms.

First, under American law the crime of terrorism is currently defined as 'Premeditated, politically motivated violence perpetrated against non-combatant targets by subnational groups or clandestine agents, usually intended to influence an audience.'[4] After reviewing the academic literature on the subject, the RAND Corporation analyst Bruce Hoffman advocates that we define terrorism as 'The deliberate creation and exploitation of fear through violence or the threat of violence in the pursuit of political change'. Hoffman goes on, 'Terrorism is specifically designed to have far-reaching psychological effects beyond the immediate victim(s) or object of the terrorist attack'.[5] Both the legal and academic definitions emphasize that terrorism is a kind of violence intended to have wide-ranging psychological effects on an audience(s) observing its manifestations. For the purposes of illustration, one could do worse than note the emotions unleashed in the USA as the result of a handful of threatening letters containing anthrax spores in the fall of 2001.

Next, if terrorism is characteristically defined in terms of an activity, analysts typically regard democratization as a process happening at national level. This process begins with the internally or externally caused breakdown of an authoritarian regime, and passes through a transitional period to the possible, although not necessarily eventual, consolidation of democratic rule. Huntington puts it more succinctly than most. Democratization 'involves bringing about the end of the non-democratic regime, the inauguration of the democratic regime, and then the consolidation of the democratic regime.'[6] How do we know when the end of the line has been reached, a transition completed and a consolidated democracy achieved? Linz and Stepan make useful observations. In their view, democracy has been consolidated when widespread agreement has been reached about the procedures involved in choosing an elected government; when such a government comes to power as the consequence of free and open elections; and when this government – both *de jure* and *de facto* – formulates public policy and exercises control over the various institutions of the State.[7] We might add that this arrangement must, in a consolidated democracy, last over some time. Democracy itself refers to a situation where there is open 'contestation' among contending groups and individuals for public office and where all or most adults have the right to participate in the political process.[8]

Finally, 'globalization' seems an equally elusive term, one frequently employed as a catch-all for such developments as the rapid world-wide spread of AIDS, McDonalds, Sushi bars, democracy and/or the International Monetary Fund (IMF). Given the substantial heterogeneity of phenomena the concept has been stretched to cover, the best way of proceeding seems to be: to suggest, first, an overall definition; and then, second, to divide the notion into several constituent elements. The economist Joseph Stiglitz defines globalization as

> The closer integration of the countries and peoples of the world which has been brought about by the enormous reduction of costs of transportation and communication, and the breaking down of artificial barriers to the flows of goods, services, capital, knowledge ... and people across borders.[9]

The political scientist Joseph Nye suggests that globalization refers to 'world-wide networks of interdependence' which have come to prominence after the Cold War.[10] Neither Stiglitz nor Nye regard the phenomenon as completely beneficial. They call attention to its effects on widening gaps between rich and poor and on accelerating the pace of environmental degradation, for example.

Some observers regard the phenomenon as sufficiently complex to warrant referring to globalizations in the plural, not globalization in the singular.[11] Writers not only refer to the complexity of globalization(s); they also commonly stress that it is not a completely new development in human history. They note that there have been heightened interactions between different civilizations at different points in the past. Observers often mention the European voyages of discovery during the sixteenth and seventeenth centuries as an example. And Nye reports that economic globalization accelerated dramatically during the nineteenth century. He goes on to quote the *Communist Manifesto*: "'All old-established national industries have been destroyed or are being destroyed ... In place of the old local and national seclusion and self-sufficiency, we have intercourse in every direction, universal interdependence of nations'".[12]

This may be the case, but what does globalization(s) mean at the advent of the twenty-first century? First, the general direction of national level public policy in the post-Cold War world has been towards the Right and the triumph of capitalist ideas. Governments in most parts of the world have pursued policies of privatization and deregulation. State enterprises have been transformed into private corporations. Rules governing the conduct of business activity in general have been loosened.[13] If we consider the matter from an institutional perspective, such organizations as the IMF, World Bank, World Trade Organization (WTO), and various agencies of the United Nations have come to play increasingly significant roles. At the regional

level, the Commission of the European Union has become the principal vehicle for European-wide economic and political integration.
Non-Governmental Organizations (NGOs) – such as Médecins sans
Frontières (or 'Doctors without Borders'), Amnesty International, and
Green Peace – have undergone their own globalizing trends. Further,
and most clearly, multi-national corporations, many of them with
corporate headquarters in the USA, have often been the engines driving
the process.

Then there is the matter of culture. For some – for example, French
intellectuals or Islamist militants – the trend towards a globalized
culture is synonymous with Americanization. The power of the
American-dominated mass media is such that, *inter alia*, American pop
music, films, television shows, English-language idioms, computer
software and many forms of attire have become pervasive around the
globe. Illustratively, in his Pulitzer Prize winning volume, *From Beirut to
Jerusalem*, Thomas Friedman reports that at the height of the Lebanese
civil war during the 1980s the most widely viewed show on Beirut TV
was *Dallas*. Friedman recalls that he and a fellow reporter (from the
Dallas Morning News) were stopped one day in the Shouf Mountains by
Druze militiamen who demanded to know at gun point who had killed
J.R.?[14] Or, to put it somewhat differently:

> By far the most visible manifestations of the emerging global
> culture is in the vehicle of popular culture. It is propagated by
> business enterprises of all sorts ... Although control of these
> enterprises is exercised by elites, popular culture penetrates broad
> masses of people all over the world. The vast scope of this penetra-
> tion can hardly be overestimated.[15]

Whether or not the trends towards cultural globalization are indistin-
guishable from American influence remains open to question.
American popular culture itself is, after all, a mix of cultures from virtually all parts of the world. But the more general phenomenon, as
described by Peter Berger, seems hard to deny.

Now, having defined our terms, at least to some extent, the questions
become: What is the relationship(s) between terrorism, democracy and
globalization? How should we go about confirming, or denying for that
matter, the existence of such a linkage? The first procedure that comes
to mind is the investigation of the historical record. When we do this,
what do we find?

First, although the word itself derives from the French Revolution

(The Reign of Terror), the first wave of politically motivated terrorism in the Western world dates from the last third of the nineteenth century. As David Rapoport, Walter Laqueur and other writers note, modern terrorism appears in the Russian Empire during the 1870s and is committed by groups, notably the People's Will organization, committed to bringing an end to the tsarist autocracy and the appalling injustices associated with it.[16] It may have been initiated by Russian groups but the philosophy of the bomb was adopted elsewhere by other organizations with different goals. By the end of the nineteenth century many European countries, as well as some countries of the Americas, had experienced what the Italian revolutionary Carlo Pisacane labelled 'Propaganda by Deed'. Anarchist circles and individual anarchists had assassinated or attempted to assassinate a long list of prominent figures – monarchs, presidents, prime ministers, police officials, powerful businessmen – who were targeted in the hope that their deaths might ignite popular revolutionary fervour and bring about the disintegration of the oppressive Capitalist State. At approximately the same time that anarchists were using the bomb and the gun towards this objective, nationalist groups began employing the same tools to further their objectives. Irish Dynamiters waged a terrorist campaign to detach Ireland from the UK. Their most spectacular achievement was the Phoenix Park (Dublin) murders in 1881. In addition, groups – for example, The Armenian Revolutionary Federation (ARF) and the Inner Macedonian Revolutionary Organization (IMRO) – seeking to win independence for Armenian and Macedonian populations from the Ottoman Empire used terrorism, as did Polish socialists attempting to separate their homeland from the Russian Empire.

Second, according to Samuel Huntington's well-known account, the world's first wave of democratization occurred over an extended period, from 1828 to 1926, as some 33 countries underwent the transition to popular government. In the majority of cases where democracy achieved consolidation, the countries underwent the changes gradually during the nineteenth century. Huntington mentions Australia, Canada, Finland, Iceland, Ireland, New Zealand, Sweden, Switzerland, UK, USA and Chile. 'The first wave had its roots in the American and French revolutions. The actual emergence of national democratic institutions, however, is a nineteenth-century phenomenon.'[17] Cases where the transition to democracy took place shortly before or in the aftermath of the First World War tended not to take, as the breakdown of democracy and rise in fascism in Italy, Germany and the various European successor states illustrate.[18]

The third subject of our inquiry, globalization, also appears to have reached a high point during the second half of the nineteenth century as Europe became what Norman Davies has labelled, 'The powerhouse of the world'.[19] European ideas, languages, cultural expressions, and forms of economic, military and political organization came to dominate much of the world. This dominance was achieved to a large extent through imperial conquest, with the British and French taking the lead. In any case, as noted in *The Economist*'s 1997 world economic survey, 'the world was more closely integrated before 1914 than it is now; in some cases much more so'.[20] That is, what we have come to call globalization was an exceptionally powerful integrative force in the world at approximately the same time as the first wave of democratization was underway, and when some countries were also the sites of terrorist violence: the 'era of the attempts', or what Rapoport defines as the first wave of modern terrorism.

In saying that terrorism, democratization and globalization were significant forces at work in the world at roughly the same time, during the latter half of the nineteenth century and in the years leading up to the First World War, we raise interesting questions of causality. The fact that events, or even complex sequences of events, occur simultaneously does not necessarily mean they are related to one another in a causal sense. Social scientists warn each other frequently that 'correlation is not causation', and note the fact that there was at one time a strong association in rural Sweden between the number of storks per acre and the birth rate – which however does not mean that the birds somehow delivered babies.[21] So, in the particular instance we confront at present, it is entirely possible that the three developments were unrelated to each other. The historical record, however, suggests this was not the case and that a linkage did exist.

It seems unlikely that nineteenth century terrorism – largely meaning assassination campaigns directed at economic and political notables – caused democratization and globalization to gather momentum. In most instances, although one could make a different case regarding tsarist Russia, ideas about national self-determination, mass participation in political life, estimates of the inherent potential of small clandestine bands to shape history, and theories of racial supremacy and social justice played a role in setting the conditions necessary, though hardly sufficient, for the initiation of terrorist violence.[22] The circulation of these ideas via enhanced means of mass communication and travel, along with elevated rates of literacy and the invention of dynamite, also appear to have made significant contributions. In short, the first wave of modern terrorism appears to have been an outgrowth of changes unleashed by the first wave of democratization and the trend towards globalism stimulated by European imperial expansion.

If that was the case then, what is the case now? We intend to investigate the contemporary relationship(s) or potential relationship(s) between terrorism, democratization and globalization by transforming each of these subjects into variables amenable to statistical analysis of a relatively simple straightforward kind. In measuring terrorism we employed data covering international terrorist events between 1990 and 1997. (These data were derived from the RAND-St Andrews Chronology of International Terrorism, the US Department of State's Patterns of Global Terrorism and the international terrorist event database ITERATE III.[23]) Events were coded, based on the nationality of the perpetrator, the country in which the event took place and the nationality of the victim(s). Next, we used the A.T. Kearney/Foreign Policy™ composite Globalization index and coded 62 countries based on their rankings on this measure: the degree of their globalization.[24] We coded countries not ranked by the index as 'not globalized'.[25] The countries so coded were sub-divided into fifths, from most globalized to least. The composite index itself includes indicators of technological development, political engagement, personal contacts, and economic integration.[26]

In dealing with the issue of democratization, we relied on Huntington's own classification based on three distinct waves. In other words, we classified countries based on whether they belonged to the first (1828–1926), second (1943–63) or third (1974–90) waves of democratization. We regarded any countries not listed under one of these three categories as undemocratic. Countries that began their transitions to democratic rule after 1990, notably those formerly part of the ex-Soviet Union, were coded as belonging to the latter category.[27]

Overall, our strategy was to treat the distribution of international terrorist events between 1990 and 1997 as a dependent variable and seek to understand how much this distribution (perpetrators, victims and venue) varied with the countries' globalism ranking and the recency of its democratic transition. Given the historical experiences we described earlier, we might hypothesize that recent international terrorism would be positively related to high levels of globalization and recent experiences with democratization. Do our data confirm our suspicions?

RESULTS

Table 5.1 presents Spearman Rank Correlations among the six variables in our analysis. The first three are measures of globalization rank of the perpetrator, the victim, and the locale of each terroristic event; and the next three are the measures of wave of democracy: first, second or third, as described by Huntington.[28]

The most obvious thing to note in this table is the direction of the statistics; in all but two instances, they are positive; and in all but one case (0.03), they are moderate (0.10–0.30) to large (0.31–0.50) in size. What this indicates is that the rank of the perpetrator, victim and venue of the event are related to each other. Substantively this can be interpreted to mean that there is a direct relationship between the wave or level of globalization from which the perpetrator or victim come, and the place in which the event takes place. Put differently, *if* a person is in a first-wave country, it is more likely than not that *if* s/he is the victim of an act of international political violence/terrorism *then* the attack is most likely to come from someone from another first-wave country and to be carried out in a first-wave, highly globalized country. Similarly, one would also expect to find persons in the least-democratized, least- globalized nations attacking each other and being the victims of each others' attacks.

This interpretation was corroborated by further systematic analysis of the data which revealed the following.[29] First, and most importantly, most of the events take place in the least-globalized and least-democratic countries and are inflicted on individuals from those countries by those from similar nations. In the data, the largest cell count is in the 'not democratized/not democratized', 'non-

Table 5.1. Relationship between Waves of Democratization and Level of Globalization

	*perp rank**	*vct trank*	*evnt rank*	*perp wave*	*vct wave*	*evnt wave*
perp rank	1.0	0.03[†]	0.38	0.42	–0.13	0.15
vct trank		1.0	0.39	–0.10	0.29	0.13
evnt rank			1.0	0.16	0.16	0.45
perp wave				1.0	0.12	0.43
vct wave					1.0	0.32
evnt wave						1.0

★ Variable labels are: perp rank = the globalization rank of the country of the perpetrator; vct rank = the globalization rank of the victim; evnt rank = the globalization rank of the country in which the event took place; perp wave = the Huntington wave of democratization of the perpetrator's country; vctm wave = the victim's country's wave; and evnt wave = the wave of the county in which the event took place.
[†] All correlations are significant at the p < 0.001 level.

globalized/non-globalized' or 'not democratized/non-globalized' cell, and in the 'non-globalized' and 'not democratized' column or row. It is beyond dispute that most of the post-1990 activity takes place in these countries.

Next, when we search for systematic sources of variation, we find them first in three locations among the non/globalized – not democratized nations, then among the first- and second-wave democracies and the upper two-fifths of the globalized world. In short, the majority of international terrorist activities takes place in the extremes of the world: the least well-connected and democratized, and the most-connected and democratized. The third pattern that draws our attention is found among the first and second wave and the upper two fifths of the globalized world; also in the fifth and non-globalized and non-democratic perpetrators, victims and locales. It is in this area that the third source of variation is found. Here it seems that these events are carried out by those from non-globalized societies against largely second-wave, and then first-wave, democracies.[30]

Finally, there is a clear tendency for the majority of the deviation to lie on the major diagonal of the tables.[31] We systematically find that the residuals in the cells constituting the major diagonal tend to be positive and large. This means there are a greater than expected number of events in these levels of the variables. Substantively, this means that the international political terrorism and violence encompassed by these variables is more prone to be restricted within each category than not. In short, first-wave perpetrators attack first/fifth victims in first-wave democracies and first/fifth globalized countries; and so on, throughout the tables. The only exception to this is the least globalized attacking the most democratic.

To coin a phrase, we call this stratified terrorism. It seems, in the post-1990 era, that international political terrorism is carried out among those countries which are most like each other, and less likely to be carried out among countries and people who are less alike. Terrorism is confined to its own neighborhood. This finding, if borne out by additional research, may have important implications in understanding why, in the post-1990 world, international terrorism exists, and where to find it.

CONCLUSIONS

Such evidence as we have been able to assemble does not support the hypothesized links either between international terrorism and globalization or between the violence and the process of democratization. For reasons that remain hidden, at least to us, the convergence of terrorism, globalism and democratization at the end of the nineteenth century is not repeated at the end of the twentieth. In fact, the preponderance of the evidence suggests something quite different. First, during most of the 1990s, international terrorist attacks tended to be carried out by individuals from the world's least-globalized countries against targets (that is, persons or property) that fall into the same category and located in the same non-globalized type of country. An argument to the effect that international terrorist attacks represent a kind of backlash against globalization carried out either by groups from the least globalized parts of the world – for example, as a reaction against exploitation at the hands of multinational corporations, or by groups drawn from the most-globalized regions seeking, for example, to reverse the process of environmental degradation – is not supported by the analysis of the data at our disposal. This dynamic may be at work in approximately a quarter of the cases (see above), but the central tendency points in a different direction.

We need to introduce an obvious qualification. Since our collection of international terrorist events extends only up until 1997, most terrorist attacks carried out, for example, by groups linked to the al-Qa'eda network and directed against American and other highly globalized targets are not included in our calculations. On the other hand, if we glance at the US Department of State's *Patterns of Global Terrorism 2001*, it still appears even in the year of 9/11 that a substantial proportion of 'significant' terrorist incidents occurred in such low globalization countries as Yemen, Angola, Bangladesh, Burundi and Somalia; and, except for Greece and Spain, the highly globalized countries of the European Union are missing from the list.[32] Some observers have argued that the Department of State's chronologies are biased, in the sense that they over-report attacks against Americans and other westerners. But, in this case, if there is a bias, it appears to run in the opposite direction from the one these observers would have predicted.

Next, there is a body of literature that links the process of democratization to high levels of domestic political violence; civil wars especially.[33] Such conflicts decline as democracies achieve consolidation. The transition process takes place during a time of great uncertainty where the new 'rules of the game' are poorly understood or not accepted by many players. This logic may apply to high-intensity domestic conflicts but it does not fit the case with which we are concerned. If we are willing to regard the countries included in Huntington's list of third-wave democracies (1975–90) as undergoing the process of transition, then democratization and international terrorism are largely unrelated. Instead it is countries at opposite ends of the spectrum that proved most susceptible to this particular type of violence. The 'non-democracies' of the Middle East, North and Sub-Saharan Africa and elsewhere have been the venues for many international terrorist incidents, often events involving attacks by perpetrators on targets from the same countries. At the other end of the spectrum, democratic consolidation hardly poses a barrier to international terrorism: far from it. India, the world's largest democracy, has been exceptionally vulnerable to this type of violence. But it was hardly alone. After the attacks of 11 September, the USA has made the goal of defeating international terrorist groups its highest national priority. It has been observed to the point of becoming a cliché that free societies, where the rule of law prevails and people are able to come and go as they please, are vulnerable to international terrorist activity. Illustratively, in August 2001, literally millions of people entered and exited the USA with the application of, at best, modest border control procedures. We should also consider the fact that consolidated democracies are frequently the venues for a kind of émigré terrorism, as groups or agents from third countries carry out attacks on fellow nationals on the territory of an established democracy. We should not forget, however, that in the case of émigré terrorism we are dealing with situations in which both the perpetrators and victims of the violence frequently come from 'non-democracies'.

We conclude with an over-worked phrase; our findings appear 'counter-intuitive'. It makes sense to believe, particularly in light of the nineteenth-century developments, that international terrorism should go together with the forces unleashed by the social and economic changes of democratization and globalization. However, within the limits imposed by our data collection, these predicted interactions do not appear to fit the flow of events at the end of the twentieth century. Of course, the interactions may exist in the hypothesized ways. Our analysis may not have been sufficiently subtle to detect them or the data employed may not have been up to the tasks we assigned them. But to the extent that we were able to measure the relationships between terrorism and the massive trends towards democratization and globalization, they are much weaker or, perhaps, more complicated than we expected.

NOTES

1. The Graduate School of the University of Nevada provided support for the construction of

the data set which serves as the basis of the analysis presented in this paper. David Roland and Petra Plajbes contributed to building this data set. Kristen Kabrin assisted in the completion of the text. We are grateful to all for their assistance.

2. Illustratively, when we searched by subject in our university's library catalogue for works on these topics we discovered 1,126 references to books about globalization, 1,228 devoted to terrorism and 578 to democratization.

3. See, for example, William Connolly, *The Terms of Political Discourse* (Lexington, MA: DC Heath, 1974), pp. 10–41.

4. Title 22 of the United States Code, Section 2656f(d).

5. Bruce Hoffman, *Inside Terrorism* (London: Victor Gollancz, 1998), pp. 43–4. For a review of some 109 separate academic attempts at definition, see Alex Schmid and Albert Jongman, *Political Terrorism* (New Brunswick, NJ: Transaction Books, 1988), pp. 1–38.

6. Samuel Huntington, *The Third Wave* (Norman, OK: University of Oklahoma Press, 1991), p. 9.

7. Juan Linz and Alfred Stepan, *Problems of Democratic Transition and Consolidation* (Baltimore, MD: The Johns Hopkins University Press, 1996), p. 3.

8. See, for example, Robert Dahl, *On Democracy* (New Haven, CT: Yale University Press, 1998), pp. 37–8.

9. Joseph Stiglitz, *Globalization and its Discontents* (New York: W.W. Norton, 2002), p. 9.

10. Joseph Nye Jr, *The Paradox of American Power* (New York: Oxford University Press, 2002), p. 81.

11. See, for example, the various perspectives in Peter Berger and Samuel Huntington (eds), *Many Globalizations* (New York: Oxford University Press, 2002).

12. Nye Jr, *The Paradox of American Power*, p. 78.

13. See, for example, Theodore Lowi, 'Think Globally, Lose Locally', *Globalization, Governance and Identity* (Montreal: Les Presses de l'université de Montréal, 2000), pp. 20–31.

14. Thomas Friedman, *From Beirut to Jerusalem* (New York: Farrar Strauss Giroux, 1989), p. 219. J.R. was a major character in this vastly popular American-made TV series.

15. Peter Berger, 'Introduction', in Berger and Huntington, *Many Globalizations*, p.4.

16. David Rapoport, 'Modern Terrorism: The Four Waves', Paper prepared at the Santander Conference, July 2002, pp. 4–7; Walter Laqueur, *Terrorism* (Boston, MA: Little, Brown and Company, 1977), pp. 11–18.

17. Huntington, *The Third Wave*, p. 16.

18. See, for example, Juan Linz, *The Breakdown of Democratic Regimes* (Baltimore, MD: The Johns Hopkins University Press, 1978), pp. 75–86.

19. Norman Davies, *Europe: A History* (New York: Oxford University Press, 1996), pp. 759–896.

20. Quoted in Lowi, 'Think Globally, Lose Locally', p.17.

21. For a discussion, see Gary King, Robert Keohane and Sidney Verba, *Designing Social Inquiry* (Princeton, NJ: Princeton University Press, 1994), pp. 75–6.

22. See, for example, Martin Miller, 'The Intellectual Origins of Modern Terrorism in Europe', in Martha Crenshaw (ed.), *Terrorism in Context* (University Park, PA: Pennsylvania State University Press, 1995), pp. 27–62.

23. There are differences between the types of events recorded in each data set, the major one being the total number of events recorded in the Iterate set compared to the State Department of RAND-St Andrews Chronology. We compared these data sets to each other in a separate analysis, to determine if there was a bias between them. The results indicated that, beyond a difference in the number of events, there are no differences among the data sets. Each set yielded results virtually identical to those described below, and complimentary to the conclusions reached here.

24. No author, 'Globalization's Last Hurrah?', *Foreign Policy*, 128 (January/February 2002), pp. 38–51. The original measure is found in 'Measuring Globalization', *Foreign Policy*, 122 (January/February 2001), pp. 56–64.

25. The effect of this is to constrain the variance in the measure accounted for by the remaining countries (nearly 100) into one category. Should the countries in the category 'not globalized' subsequently be ranked, the magnitude of the correlation will change.

26. Technology includes: number of internet users, internet hosts and secure servers. Political Engagement includes: number of memberships in international organizations, UN Security Council missions participated in, and number of foreign missions in the country. Personal Contact includes: international travel and tourism, international telephone traffic and cross-

border transfers. Economic Integration includes: trade, foreign direct investment and portfolio capital flow, income payment and receipts. See *Foreign Policy*, 128 (January/February 2002), p. 40.

27. Huntington, *The Third Wave*, pp. 16–30.
28. In all cases, the statistic is significant beyond the $p < 0.001$ level. This is due to the size of the N, which is generally greater than 2,200. Spearman's measure is of the correlation among the rank of observations, pair-wise. We selected this measure because, unlike say gamma or the measures from the tau family, all observations, including ties, are used. This becomes an important feature in the analysis that follows.
29. An appendix of 14 tables which detail this additional analysis is available on request from the authors.
30. These tend to be the most-globalized countries, but it is important to keep in mind that there are less-globalized nations, and victims and perpetrators arising among first- and second-wave democracies. Also there is comparatively no terrorism carried out by third-wave perpetrators or on third-wave victims and in third-wave countries. Violence is confined to the oldest democracies or to the non-democracies circa 1990.
31. The major diagonal, or cells 1,1 2,2 3,3 4,4 of a 4 x 4 table, in any table, is directly analogous to the regression line. In a table with independent variables, we would expect no residual in any cell, and a zero correlation and slope. In a table with systematically large and positive residuals along the major diagonal we would expect moderate to large correlations and slopes. This would indicate a non-zero relationship.
32. US Department of State, *Patterns of Global Terrorism 2001* (Washington, DC: US Department of State), pp. 69–84. To be fair, India, which ranks high on the globalization index, is the most common country site of terrorist incidents.
33. See, for example, Havard Hegre, Tanja Ellingsen, Scott Gates *et al.*, 'Toward a Democratic Civil Peace? Democracy, Political Change and Civil War, 1816–1992', *American Political Science Review*, 95/1 (March 2001), pp. 33–48; Jack Snyder, *From Voting to Violence* (New York : W.W. Norton & Company, 2000), pp. 15–43.

6

Terrorism and Knowledge Growth: A Databases and Internet Analysis

AVISHAG GORDON

INTRODUCTION

WHAT IS knowledge growth? In terms of scientific areas of study, knowledge growth refers to the number of items about the subject area which appear in databases of books, articles and journals. Knowledge growth thus provides a reflection of the state of the art of any scientific discipline and it has a direct bearing on the evolution and formation of a scientific discipline. Garvey enumerates several changes that are taking place in a scientific field following knowledge growth:

- Increased specialization and smaller subject-areas.
- Increased team research.
- Increased number of specialisms, which are developing out of the disciplinary boundaries, and between disciplines.[1]

The growth of knowledge in a scientific discipline reflects its developmental stage, its interdisciplinarity and the existence of different schools of thought and various approaches in this subject area. The fluctuations in knowledge growth in a discipline indicate changes occurring in the field: for example, a major breakthrough or a period of controversy. Accelerated literature growth in a field of study may indicate a higher level of interactions between researchers during a period of a major debate. Another indicator of a change is the lack of cited literature in a research field during a paradigm shift.

The growth of knowledge in a specialism is a cause of fragmentation of the field, and the creation of 'pocket specialism' which mark a period of creativity and innovation in the specific field of study. This fragmentation channels the research into different directions, thus bringing about additional growth in the number of books, articles, journals and documents published in the area.[2] The same growth could bring about an increased consolidation and synthesis in the field.

The debate on the question of whether terrorism could become a discipline in the near future, or not, is also related to its knowledge growth. The increasing number of different types of published material about terrorism calls for more co-ordination and control of this growth. Thus, providing co-ordination and control is actually the function of a discipline which establishes the publication channels for the dissemination of research results and furnishes the researchers with their own body of knowledge and problems.

The growth of scientific knowledge is sometimes analogous to the life cycle of a living organism.[3] Scientific knowledge as it grows becomes more and more fragmented into specialism, bringing together pieces of knowledge previously isolated from the mainstream of the literature. This process rejuvenates the field with more relationships which brings about more information and solutions to the field's research. With regard to the study of terrorism, in this process the changing definition of the term plays an important role, which actually signifies a new life cycle each time a new definition arises, since this new definition brings into the field new events, new realities and new research projects and analyses.

This chapter maintains that the growth of terrorism publications calls for a creation of a disciplinary framework within which the field boundaries could be delineated, and its literature co-ordinated and organized.

SENGUPTA'S LAW AND PERIODS OF RAPID KNOWLEDGE GROWTH

Sengupta's Law of Bibliometrics states that: 'During phases of rapid and vigorous growth of knowledge in a scientific discipline, articles of interest to that discipline appear in increasing number in periodicals distant from the field'.[4] Research on terrorism traditionally belongs to the social sciences. An indication of rapid growth in knowledge in this field is, therefore, the appearance of articles on the subject in disciplines remote from its original 'birthplace', for example in the periodicals *Life Science* and *Engineering*.

In the 1970s, there were six core journals which published material about terrorism, and all of them were in the Political Science and International Relations domains.[5] Yet, as time progressed, articles on terrorism began to appear in other areas. For example, in the mid-1990s a number of terrorism research papers started to appear in *Aviation Week and Space Technology*, which is an aeronautics journal. The number of articles about terrorism appearing in this journal during the period 1995–1998 grew by 80 per cent compared to the number of terrorism articles that appeared between 1988 and 1995.[6]

The growth of terrorism literature during the 1990s was also reflected in the Science, Technology and Medicine (STM) databases, which are remote from the traditional mainstream research on terrorism. This trend indicates an information overload and a spillover to both close and remote disciplines.

THE GROWTH OF THE LITERATURE ON TERRORISM

The growth of terrorism literature has been discussed in several studies.[7] The authors dealing with this issue generally judged that the literature in this field was dispersed and uncoordinated. Its spread, on the one hand, and the increase of the quantity of material published about terrorism, on the other, seemed to delay the formation and structuring of terrorism as a mature research discipline.

Figure 6.1 shows the relationship between the rise in international terrorism events and the growth of the literature in this subject area. Interestingly, the figure shows that the apex of terrorism occurrences (1984–88) is not the same as the peak years of the publication of monographs (1994–98) or the peak years of articles published about terrorism (1978–83). Although the trends illustrate the rate of knowledge growth on terrorism and the size of the growth of the phenomenon itself, the figure shows that the written output does not necessarily match the incidence of terrorism in the wider world. While the literature does appear to be steadily growing in volume, the figure suggests that the incidence of terrorist acts themselves has been declining. As a counter-balance to this trend, however, there is some evidence that the severity and the lethal nature of terrorism events has been increasing over the past two decades even while the number of events has been falling. In short, there have been fewer attacks, but these have been more vicious and deadly than those seen in the past.[8] The mortality rate from terrorism activities jumped by 81 per cent from 1995 to

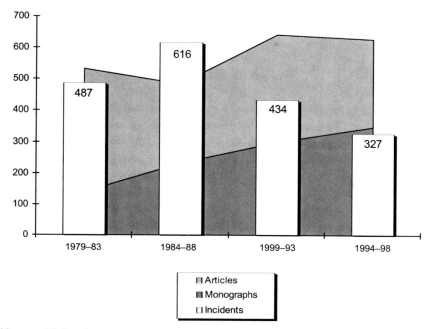

Articles
Monographs
Incidents

*Sources: US State Department 'Patterns of Global Terrorism'

Figure 6.1. Comparing the Level of International Terrorist Incidents with Publications on Terrorism (Monographs and Articles), 1979–98*

1996. As the 1990s progressed, it became more and more obvious that terrorists were targeting the public at large rather than the immediate victims.

While the literature on terrorism certainly appears to be growing fast, it nevertheless remains clear that it is still not being controlled or co-ordinated at an academic or professional level. Instead, at the heart of the burgeoning literature, there is a tiny core of specialist journals in the field among the core publications, surrounded by a miasma of many more journals on the periphery which publish literature in this subject area.

A model of a dispersed uncoordinated literature characterizes any young, immature research field.[9] The process of controlling and co-ordinating scientific literature is designed to link and integrate research work around common interest issues. It is also intended to reduce intel-lectual conflicts. The vast spread of terrorism literature is illustrative of a research field striving for academic recognition as a mature discipline, although it is not yet stable enough to be fully classified as a scientific research field. This chapter presents knowledge growth as a given, which is the reason why it is given prominent presentation as part of the introduction.

SOME ASSUMPTIONS

This chapter assumes that there is a greater growth in terrorism literature in comparison to other, more established, social sciences, and also a growth in terrorism literature in the STM disciplines. Another assumption is that this growth is reflected in the increasing number of definitions of terrorism over time. Each new type of violent action which is defined as terrorism adds new literature and research papers which makes it even harder to delineate the field's disciplinary boundaries. It was assumed that a relationship exists between knowledge growth in a discipline and its use of empirical research methods.[10] This hypothesis has to be checked, since, on its face value, most research on terrorism is qualitative and, at the same time, the amount of knowledge on terrorism is constantly increasing.

ERL databases were chosen for the present analysis since they divide the material indexed into two large time periods and their coverage goes back to the 1960s. These databases cover the STM areas as well as the social sciences, thus enabling the possibility of comparisons. The American National Criminal Justice Reference Service (NCJRS)[11] was also searched, as was the US Government Publication Office database (GPO).[12] The growth in the number of documents in these databases was recorded, and the unit of measurement was an article or a document indexed in a database (although reference was also made to reports from government and research institutions).

The ERL databases showed that even in the period immediately prior to the 11 September attacks, there was considerable growth in the number of papers being published on terrorism. This reflected the increasing prominence of terrorism material in fields that were originally far from the source of terrorism literature, that is, far from the discipline of the social sciences. The average growth rate across the databases observed was 58 per cent, with Medline in particular showing a massive increase of 82 per cent. This latter phenomenon is understandable in view of the growing interest in bio-terrorism and the literature about various post-trauma treatments in recent years.

Within the social sciences – a more traditional home for articles on terrorism – the growth over the past 40 years has also been considerable. Table 6.1 shows the average growth of the number of terrorism papers in a number of social science disciplines since 1987. Combined, the disciplines have seen an increase in terrorism articles of over 234 per cent. The fastest growing subject area has been 'Peace Studies', which is a relatively young research field whose literature in general has been growing at an accelerated rate. The 'Mass Communication' discipline also demonstrates impressive growth. This discipline has now been established within academia as an autonomous legitimate research and teaching field. The 'terrorism' research field follows, with 151 per cent growth from the end of the 1980s to 2001. 'Comparative Politics', however, shows a relatively moderate growth of 103 percent over the years, a rate which indicates that this subfield reached maturation long ago.

Table 6.1. Growth of Terrorism Literature in the Social Science Database*

Field	No. of records 1963–87	No. of records 1988–2001	Growth rate
Terrorism	312	784	151%
Mass Communication	434	2001	361%
Comparative Politics	122	247	103%
Peace Studies	7	81	1,057%
Education	93	129	39%
Economics	5	66	1,220%
Psychology	119	340	186%

*Source: Social Science Abstracts in the ERL Databases.

Ulrich's Guide to Periodical Literature, on disk or online, helps delineate the borderline of disciplines by identifying journals in the subject areas. This database was searched, as was the Journal Citation Reports (JCR) on the Web of Science. The JCR is an index of the most cited journals in each field, and therefore highlights the core of the published literature in many research fields. In the Ulrich's Guide and the JCR searches, the unit of measurement was a journal. Ulrich's Guide defines a terrorism journal according to the 24 criteria by which this database delineates subject areas. Some of these criteria are: the journal's own statement about its purpose and objectives; the journal's name, its editors and publisher; the Library of Congress (LC) and its Universal Decimal Classification (UDC), etc.

The Ulrich's Guide identified 42 journals as belonging to the terrorism research field. The first of these, *Veterans of Foreign Wars of the United States (VFW Magazine)*, started publication in 1912 and is still active today. The most recent journal, founded in 1999, is *Faultlines*, published by the Institute of Conflict Management in India. The JCR includes in its database only one of the 42 journals identified in the Ulrich's Guide

database as terrorism publications: *Kyklos,* which is a peripheral journal
in the terrorism research area.

Between 1910 and 1970 there were one or two terrorism journals
published per decade. In the first half of the 1970s, three new journals
appeared. From 1970 to 1975, three journals started publication; two of
which ceased to appear after a short time. Between 1975 and 1980, five
more journals started publication and four are still active. In the 1980s,
13 journals started publication and four ceased, leaving nine more active
journals. In the 1990s, 11 more terrorism periodicals appeared, and only
one ceased.

It is possible to observe a trend here, in which the 1970s formed the
'take off' years in terrorism scholarship, the 1980s followed this trend,
and the 1990s saw the stabilization of the growth of terrorism journals,
with 91 per cent of the publications inaugurated remaining active. This
model follows, to some extent, the 'S-Shape' Growth Curve Theory,
which states that as soon as the literature growth becomes very rapid, an
opposite trend starts, causing the death of the growth process (a kind of

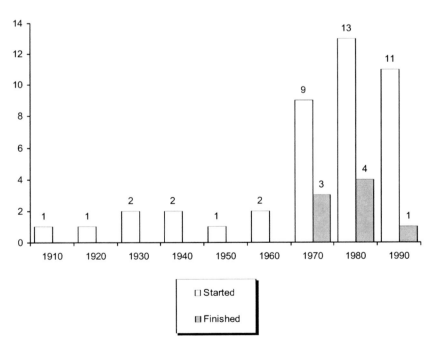

*Source: Ulrich's Guide to Periodical Literature.

Figure 6.2. Number of Terrorism-Related Journals in Circulation

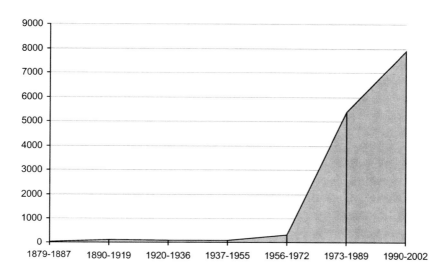

*Source: WorldCatalog Database.

Figure 6.3. The Growth in Terrorism Publications*

fall after saturation). The growth pattern here looks rather like an elongated letter 'S'.[13] This pattern was observed generally in the growth of terrorism literature as seen in Figure 6.3.

THE GROWTH IN THE NUMBER OF TERRORISM DEFINITIONS

How terrorism is defined has differed enormously between and among people, nations, cultures, and time periods. Even in a world post-11 September, where there is enormous pressure to try and reach more international agreement on the meaning of the term, there still remain significant differences in how the term is defined. For the scientific community, the growth in the number of definitions of terrorism can, however, be an indication of a growth of knowledge in the field and may represent developmental stages through which this field has passed. Each new definition adds new categories to the study of the terrorism, new research avenues and new perspectives, and all this contributes to the fragmentation and subdivision of the field of study on terrorism, and thus, to more literature dispersion and less control on knowledge growth.

A Sociological Abstract database search, using the key words 'terrorism and definition', yielded five records during the coverage years of

1963–85, and 23 records during the period 1986–2001. In 1988, Schmid and Jongman found 109 definitions of terrorism while collecting material for their monumental book, *Political Terrorism*.[14] Another search, this one of the NCJRS in 2001, retrieved 311 documents dealing with the definition of terrorism. Reid mentioned that the CIA defines terrorism anew each time a new president is elected.

A search of the Dissertation Abstracts online (UMI) found 20 theses dealing with the definition of terrorism; and the World Catalogue in the 2000s indexed nine books in German, French and English (published during 1973–97) dealing with the issue of defining terrorism. A number of researchers thought that building a typology of terrorism would make the process of formulating a definition of terrorism easier.[15] Several attempts were made, with some success, to define terrorism from a legal standpoint.[16] On the other hand, researchers who deal with terrorism from the legislative angle found that its definition was not judicially clear and unambiguous, probably because there were too many political considerations.

It is clear, therefore, that the growth in terrorism activities, as well as in the literature published about it, is reflected in an increasing number of definitions of this phenomenon. The constantly changing definition of terrorism, however, makes it difficult to delineate this subject area and initiate research into its events and trends.[17]

The attempts to 'understand' motivations for the terrorists' activities do not help define this phenomenon, since the history of terrorism shows that these have changed over time from political to economic, and, more recently, to religious motivations. These changes in justifications enlarge the support-base of terrorism from regional to global advocacy. They also increase the severity of terrorist actions, which are now backed by religious convictions and justifications.[18]

KNOWLEDGE GROWTH AND RESEARCH METHODS

Several researchers have suggested that a relationship exists between the commitment of an academic subfield to empirical research methods and faster knowledge growth within this subfield.[19] It was also observed that a definite research approach in a field has a direct impact on knowledge growth.[20] In short, the use of more rigorous methods has been associated with an increase in the quantity of research output.

Chapter Three in this volume has already raised the issue that the research methods being used to study terrorism appear to be inadequate.

The point was made that the use of statistics in terrorism-related research was relatively uncommon and, indeed, was used far less than in other academic disciplines. Table 6.2 below certainly supports the view that statistics are used very infrequently in terrorism research. Compared to six other fields, terrorism clearly uses statistics the least. Table 6.2 includes both of the fields considered in the assessment in Chapter Three (criminology and forensic psychology) and also incorporates an assessment of terrorism, mass communication, comparative politics and peace studies. The literature growth rate of all six areas was matched against the use of statistics in the period running from 1992 to 1998.

The table shows, however, that there was no clear relationship between the use of statistics used in a subfield and the knowledge growth of this subfield (the Spearman's rho rank order correlation showed negligible positive relationship of $r=0.086$). The findings then suggest that the very low percentage of statistical studies in terrorism has not seemed to delay the growth in terrorism literature. By comparison, the extensive use of statistics in criminology does not seem to have accelerated its literature growth. Of course, the major problem with this assessment – and indeed with considerations of 'knowledge growth' as defined in this chapter – is that it is essentially a measure of quantity. It is very clear that a great deal continues to be written about terrorism. What is not clear is whether the quality of this material is improving in any significant manner.

Nevertheless, the picture emerging is definitely one of the scientific communities showing a growing and wider interest in terrorism in recent decades. This was a trend already well in place before 11 September 2001 and one suspects that interest will only be heightened further in the aftermath of these attacks. An indication of the wider interest in terrorism can be seen in the range of periodicals which now include articles on the subject. The spread pattern of terrorism publications in the 1990s identified two core journals in the field of terrorism: *Terrorism and Political Violence* and *Studies in Conflict and Terrorism*. The rest of the published material about terrorism is scattered among other journals in which terrorism is only one of several topics covered. The terrorism material, which follows the growth dynamics of this field, appears in several forms:

- Many non-terrorism journals publish about this phenomenon only occasionally.
- Articles and research papers appear in specific (though not necessarily academic) journals, such as *The Economist*, whose main interest is

Table 6.2. Knowledge Growth and the Use of Statistics

Field	Knowledge growth★	Rank	Statistics†	Rank
Terrorism	151%	5	8.4%	6
Mass Communication	361%	2	32.5%	3
Comparative Politics	103%	6	31%	4
Peace Studies	1,057%	1	26.2%	5
Criminology★	206%	4	86%	1
Forensic Psychology★	269%	3	60%	2

★ As recorded in ERL databases 1966/87–2001.
† Percentage of articles which used statistics in two core journals in each field during the 1990s.

economy, but which frequently, and consistently, covers terrorism issues.

- Several academic journals in various disciplines have dedicated a whole issue to terrorism. *Current History,* for instance, devoted 99/636 (2000) to various aspects of terrorism, such as biochemical terrorism, nuclear terrorism, religious terrorism, counterterrorism, the role of the press in terrorism events, and cyber-terrorism. The other issues published that year did not deal with terrorism at all.
- Finally, there are also peripheral journals, such as *Aviation Week* and *Space Technology*, which react to certain terrorist events by reporting about technological counterterrorism devices entering the market. Similarly, tourism journals react to the harm caused to tourism by terrorism.

In sum, there is a small core of terrorism journals, and a large spread of terrorism literature in peripheral journals. The development of computerized databases has increased exposure to material about terrorism, and this has now infiltrated into STM fields, thus increasing the interdisciplinarity of this subfield.

Although the unit of measurement of this study is a journal article, it is important to also observe the growth of other kinds of terrorism literature. This creates a more complete picture of knowledge growth and information flow in this subject area. For example, Table 6.3 illustrates the growth of government reports and monographs on terrorism. In a by now familiar pattern, the table shows an accelerated growth of monographs during the period measured and a considerable growth in government documents about terrorism in a subject-bound government database – NCJRS – which reports on crime, violence and legislation connected with these issues. The GPO, which is a general database for all kinds of government documents, showed only a moderate knowledge growth during the period measured (1980–2001).

Table 6.3. The Growth of Terrorism Monographs and Government Reports in Online Databases, 1980–2001

Period/Database	1980–91	1992–2001	Growth rate
GPO	234	285	21.8%
NCJRS	394	642	62.9%
Books in print	497	892	79.5%

DISCUSSION

Terrorism literature has grown rapidly since the 1970s, especially in the social sciences. Following Sengupta's Law, material about terrorism has infiltrated distant disciplines in the life sciences and technology. The introduction of computerized databases and the accessibility data on the Internet accelerated this process, allowing researchers to become exposed to already existing information that was not previously available.

The variety and multitude of material published about terrorism has created 'pocket specialities' in this research field, such as 'law and terrorism' and 'media and terrorism'. The growth of data about terrorism has found a circulation outlet in the form of scientific and popular articles, books, government reports, conference proceedings and online articles.

The peak years of terrorism events, according to information accumulated by the US Department of State in its database 'Patterns of Global Terrorism', were 1984–88. Yet the peak years so far for the growth of monographs about terrorism have been 1994–98; while the period from 1979 to 1984 was the apex for articles published in this subject area.

It is possible that the growth in terrorism literature was influenced to some extent by the dynamics of terrorism events, even though the peak years of the frequency of the events and of the number of publications do not coincide. It is safer to assume that this growth was due to several factors, such as the growth in R & D investment, and the growth in the number of scientists who study terrorism.[21]

The results show a positive, although negligible, relationship between knowledge growth and the research methods used by researchers coming from different fields. The fact that terrorism researchers publish mostly qualitative material has not stood in the way of knowledge growth in this field. The number of terrorism definitions, however, was affected by the growing amount of material published in this subject area, on the one hand, and the spread of terrorism, its changing form, and the infiltration of this phenomenon into many aspects of our lives, on the other.

The literature of terrorism is still comprised of dispersed and uncoordinated publications, which lack the control of a highly developed research field. There is no clear-cut distinction between popular and scientific studies in this field. The model of the published literature is that of a very small core and a very large periphery, which characterizes a young research field that has not yet reached the status of an established research discipline. Nevertheless, the rapid growth of knowledge in this area indicates that terrorism is a vital research field. With some control and coordination of its literature, it can develop into a mature, stable scientific discipline.

What then are the future directions of terrorism studies as a discipline? The growing amount of terrorism publications, popular, semi-academic and academic, should allow it to become an academic discipline. The potential is certainly there, if its literature can be better organized and controlled, and if the university authorities can provide financial support for such a development and allocate the necessary resources for this process.

The establishment of academic departments for terrorism studies within the university sector would be an important milestone for the delineation of the field's boundaries. If realized, such a development could integrate the research community's interests around key issues on terrorism, and could do much to minimize unnecessary intellectual conflicts which have been so prominent in recent decades.

It is also possible that the current subject of terrorism could become a discipline as a result of a pressure from below: either from a social movement, or as a result of impetus from a spectacular event. 11 September certainly provides a candidate for the latter, though it remains to be seen what lasting impact the attacks against New York and Washington will have in this regard. It is also possible – if not likely – that change may come about as a result of a pressure from above: namely, from the university authorities.

Ultimately, there are several factors which could accelerate the evolution and emergence of terrorism as an academic discipline:

- First, as already indicated, the destructive attacks of 11 September have profoundly changed perceptions of the scope, significance and direction of terrorism, and has added an important dimension to the research that followed this event.
- Even prior to 11 September, knowledge in this subject area was growing and there is no reason to expect this trend will change.
- This field was already fragmented into pocket specialisms even

before its literature was co-ordinated and organized in some respects. As a result, the growth of knowledge in this field has become even more emphatic.

• There exists a core of terrorism researchers whose main interest is to do more research on the field and to push even further the idea of terrorism as an autonomous discipline.
• The Ulrich's Guide identified a body of 42 terrorism journals, and this is a solid knowledge-base that can serve an evolving new discipline.

Only time will tell if the field can develop sufficient strength and coherency to make the leap. One suspects that if the transition is not made in the coming decade, it may not again find a more favourable time to do so.

NOTES

1. W.D. Garvey, *Communication: The Essence of Science* (New York, Oxford: Pergamon Press, 1979).
2. H. Small and E. Greenlee, 'Citation Study of Aids Research', in C.L. Borgman (ed.), *Scholarly Communication and Bibliometrics* (Newberry Park CA: Sage, 1990), pp. 166–93.
3. D.R. Swanson, 'Intervening in the Life Cycle of Scientific Knowledge', *Library Trends*, 41/4 (1993), pp. 606–31.
4. I.N. Sengupta, 'The New Parameters of Bibliometric Research and their Application to Research Periodicals in the Field of Biochemistry', *Scientometrics*, 10 (1986), pp. 235–42.
5. E. Reid, 'An Analysis of Terrorism Literature: A Bibliometric and Content Analysis Study', PhD dissertation, University of Southern California, Los Angeles, 1983.
6. Avishag Gordon, 'The Spread of Terrorism Publication: A Database Analysis', *Terrorism and Political Violence*, 10/4 (1998), pp. 190–93.
7. For example, see Avishag Gordon, 'Terrorism Dissertations and the Evolution of a Specialty: An Analysis of Meta-Information', *Terrorism and Political Violence*, 11/2 (1999), pp. 141–51; Ariel Merrari, 'Academic Research and Government Policy on Terrorism', *Terrorism and Political Violence*, 3/1 (1991), pp. 88–102; E. Reid, 'Terrorism Research and the Diffusion of Ideas', *Knowledge Policy: International Journal of Knowledge Transfer and Utilization*, 6/1 (1993), pp. 17–37; E. Reid, 'Evolution of a Body of Knowledge: An Analysis of Terrorism Research', *Information Processing and Management*, 33/1 (1997), pp. 91–106; Alex Schmid and Albert Jongman, *Political Terrorism, A New Guide to Actors, Concepts, Databases, Theories, and Literature* (Amsterdam: SWIDOC, 1988); and Andrew Silke, 'The Devil You Know: Continuing Problems with Research on Terrorism', *Terrorism and Political Violence*, 13/4 (2001), pp. 1–14.
8. See Bruce Hoffman, *Inside Terrorism* (London: Victor Gollancz, 1998).
9. Gordon, 'The Spread of Terrorism Publication'.
10. J. R. Platt, 'Strong Inference', *Science*, 146/3642 (1964), pp. 347–53.
11. See http://www.ncjrs.org/ncjhome.htm
12. See www.access.gpo.gov
13. A.J. Meadows, *Communicating Research* (London: Academic Press, 1998).
14. Schmid and Jongman, *Political Terrorism*.
15. See Reid, *An Analysis of Terrorism Literature*; V.Y. Fedianin, 'The Problem of Creating a Universal Definition of Terrorism', *Moscow Journal of International Law*, 4/1 (1998), pp. 6–14; and B. Ganor, 'Defining Terrorism: Is One Man's Terrorist Another Man's Freedom Fighter?' Http://ict.org.il/articles/define, 19 March 2000.
16. See L.R. Beres, 'The Meaning of Terrorism Juriprudential and Definitial Classification', *Vanderbilt Journal of Transnational Law* (1995), pp. 239–49; and L.R. Beres, 'Terrorism, Law and Special Operations: Legal Meaning for the SOF Commander', *Special Warfare, Fort Brag*, 11/1

(1998), pp. 28–36.

17. Reid, 'Evolution of a Body of Knowledge'.

18. C. Dishman, 'Trends in Modern Terrorism', *Studies in Conflict and Terrorism*, 22 (1999), pp. 357–67.

19. Platt, 'Strong Influence'.

20. M.S. Stephenson, 'Research Methods Used in Subfields and the Growth of Published Literature about those Subfields: Vertebrate Paleontology and Geochemistry', *Journal of the American Society for Information Science (JASIS)*, 51/1 (1985), pp. 147–62.

21. M. Mabe and A. Mayur, 'Growth Dynamics of Scholarly and Scientific Journals', *Scientometrics*, 15/1 (2001), pp. 147–62.

7

What Do We Know About the Substitution Effect in Transnational Terrorism?

WALTER ENDERS AND TODD SANDLER

THE SUCCESS of the terrorist attacks on the World Trade Center and the Pentagon, on 11 September 2001 (henceforth, 9/11), has resulted in profound economic and social consequences for the United States. In addition to the loss of life and property, the total cost of the attacks is staggering. With the economy already on the brink of recession, the unemployment rate rose by almost one per cent.[1] Some sectors bore the brunt of the loss in business and consumer confidence. Wall Street closed for a week; on its re-opening, various stock market indices fell substantially and investment funds seemed to dry up. The airline industry was temporarily shut down, the tourism industry was especially hard hit, and several airlines never recovered. The opportunistic anthrax attacks that followed caused major disruptions of the mail.

The world-wide response to fighting terrorism has been equally dramatic. The US-led coalition known as 'Operation Enduring Freedom' quickly achieved its aim of eliminating the Taliban regime in Afghanistan. In total, 17 nations contributed more than 16,500 troops to the initial operation. Other efforts included the enhancement of airport security and directives from nearly 150 countries to freeze terrorist assets totaling at least $104.8 million.

Within the USA, President Bush created the Office of Homeland Security and the National Defense Authorization Act (S. 1438, 8

December 2001). This Act earmarked funds for extending the 'War on Terrorism', which includes countermeasures against potential biological and chemical attacks. Future years promise even greater anti-terrorism measures. President Bush's proposed budget for 2003 directs $37.7 billion to homeland security (an $18.2 billion increase over 2002). In particular, the budget proposal includes $11 billion for border security, $6 billion to defend against bioterrorism, $3.5 billion (a 1,000 per cent increase) for police, firefighters and Emergency Medical Teams, and $700 million to co-ordinate the anti-terrorism measures of the various government branches.

Undoubtedly, a massive anti-terrorist campaign will reduce the overall level of terrorism. Nevertheless, an important strategic question remains, since some anti-terrorism policies are apt to be more success-ful than others. As surveyed in this paper, economists and political scientists have investigated the effectiveness of alternative policy responses (for example, toughening punishments, retaliatory raids, installing technological barriers). Each anti-terrorism policy can influ-ence a terrorist group's choice of operations by either affecting their resources or the relative costliness of different kinds of attacks. Such policies can have an 'income effect' or 'substitution effect', or both. The income effect involves the overall level of available resources – for example, freezing terrorists' assets reduces their 'war chest' and their overall ability to conduct a campaign of terror. If a government action increases the resource outlays necessary to undertake a particular type of operation, then there is a motive to substitute into some less costly operation that achieves a similar outcome at less cost. For example, the installation of screening devices in US airports in January 1973 made skyjackings more difficult, thus encouraging terrorists to substitute into other kinds of hostage missions or to stage a skyjacking from an airport outside of the USA.

Unlike the two examples above, the income and substitution effects of an anti-terrorism policy are often interrelated. For example, the seizure of a cache of explosive devices has a clear income effect (since resources decline) and a substitution effect (since terrorists are less likely to stage incidents that rely on explosives). The essential point is that the overall effectiveness of any anti-terrorism policy depends on the direct *and* indirect effects that arise through various substitutions. The purpose of this chapter is to provide a careful examination of the terrorists' decision-making process, so as to understand and predict the likely responses.

TRANSNATIONAL TERRORISM

Since the events of 9/11, the popular press has run articles arguing over the precise meaning of 'terrorism'.[2] We define terrorism as the premeditated use, or threat of use, of extranormal violence to obtain a political objective through intimidation or fear directed at a large audience. An event, no matter how brutal, is not a terrorist incident unless it involves the presence of a political objective. Incidents that have no specific political motive are criminal rather than terrorist acts: a bar-room shooting is a criminal act, while the assassination of an ambassador to coerce political change is a terrorist act. Another fundamental ingredient in the definition is the creation of widespread intimidation or fear. Unlike warfare, where the aim is to destroy opposing combatants, terrorists also seek to affect those not immediately involved with the political decision-making process. The 9/11 attack on the World Trade Center clearly fits this pattern.

As part of the attempt to create a general climate of intimidation, terrorists strike at a variety of targets using attack modes ranging from skyjackings to simple threats and hoaxes. The mix of operations makes it difficult for the authorities to predict the nature and location of the next incident. From the perspective of the authorities, terrorist incidents appear to be random, so that society must expend relatively large amounts of resources to protect against all forms of potential attacks.

Most terrorist events directed against the USA do not occur on US soil. The kidnapping and murder of reporter David Pearl, in Pakistan; the destruction of the Al Khubar Towers housing US airmen in June 1996 near Dhahran, Saudi Arabia; and the bombs destroying the US embassies in Kenya and Tanzania in August 1998, are but three gruesome examples of *transnational* terrorism. Terrorism is transnational when an incident in one country involves perpetrators, victims, targets, institutions, governments, or citizens of another country. Obviously, the four skyjackings on 9/11 constitute transnational terrorist attacks since the events were staged by individuals who crossed into the USA from abroad and because victims came from many countries. However, the bombing of the Murrah Federal Building in Oklahoma City by Timothy McVeigh, in April 1995, was not a transnational terrorist incident.

From the late 1960s until the late 1980s, transnational terrorism was primarily motivated by nationalism, separatism, Marxist ideology, anti-racism, nihilism and the desire for economic equality.[3] In the 1990s, a driving motivation of terrorism changed with 'the emergence of either obscure, idiosyncratic millennium movements' or religion-based groups.[4] When religion provides the dominant objective of a group that employs terrorist tactics, it is identified as a religious terrorist group (for example, Hamas, Algerian Armed Islamic Group (GIA), Hezbollah, Egyptian Gamat al-Islamiya). Since the beginning of 1980, Bruce Hoffman reports that the number of religion-based groups has increased as a proportion of the active terrorist groups: 2 of 64 groups in 1980; 11 of 48 groups in 1992; 16 of 49 groups in 1994; and 25 of 58 groups in 1995.[5] This increase can be attributed to a growth of religious fundamentalism world-wide, the diffusion of the Islamic revolution from Iran, and the approach of the millennium. With this motivational change for some terrorists, both Hoffman[6] and Juergensmeyer[7] view the new generation of terrorists as posing a more deadly threat than earlier groups.

The demise of many leftist groups in the late 1980s and 1990s is attributable to at least three factors: (1) domestic efforts by some terrorism-prone countries (for example, France, Germany, Spain, the UK) to capture and to bring to justice group members; (2) reduced state sponsorship of left-wing groups by East European and Middle Eastern countries;[8] and (3) the reduced interest in Marxism following the collapse of many communist regimes. These factors were bolstered by collective initiatives by the European Union to foster co-operation in terms of extradition, shared intelligence and accreditation of foreign diplomats.[9] In recent years, NATO has also begun a programme to collectively address the risks posed by transnational terrorism.[10] Another recent development in terrorism has been the increase in 'splinter' groups which are less disciplined, often more violent, and more nebulous than the parent group.[11] The IRA splinter group responsible for the Omagh bombing in Northern Ireland on 15 August 1998 is a clear-cut example. They did not follow standard IRA procedures and issued a warning that herded people nearer to the subsequent blast. Some days later, the group apologized and suspended their bombing operations for almost two years. If members' actions are not constrained, then a few fanatical individuals can cause great carnage.

The greater prevalence of religious groups has apparently increased the lethality of post-Cold War terrorism, because such groups view civilians as legitimate targets of a 'decadent' society. Religious groups that declare a jihad, or holy war, against another nation consider its people, not just its officials, as the enemy. Moreover, religious terrorist groups act out of a desire to satisfy their own goals (for example, ascend to heaven) rather than to win favour with an external constituency. Violence may be viewed as a purifying act. Although it is tempting to attribute the increased casualties per incident, documented below, to better technology available to terrorists, most of the incidents have not really relied on new technologies. Old-fashioned bombs were used both in Oklahoma City and Nairobi, and against most other targets. The difference today is that these bombs are set to explode where and when maximum carnage will result.

THE CHOICE-THEORETIC MODEL OF TERRORISM

The choice-theoretic model of rational terrorists considers a terrorist group as choosing how to allocate scarce resources to maximize the expected value of its objective function. The model developed by William Landes considers a potential skyjacker contemplating the forcible diversion of a commercial aircraft for political purposes.[12] A simplified version of the Landes' model considers three states of the world: there is no skyjacking; the skyjacking is successful; and the skyjacking fails.

In order to highlight the risky nature of terrorism, we assume that utility in the no-skyjacking state is certain; if the terrorist decides not to attempt to undertake the skyjacking, utility is given by U^N. If, however, the skyjacking occurs, the outcome is uncertain. Expected utility can be represented by:

$$EU^{SKY} = \pi U^S + (1 - \Pi)U^F, \tag{1}$$

where EU^{SKY} = expected utility if there is a skyjacking

     π = skyjacker's subjective estimate of the probability of a successful skyjacking;

     $1 - \pi$ = skyjacker's subjective estimate of the probability of a failed skyjacking;

     U^S = utility if the skyjacking is successful;

     U^F = utility if the skyjacking fails.

The terrorist will attempt the skyjacking if the expected utility derived from undertaking the skyjacking exceeds the utility level U^N when there is no skyjacking:

$$U^N < EU^{SKY} = U^S + (1 - \pi)U^F. \tag{2}$$

Thus, anything that lowers U^N or raises EU^{SKY} increases the probability of a skyjacking.

Landes' model is useful for understanding the choice between legal and illegal terrorist activities. Given that utility from success exceeds utility from a failure [that is, $U^S > U^F$], it follows that an increase in the probability of a success will make it more likely that the skyjacking will occur. Formally, the change in expected utility from a skyjacking due to a change in π is:

$$dEU^{SKY} / d\pi = U^S - U^F > 0. \tag{3}$$

Hence, if the authorities undertake a policy (such as enhanced airport security) that reduces the probability of a successful skyjacking (lowering Π), the Landes' model predicts that the terrorists will be more likely to forego the skyjacking, owing to the associated reduction in EU^{SKY}. Policies that lower the utility from a skyjacking failure, such as longer jail sentences, also reduce the expected utility from skyjackings, thus decreasing the likelihood of such events. Moreover, policies that limit the utility from success, such as reduced media coverage, also reduces the number of skyjackings.

Although some Hamas and al-Qa'eda terrorists engage in suicide missions, the vast majority of terrorists do not resort to such attacks and respond predictably to security enhancements and other policy actions. Nevertheless, the model is capable of addressing suicide attacks. If a terrorist is concerned with living, then U^F is likely to be low, thereby inhibiting EU^{SKY} from exceeding U^N – the necessary requirement for an attack. A fanatical terrorist, who does not fear death and may welcome it, has a higher U^F, which makes an attack more likely in (2). Fanaticism brings U^F closer to U^S in (3); thus the policy effectiveness of lowering the success probability diminishes. If, for example, $U^F = U^S$ in (3), then efforts to lower π have no effect on EU^{SKY}. Consequently, policy becomes completely ineffective. Fanatical terrorists must be apprehended or killed for attacks to stop.

Landes presented two regressions for US skyjackings based on US Federal Aviation Administrative data on skyjackings for the 1961–66 period. The first regressed the quarterly total of skyjackings on the probability of apprehension, conviction, sentencing, and other policy efforts. The second regressed the time interval between skyjackings and the same set of variables. Both regressions found the length of sentence and the probability of apprehension to be significant deterrents. For most regressions, the probability of conviction was marginally significant. Landes also estimated that between 41 and 50 fewer skyjackings occurred in the USA from the start of 1973 following the installation of metal detectors in US airports.

More generally, substitutions can be analysed with a household production function (HPF) approach for which the utility of a terrorist group is a function of a shared political goal. The HPF model was first applied to transnational terrorism by Enders and Sandler in 1993.[13] Given transnational terrorist groups' budget constraints, this shared goal is produced from a number of *basic commodities* that may include both terrorist and non-terrorist activities. To be more specific, basic commodities may include political instability, media publicity, an atmosphere of fear, or extortion. Alternative terrorist attack modes can be substitutable if they produce the same basic commodities. Substitution possibilities are augmented when attack modes are logistically similar and yield the same basic commodities in nearly identical proportions. An assassination of a key public official or a skyjacking might be substitutes if they provide a terrorist group with similar amounts of media attention. Complementarity results when a *combination* of attack modes is required to produce one or more basic commodities, or when the success of one type of attack reinforces the effects of a second type of attack. For example, in the wake of 9/11, the anthrax mailings had an especially demoralizing (complementary) effect on a public already sensitized to terrorism.

The advantage of the HPF approach is that it allows for substitutions between legal and illegal activities *and* for substitutions within the set of illegal terrorist activities. Choices within the set of terrorist activities are many and include the intended lethality of the act, its country of location, and whom or what to target.[14] In each period, an overall resource constraint limits the terrorist group's expenditures to a magnitude not exceeding its monetary and non-monetary resource endowments. The expenditures on any activity consist of the product of the activity's level and its per-unit price. Each terrorist and non-terrorist tactic has a per-unit price that includes the value of time, the use of personnel, funding and capital equipment, including weapons. A skyjacking is a high-priced incident because it is logistically more complex to plan and execute and thus requires more resources than do many other types of incidents. At the other extreme, threats and hoaxes require few resources and are low-priced incidents. Nevertheless, such incidents can add to the overall level of fear and intimidation. The recipients of various powders disguised as anthrax felt the same initial fear and undertook the same precautions as did the recipients of the real thing.

In addition to such technological considerations, the prices terrorists pay for each tactic are influenced by anti-terrorism policies. If, for instance, the government were to secure its embassies or military bases, then attacks against such facilities would become more costly on a per-unit basis. If, moreover, the government were not at the same time to increase the security for embassy and military personnel when outside their facilities, then attacks directed at these individuals (for example, assassinations) would become relatively cheaper.

The HPF approach yields a number of important predictions concerning the substitution phenomenon. The critical result is that a government policy that increases the relative price of one type of terrorist tactic produces a substitution out of the now-more-costly tactic into those terrorist and non-terrorist activities whose prices are now relatively less costly. If, for example, embassies are fortified, then attacks against embassy personnel and property *within* the mission's ground become more costly for the terrorists – that is, there is a rise in the price of such attacks. Similarly, in choosing a venue, the price is anticipated to differ based on security measures taken by the authorities; therefore, a country with more porous borders will be the staging ground for attacks against targets from other, more secure, countries. A further prediction of the model is that complementary tactics would respond in a similar fashion to relative price changes. For example, assassinations and bombings tend to be substitutes, while bombings and threats are complementary. Thus, the model predicts that a policy that makes it more costly to obtain assault weapons (an important input in an assassination) will reduce the number of assassinations but increase the number of bombings and threats. In contrast, government interventions that raise the price of all terrorist tactics or that reduce terrorists' resources will cause non-terrorist activities to increase relative to terrorist actions. However, there is no reason to suppose that this type of policy will induce substitutions among the various attack models.

To be more formal, suppose that a group only uses two kinds of operations – hostage taking (h) and bombings (b). Further, suppose that the per-unit costs of each kind of operation are P_h and P_b for hostage taking and bombings, respectively. In general, these unit costs will depend on the level of operations and on the anti-terrorism expenditures of the authorities:

$$P_h = P_h(h, g_h) \, , \, \delta P_h/\delta h \geq 0 \text{ and } \delta P_h/\delta g_h \geq 0, \tag{4}$$

$$P_b = P_b(b, g_b) \, , \, \delta P_b/\delta h \geq 0 \text{ and } \delta P_b/\delta g_b \geq 0, \tag{5}$$

where g_h and g_b are the government's anti-terrorism expenditures on hostage-takings and bombings, respectively.[15]

Taking as given the government's anti-terrorism expenditures and their own total level of resources (R), the terrorists choose h and b to maximize their utility:

$$U(h, b),\tag{6}$$

subject to:

$$R = P_h(h, g_h)\, h + P_b(b, g_b)\, b.\tag{7}$$

Under the standard assumptions, it is possible to show that hostage taking and bombings decrease when the authorities manage to limit the terrorist's resource base R. Moreover, actions by the authorities to increase the unit cost of, say, hostage taking cause terrorists to switch some operations to the now relatively cheaper bombing events.

A third choice of terrorists involves an intertemporal allocation of resources. Analogous to other investors, terrorists can invest resources to earn a rate of return, r, per period. When terrorists want to augment operations, they can cash in some of their invested resources. Suppose that terrorists have a two-period horizon and must decide terrorist activities today (T_0) and tomorrow (T_1) based on resources today (R_0) and tomorrow (R_1). The intertemporal budget constraint is:

$$T_1 = R_1 + (1+r)(R_0 - T_0),\tag{8}$$

where tomorrow's terrorism equals tomorrow's resource endowment plus (minus) the earnings on savings (the payments on borrowings) from the initial period. Terrorists maximize an intertemporal utility function, $U(T_0, T_1)$ subject to (8) and, in so doing, decide terrorist activities over time. Thus, terrorists can react to shocks by augmenting operations not only from curbing non-terrorist activities, but also through an intertemporal substitution of resources.

Unlike a standard intertemporal optimizing framework, the capital market is not perfect – terrorist groups cannot fully borrow against their expected future income levels. As such, there may also exist a liquidity constraint. If high-terrorism periods are to be supported by an intertemporal substitution, it may be difficult for terrorists to maintain a prolonged campaign. In this way, particularly long and intense terrorist campaigns are not as readily sustained as lower levels of conflict. This prediction may not characterize non-resource-using threats and hoaxes.

We can summarize some of the key predictions and implications of the household production approach as follows:

- *Substitutions across attack modes:* an increase in the probability of success, a decrease in the relative price, or an increase in the payoff of any one type of attack mode will increase that type of attack.

• *Effects of government policies*: government policies aimed at a single type of terrorist event (for example, the installation of bomb-sniffing equipment in airports) adversely changes its relative price and results in a *substitution* into now less expensive modes of attack. Thus, Landes' measure[16] of the success of metal detectors, in terms of fewer skyjackings, does not go far enough, because the application of this technology may have induced a large number of other kinds of events.

• *Substitutions across countries:* a decrease in the probability of success or a reduction in the payoff in successfully attacking any one country will reduce the number of attacks on that country. Given their available resources, terrorists will move planned attacks into similar, relatively less-protected countries.

• *Intertemporal substitutions*: high-terrorism states deplete resources and so are followed by low-terrorism states. Particularly long and intense terrorist campaigns are not as readily sustained as are lower campaign levels.

EVIDENCE OF THE SUBSTITUTION EFFECT

The data we use is constructed from the source files of ITERATE (International Terrorism: Attributes of Terrorist Events). ITERATE was originally developed by Edward Mickolus.[17] ITERATE uses information from publicly available sources to construct a chronology of transnational terrorist events. The sources for ITERATE include the Associated Press, United Press International, Reuters tickers, the Foreign Broadcast Information Service (FBIS) *Daily Reports*, and major US newspapers (for example, the *Washington Post* and *New York Times*).

Figure 7.1 displays the quarterly totals of all transnational terrorist events over the 1968:1–2000:4 period. In contrast to the impression given by the media, the number of transnational terrorist incidents has been declining since 1993. Bombings are the favourite mode of operation of terrorists, accounting for about half of all transnational terrorist incidents on average in any given year. As is evident from the figure, transnational terrorism displays a number of sharp peaks and troughs. Some of the fluctuations are due to landmark political events. The jump in 1979 can be attributed to the political ramifications surrounding the

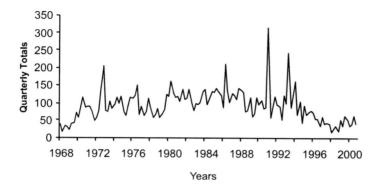

Figure 7.1. All Incidents

takeover of the US embassy in Tehran.[18] The spike in 1986 is associated with the US retaliatory raid against Libya that occurred on 15 April 1986. The latter half of the 1990s represents a downturn in transnational terrorism due, in large part, to fewer states sponsoring terrorism in the post-Cold War era.[19]

SUBSTITUTIONS AND RELIGION-BASED TERRORISM

Despite the decline in overall terrorism, Figures 7.2 and 7.3 paint a grim picture. Figure 7.2 shows the number of individuals *killed* per quarter in all transnational events, and Figure 7.3 shows the quarterly proportion of incidents with *casualties* and the proportion with deaths. Notice that

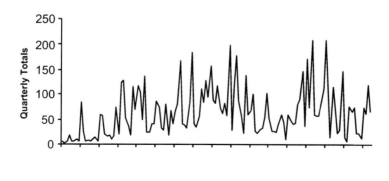

Figure 7.2. Individuals Killed

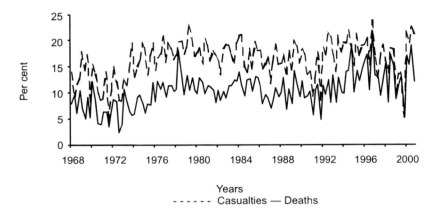

Figure 7.3. Proportions of Incidents Involving Casualties and Deaths

the values of the *killed* series have generally increased since 1993. Over the entire sample period, an average of 63 individuals have been killed in each quarter. Beginning in 1993, the average number of deaths has increased to 79 per quarter. This pattern is reinforced by the data shown in Figure 7.3. The proportion of incidents with *casualties* (the dashed line in the figure) has remained fairly stable since 1973; however, the proportion of incidents with deaths has more than doubled over the same period. In fact, the proportion of casualty incidents without deaths (that is, those with only wounded individuals) has declined. In recent years, there has been little difference between the proportion of incidents with casualties and the proportion of incidents with deaths. The strong impression from Figures 7.1–7.3 is that the number of incidents has been declining while the typical incident is becoming much more lethal. The increase in the proportion of deadly incidents is consistent with the HPF model. Enders and Sandler trace the increase in the severity of a typical terrorist incident to the takeover of the US Embassy in Tehran.[20] The change in the composition of terrorists from less leftist groups to more religious groups means that terrorists no longer fear death. Moreover, fundamentalist terrorist groups purposely seek out mass casualties, viewing anyone not with them as a legitimate target. As such, the typical incident is more likely to involve the death of a terrorist and/or the public.

The assassination series shown in Figure 7.4 includes both successful and failed assassinations. As such, the values shown exceed the number

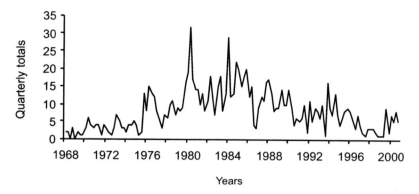

Figure 7.4. Assassinations

of assassinations resulting in deaths. Notice that the overall pattern of the series follows the pattern of transnational incidents shown in Figure 7.1. The disturbing feature is that assassinations are declining while the number of incidents with deaths is increasing; as such, more *deadly* incidents involve non-protected persons and multiple victims.

Substitutions and government policy interventions

Enders and Sandler applied vector autoregression (VAR) analysis to capture the potential interactions among various terrorist attack modes (for example, skyjackings and other hostage events) in response to government policies.[21] They find that the installation of metal detectors in airports (begun in 1973) decreased skyjackings and threats, but increased other kinds of hostage incidents, not protected by detectors. Specifically, metal detectors were estimated to reduce skyjackings and threats and hoaxes by 13 and 9.5 incidents per quarter, respectively. However, the number of other hostage-taking incidents and assassinations rose by almost 10 incidents per quarter. The measured trade-off between skyjacking and other logistically complex events was nearly one for one.[22] In terms of the HPF approach, the installation of metal detectors in US airports increased the relative price of a skyjacking. Skyjackings fell and so did the complementary threats and hoaxes. This policy intervention had primarily a substitution effect, because it did not deplete the resources, knowledge, or wherewithal of the terrorists. Substitutions across attack modes were also found to be important when the USA fortified its embassies in 1985 in accord with public law

98-533. Although direct attacks on embassies were reduced, an indirect consequence was that the number of political assassinations was increased by 5.4 incidents per quarter.

Intertemporal Substitutions

Both Brophy-Baermann and Conybeare[23] and Enders and Sandler[24] examine the effects of retaliatory raids on intertemporal substitutions. Brophy-Baermann and Conybeare find that retaliations by Israel against Palestinian terrorists had no lasting effects on the level of terrorism. They posit a model in which rational terrorists select a long-run or 'natural' rate of attacks. The actual level of attacks will differ from the 'natural' level only in the presence of an unanticipated event. In 1972, Israel conducted nine air raids against PLO camps in Syria in retaliation for Black September's attack on Israeli athletes in the 1972 Munich Olympic games. These attacks were estimated as *increasing* the number of PLO attacks against Israel by 9.39 incidents on impact. After three quarters, the PLO attacks were only 0.5 incidents above the natural rate. Five other Israeli attacks were found to have no long-run statistical effect on PLO terrorism.

Similarly, Enders and Sandler establish that the US retaliatory raid against Libya on April 1986 (for its suspected involvement in the bombing of the La Belle Discothèque in West Berlin on 4 April 1986) was associated with an immediate increase in terrorist attacks against US and UK interests.[25] The raid involved 18 US F-111 fighter-bombers being allowed to take off from UK airbases in Lakenheath and Upper Heyford. The planes were deployed from UK airbases because European nations, geographically closer to Libya, refused to allow the USA to use their airbases or their airspace. This endangered the raid since it forced the US fighters to refuel in mid-air after flying through the Straits of Gibraltar.

As a result of the raid, terrorist attacks against US and the UK interests were estimated to have increased by 39 incidents. However, the attacks did not persist for long as there was a temporary lull while terrorists built up depleted resources. In the long run, the mean number of attacks directed against US and UK interests was found to be unchanged. The evidence seems to be that retaliatory raids induce terrorists to *intertemporally* substitute attacks planned for the future into the present to protest against the retaliation. Within a relatively few quarters, terrorist attacks resumed the same mean number of events.

However, the Israeli raids against the PLO and the US raid against Libya did destroy some of the terrorists' resource base, so that one must wonder why terrorism did not diminish overall as a result of the raids. One answer is that the retaliations were not sufficient to destroy a significant portion of the terrorists' bases or personnel. A second answer is that the raids actually made it easier for terrorists to recruit new members and to raise funds. A third answer is that Libya was not responsible for a lot of transnational terrorism.

More recently, Enders and Sandler find additional evidence of intertemporal substitutions using a threshold autoregressive (TAR) model.[26] The HPF model implies that high-terrorism states are difficult to maintain if there are important liquidity constraints. In the midst of an intense terrorist campaign, weapons, funds, and personnel may be depleted. In contrast, a low-terrorism state can be maintained almost indefinitely; during this time, terrorists can recruit individuals, raise funds, and acquire weapons. As such, low-terrorism states should be more persistent than high-terrorism states. Enders and Sandler let y_t denote the number of incidents with deaths over the 1970:1-1999:4 period and estimate the TAR model (with t-statistics in parenthesis):

$$y_t = [21.53] I_t + [7.09 + 0.47_{yt-1}] (1 - I_t),$$
$$\quad (23.02) \qquad (3.12) \quad (2.41)$$

$$\text{where: } I_t = \begin{cases} 1 & \text{if } y_{t-1} \geq 18 \\ 0 & \text{if } y_{t-1} < 18. \end{cases}$$

$$(9)$$

The threshold model suggests that there is no single long-run equilibrium value for the number of incidents; instead, there are high- and low-terrorism regimes or states. In the low state (that is, when the number of incidents is fewer than 18), the system gravitates toward 13 incidents per quarter [$7.09 \div (1.0 - 0.47) \approx 13$]. If, however, the number of incidents exceeds the threshold, there tends to be an immediate jump to 21.53 incidents. Whenever the number of incidents exceeds this threshold due to a shock or event, there will be an immediate decline to 21.53 incidents in the subsequent quarter. The high-incident state can be maintained until a shock of sufficient magnitude causes a switch of regime; however, the number of events in this heightened state cannot be maintained at more than 21.53 incidents. Insofar as the estimated standard deviation is equal to 6.14, the magnitude of a typical shock is likely to cause a regime switch.

Policy Implications

The findings that substitution effects are important have a number of implications for government policy-making. Clearly, governments must act to reduce the terrorists' resource endowments (that is, their finances, leadership, and membership) if an overall decrease in terrorism is to follow. Efforts to infiltrate and undermine terrorist groups and to freeze their assets have the consequence of reducing the overall amount of terrorism.

Even some piecemeal policies that cause substitutions by focusing on only part of the overall terrorism problem may have some net positive impacts. To the extent that the US National Defense Authorization Act leads to a reduction in the likelihood of biological terrorism, substitutions into other attack modes will occur. The desirability of such policies is that they may force terrorists to substitute into *less harmful events*. Anti-terrorist policies can be most effective when the government simultaneously targets a wide range of terrorist attack modes, so that the *overall* rise in the prices of terrorist attacks becomes analogous to a decrease in resources. A government must maintain the resolve to fight terrorism. Terrorists do not have the same ability as governments to maintain a sustained offensive. A short-lived governmental effort to fight terrorism will afford the group time to regroup and replenish its resources. Success in raising the price of all modes of terrorist attacks and/or in reducing terrorists' resources would induce them to shift into legal protests and other non-terrorist actions to air grievances.

Similarly, the development of technological barriers to thwart terrorism causes a substitution into other attack modes in the short run. In the long term, terrorists will develop ingenious countermeasures to circumvent the technology. Immediately after airport vigilance was increased as a result of 9/11, Richard Reid (aka Tariq Rajah) was discovered on a flight from Paris to the USA with an explosive device in his shoes. Now that airport security routinely inspects shoes, plastic guns, electronic jamming equipment, bottles of flammable liquid or other explosive devices are predicted to be hidden on (or in) the terrorist or in carry-on luggage. Thus, there are dynamic strategic interactions; authorities must be vigilant to improve technology by anticipating ways of circumventing current technological barriers. This vigilance must lead to periodic upgrades in the technology prior to the terrorists exposing the technology's weakness through a successful attack.

WHAT WE DO NOT KNOW ABOUT THE SUBSTITUTION EFFECT

ITERATE poses a number of shortcomings that researchers must take into account when testing theories. First, since it relies on public sources such as newspaper accounts, ITERATE picks up only *newsworthy* transnational terrorist incidents. However, what is deemed 'newsworthy' changes over time as the public becomes desensitized to terrorism. For example, ITERATE contains the following incident:

> 5 November 1985 – GREECE – Police discovered a bomb in a suspicious-looking cloth bag planted between the first and second floors of an Athens building at 8 Xenophon Street. The building housed the offices of Trans World Airlines. Bomb experts removed the bomb and detonated it without mishap.

Given the increased severity of terrorist events, such an attempted bombing might not be prominently reported in the newspapers. Thus, ITERATE might suggest that certain types of terrorist events may have declined simply because they are no longer reported. Of course, this bias is more likely for threats, hoaxes, and bombings without casualties than for incidents with deaths. The bias has worsened since mid-1996, when the FBI's *Daily Reports* became unavailable to ITERATE coders. Moreover, by relying on newspaper accounts, ITERATE is better at describing the actions of terrorists than of the authorities. In some instances, government strategies are revealed and coded in ITERATE. However, anti-terrorism initiatives may have been undertaken in secret in response to an undisclosed terrorist threat. To circumvent such limitations of ITERATE, the US government should give proven researchers access to the unclassified portions of its more inclusive data sets. The same is true of the RAND-St Andrews data set on incidents, which we have tried unsuccessfully to acquire. The true biases in these data sets can only be ascertained by testing the same hypothesis with alternative data sets.

Clearly, there is much to learn about the substitution effect. Only a portion of the problem concerns data limitations. Instead of presenting a 'laundry list' of unknowns, we conclude with three useful directions for future research involving substitutions associated with terrorist negotiations, terrorist recruitment, and terrorist networks.

A significant amount of published research has examined the effects of negotiating with terrorists.[27] If terrorism becomes successful, the HPF model predicts that terrorists will devote more of their resources to terrorist activities and that new terrorist groups will emerge.

However, the extent to which a concession to one terrorist group induces additional terrorist incidents needs to be satisfactorily established.

As posited, the HPF model treats the resources of a group as given. Nevertheless, groups can obtain resources through publicity. An extremely heinous or highly visible attack may provide a signal that the responsible group is particularly influential or powerful. Such attacks may lower recruiting costs so that major campaigns become more sustainable. This means that the recruiting decisions are not independent of the mode of attack.

The HPF model analyses the choice-theoretic decision of a single terrorist group. If terrorists are tied together implicitly through similar hatreds (for example, of Israel and the USA), then multiple terrorist groups may simultaneously act as a unified whole. However, there may be important *network externalities* or interdependencies not directly captured by the HPF model of a single group. Since attack modes may be complementary, the actions of one group may affect the behaviour of other groups. For example, attacks by al-Qa'eda may make it more desirable for a second terrorist group to also attack US interests. Moreover, strikes against terrorists in Afghanistan may make it easier for terrorists elsewhere to recruit individuals and resources. Such complementarities may induce terrorists worldwide to take on the appearance of a single group even though they have no direct links with each other.

NOTES

1. All data used in this section were obtained from the official website of the President of the USA: www.whitehouse.gov.
2. Caleb Carr raises a number of issues concerning the appropriate definition of terrorism (see Caleb Carr, *The Lessons of Terror: A History of Warfare Against Civilians, Why It Has Always Failed and Why It Will Fail Again* (New York: Random House, 2002). Also, *Slate* (http://slate.msn.com//?id=2062267) contains a discussion of the premise that terrorism necessitates that the victims be non-combatants.
3. Paul Wilkinson, *Terrorism and the Liberal State* (London: Macmillan, 1986).
4. Bruce Hoffman, 'The Confluence of International and Domestic Trends in Terrorism', *Terrorism and Political Violence*, 9/2 (1997), pp. 1–15.
5. Ibid.
6. Bruce Hoffman, *Inside Terrorism* (New York: Columbia University Press, 1998).
7. Mark Juergensmeyer, 'Terror mandated by God', *Terrorism and Political Violence*, 9 (1997), pp. 16–23.
8. See Peter Chalk, 'The Liberal Democratic Response to Terrorism', *Terrorism and Political Violence*, 7/4 (1995), pp. 10–44; Richard Clutterbuck, 'Keeping Track of Terrorists after 1992', *Terrorism and Political Violence*, 4 (1992), pp. 301–6; and Albert Jongman, 'Trends in International and Domestic Terrorism in Western Europe 1968–1988', *Terrorism and Political Violence*, 4 (1992), pp. 26–76.
9. See Chalk, 'Liberal Democratic Response to Terrorism'; Paul Wilkinson, 'The European Response to Terrorism: Retrospect and Prospect', *Defence Economics*, 3 (1992), pp. 289–304; and

M. Zagari, 'Combating Terrorism: Report to the Committee of Legal Affairs and Citizens' Rights of the European Parliament', *Terrorism and Political Violence*, 4 (1992), pp. 288–300.

10. Philip Wilcox, Jr, 'The Western Alliance and the Challenge of Combating Terrorism', *Terrorism and Political Violence*, 9 (1997), pp. 1–7.

11. See Hoffman, 'Confluence of International and Domestic Trends'; and Hoffman, *Inside Terrorism*.

12. William Landes, 'An Economic Study of US Aircraft Skyjackings, 1961–1976', *Journal of Law and Economics*, 21/1 (1978), pp. 1–31.

13. Walter Enders and Todd Sandler, 'The Effectiveness of Anti-Terrorism Policies: Vector-Autoregression-Intervention Analysis', *American Political Science Review*, 87/4 (1993), pp. 829–44.

14. See Todd Sandler and Harvey Lapan, 'The Calculus of Dissent: An Analysis of Terrorists' Choice of Targets', *Synthese*, 76/2 (1988), pp. 245–61.

15. Notice that in our two-incident example, we abstract from direct substitutability and complementarity. In a more general setting, we could allow the price of bombings to depend on the number of hostage-takings and the price of hostage-takings to depend on the number of bombings. Moreover, anti-terrorism spending directed towards one type of incident might be expected to increase the price of the alternative incident types.

16. Landes, 'Economic Study of US Aircraft Skyjackings'.

17. Edward Mickolus, *International Terrorism: Attributes of Terrorist Events, 1968–1977 (ITERATE 2)* (Ann Arbor, MI: Inter-University Consortium for Political and Social Research, Mickolus, 1982). The database has been extended on a number of occassions (for example, Edward Mickolus, Todd Sandler, Jean M. Murdock *et al.*, *International Terrorism: Attributes of Terrorist Events, 1978–1987 (ITERATE 3)* (Dunn Loring, VA: Vinyard Software, 1989); Edward Mickolus, Todd Sandler, Jean M. Murdock *et al.*, *International Terrorism: Attributes of Terrorist Events, 1988–1991 (ITERATE 4)* (Dunn Loring, VA: Vinyard Software, 1993); and Peter Fleming, *International Terrorism: Attributes of Terrorist Events, 1992–1998 (ITERATE 5 update)* (Personal communication, 2001)). Todd Sandler further updated select variables through 1999–2000.

18. Walter Enders and Todd Sandler, 'Is Transnational Terrorism Becoming More Threatening?', *Journal of Conflict Resolution*, 44/3 (2000), pp. 307–32.

19. Walter Enders and Todd Sandler, 'Transnational Terrorism in the Post-Cold War Era', *International Studies Quarterly*, 43/1 (1999), pp. 145–67.

20. Enders and Sandler, 'Is Transnational Terrorism Becoming More Threatening?'

21. See Enders and Sandler, 'The Effectiveness of Anti-Terrorism Policies'; and Walter Enders and Todd Sandler, 'Terrorism: Theory and Applications', in Keith Hartley and Todd Sandler (eds), *Handbook of Defense Economics* (Amsterdam: Elsevier, 1995), pp. 213–49.

22. Also see Walter Enders, Todd Sandler and Jon Cauley, 'UN Conventions, Technology and Retaliation in the Fight Against Terrorism: An Econometric Evaluation', *Terrorism and Political Violence*, 2/1 (1990), pp. 83–105; and Eric Im, Jon Cauley and Todd Sandler, 'Cycles and Substitutions in Terrorist Activities: A Spectral Approach', *KYKLOS*, 40/2 (1987), pp. 238–55.

23. Bryan Brophy-Baermann and John Conybeare, 'Retaliating Against Terrorism: Rational Expectations and the Optimality of Rules versus Discretion', *American Journal of Political Science*, 38/1 (1994), pp. 196–210.

24. Enders and Sandler, 'The Effectiveness of Anti-Terrorism Policies'.

25. Ibid.

26. Walter Enders and Todd Sandler, 'Patterns of Transnational Terrorism, 1970–99: Alternative Time Series Estimates', *International Studies Quarterly* (forthcoming).

27. Examples of such work include: Scott Atkinson, Todd Sandler and John Tschirhart, 'Terrorism in a Bargaining Framework', *Journal of Law and Economics*, 30/1 (1987), pp. 1–21; Todd Sandler and John Scott, 'Terrorist Success in Hostage-Taking Incidents', *Journal of Conflict Resolution*, 31/1 (1987), pp. 35–53; Harvey Lapan and Todd Sandler, 'To Bargain or Not to Bargain: That Is the Question', *American Economic Review*, 78/2 (1988), pp. 16–20; Reinhard Selten, 'A Simple Game Model of Kidnappings', in Reinhard Selten (ed.), *Models of Strategic Rationality* (Boston, MA: Kluwer Academic, 1988); Muhammad Islam and Wassim Shahin, 'Economic Methodology Applied to Political Hostage-Taking in Light of the Iran-Contra Affair', *Southern Economic Journal*, 55/4 (1989), pp. 1019–24; John Scott, 'Reputation Building in Hostage Incidents', *Defence Economics*, 2/3 (1991), pp. 209–18; and Wassim Shahin and Muhammad Islam, 'Combating Political Hostage-Taking: An Alternative Approach', *Defence Economics*, 3 (1992), pp. 321–7.

8

Conflict Theory and the Trajectory of Terrorist Campaigns in Western Europe

LEONARD WEINBERG AND LOUISE RICHARDSON

THE STUDY of political terrorism has largely been an a-theoretical undertaking.[1] Psychiatrists and psychologists, from Cesare Lombroso to Fred Hacker and beyond, have offered their views identifying the personality types likely to commit acts of terrorist violence or take the lead in organizations pursuing their ends by terrorist means. Analysts drawn from other social sciences have also applied their ideas concerning the sources of unconventional warfare, human aggression, and the behaviour of individuals in small face-to-face groups to account for the operations of terrorists in different settings. During the 1970s several scholars sought to apply the lessons learned from the study of mass social and political movements to the conduct of such minuscule endeavours as the Symbionese Liberation Army in the USA or the equally short-lived Angry Brigade in the UK. These efforts led Walter Laqueur to throw up his hands and suggest that his readers consult Conrad and Dostoevski if they really wanted to understand the terrorist phenomenon.[2]

Despite these efforts to apply the theoretical insights of the various social sciences to the understanding of political terrorism, much of its study has been driven by the immediate needs of policy-makers and others charged with the responsibility of bringing a rapid end to both the violence and its perpetrators. Description and intelligence gathering have usually taken precedence over efforts at abstract explanation, particularly when lives have been on the line. When those in positions of responsibility try to determine the circumstances in which suicide bombers will strike or small bands of religious fanatics will disperse poison gas in crowded places, their interest in academic speculation and abstract theory tends inevitably to be limited.

The above suggests that the inter-disciplinary views of conflict developed in the work of various social psychologists, sociologists and political scientists may provide a successful basis for the general understanding of political terrorism. An advantage to this approach is that theories of conflict were designed to be applicable to all levels of conflict, from inter-personal to international, from small communities deciding whether or not to chlorinate their water supplies to wars between nations. Political terrorism seems to mirror conflict theory because its practitioners range from such 'lone wolves' as Timothy McVeigh to small bands operating in clandestine circumstances; from 17 November; to such large and complex organisations as Hizbollah, to national governments; or 'rogue' states offering support to various groups active in Jammu-Kashmir, the West Bank and the Central Asian republics. This paper applies conflict theory to terrorism to see whether or not it can help us to understand how and why terrorist campaigns come and go.

We are seeking a framework for understanding the general course or trajectory of social and political conflicts at the inter-group, community and international levels. In order to see if it makes sense to apply such a framework to terrorist campaigns we will attempt a coherent rendering of a framework for the analysis of conflict. Second, we will distinguish between a terrorist 'campaign' and a brief episode of politically inspired violence. Third, and most ambitious, we will apply the framework to the reality of particular campaigns.

CONFLICT THEORY

During the 1950s and early 1960s scholars from various disciplines sought to develop a general understanding of human conflict. The assumption with which they began was that all conflicts between humans shared certain traits. These traits could be understood best if they were viewed as phases or stages of a spiral, or cycle, of conflict.[3] In these early writings, conflicts were identified first on their level: intra-personal, inter-personal, intra-group, inter-group and international. Then, the stages of these conflicts, from initiation to resolution, were specified. The levels varied but the stages were thought to be constant.

The common enterprise soon split between those concerned with intra-personal and those with international conflict.[4] What remained tended to be dominated by those committed to conflict resolution and peace studies.[5] The effect of focusing on peace studies has in part led to the marginalization of the field.

There seems to be agreement that social and political conflicts may go through a series of stages. There is no causal requirement that all conflicts follow an identical path from initiation to resolution. Most conflicts are settled well before there is a resort to violence of any kind. At the other extreme, there are conflicts which become so intractable that the parties involved resist resolution.[6] Analysts also seem to agree that a conflict must be willed by at least one of the parties involved. Economic deprivation, racial discrimination and religious bigotry may be among the conditions necessary for conflicts to occur but they are not sufficient. There must be a subjective recognition that goals or interests are incompatible for conflicts to become manifest. As Louis Kriesberg writes: 'Often a conflict does not emerge simply because individuals find other means of coping with the inequalities and differences that they find unsatisfactory.'[7] In short, the framework for the analysis of conflicts may suggest a cycle but it is far from being a calendar.

Stage One

According to Kriesberg, four conditions need to be present for a social or political conflict to emerge. First, the parties involved must begin to think of themselves as having separate identities from one another. There must be an awareness of social or group difference. Whatever the basis for the difference – economic status, ethnic affinity, religious belief, national identity – it must be one that can be communicated relatively quickly and easily. Next, at least one of the parties to the emerging conflict must have a grievance to be satisfied. Third, at least one of the parties involved must be able to formulate a set of goals or a plan to change the other party in such a way as to reduce or eliminate the grievance. Last, members of the aggrieved party must believe they are capable of bringing about change in the other party that will bring about the desired results. Or, 'A conflict emerges when members of one or more potential conflict parties develop a shared identity, generate a sense of grievance, form a goal that another party, being responsible for the grievance, be changed, and come to believe they can bring about that change.'[8]

Even when these conditions have been met and a conflict has become manifest, there is no necessity that it will lead to violence. There are usually alternative means available to the parties involved. It is only when at least one of the parties involved in the conflict makes a 'strategic choice' to contend with the other that the probability of violence rises. 'When people deal with conflict by contending, each trying to do well at the others' expense, a set of moves and counter-moves tends to result that drives the conflict to increase in intensity.'[9]

Stage Two

Certain telltale signs appear as a conflict begins to escalate and contention becomes coercion. What had become a dispute over a single issue or small-scale grievance tends to become more general, covering a wide range of grievances. In Berkeley in 1964, for example, what began as a narrowly focused dispute – over the use of a public space in front of Sproul Hall to protest against the Republican Convention's nomination of Barry Goldwater – became a wide-ranging generational conflict over university governance within the space of less than nine months.[10] The conflict, in other words, gets redefined in such a way as to raise the stakes involved. Further, not only do the number and importance of the issues involved expand but so do the number of people who become drawn into the conflict. If the issues in dispute can be generalized and posed as a threat to the identity of a group to which large numbers of people belong, and with which they link their own identities, the prospect of an intractable conflict appears.[11] In the case of Sri Lanka, for example, a conflict over preferential treatment for Sinhalese in university admissions and public employment during the 1960s and 1970s led to Tamil protests which led, in turn, to anti-Tamil rioting which eventually produced a full-scale civil war as the identities of many Sri Lankans became caught up in the conflict.[12] In addition, at this early, escalated stage of the conflict something like a division of labour occurs. At this stage specialized 'struggle groups' appear, small groups of individuals seeking to champion the cause of one or both of the parties involved in the conflict. The commitment of these small groups is to the struggle itself as much as to the original cause for which they were created. In other words, as the intensity of the conflict mounts, the desire to achieve one party's ostensible goal is often displaced by the desire to harm the other party simply for the sake of inflicting injury. When this happens the conflict begins to take on a life of its own, fuelled by the growing animosities between the contending parties and especially by the 'struggle groups' formed specifically to act as a vanguard to lead the conflict.[13]

Alongside these developments, members of a party in conflict begin to perceive members of the other party involved as adversaries. There is social and psychological polarization at work as relations between the parties deteriorate; social contacts between members of the different parties in contention are reduced.[14] Likewise, information about the other side is filtered in such a way as to accentuate the negative aspects of the adversary and assume the worst about its intentions. At this point there may be virtually nothing the other party can do to dispel the negative expectations that have arisen about its intentions. Mutual suspicion and mistrust will then produce a self-fulfilling prophecy.[15] Just how powerful these processes can be is suggested by the astonishing transformation of long-time neighbours into the most savage enemies in such civil wars as those that broke out in the ex-Yugoslavia in 1991.

When most of the above conditions are present conflicts have escalated. They do so when three defining elements appear. First, there is an increase in the severity of the coercive means employed or threatened by the parties involved. There is also an increase in the frequency of violent encounters between the adversaries. Small and occasional bites in the 'War of the Flea' become bigger and more frequent.[16] More damaging weapons may be used and more often. Second, there is an expansion in the geography of the conflict. The conflict spreads to regions previously immune to violent encounters. Third, there is an increase in the number of participants in the conflict as new recruits are attracted.[17]

The dynamics of escalation are captured by the concept of entrapment identified by Brockner and Rubin:

> The individual makes some investments in the hope of achieving some goal. The process of goal attainment, however, requires the individual to make repeated investments over time. Thus, it is not uncommon for people to discover, somewhere during the course of this process, that they are in a decisional 'no man's land', in which they have made a substantial investment but have not as yet achieved their goal. At this point individuals are likely to experience considerable conflict about the prospect of making continued investments. On the one hand, they may not wish to continue investing, because the goal may no longer be seen as either readily attainable or worthy of additional costs. On the other hand, the individual may feel a strong need to continued investing, at least in part to justify the expenditures that have already been made. To the extent that they do continue investing in order to justify prior commitments, they are said to be entrapped. When taken to an

extreme, the choice to escalate commitment to a chosen course of action can produce irrational behaviour with disastrous consequences.[18]

Brochner and Rubin were writing largely about individuals with personal problems to resolve. But entrapment may be a more serious problem when the parties engaged in a conflict are large-scale groups or national governments where not only personal but group or national prestige is involved. In wars, for example, feelings of group solidarity, along with excitement, pride and pleasure in the experience of national glory may make a change of course based on reduced investments exceptionally hard to achieve. Under these circumstances, the parties engaged in an escalated conflict often come to be led by hardliners, inflexible types, whose reputations are based on finding 'light at the end of the tunnel' by increasing their party's investment in the struggle.[19]

Pruitt and Rubin suggest three models of conflict escalation. In the 'aggressor-defender' model an aggressor has a goal that places it in conflict with a defender. The aggressor begins with limited coercive tactics, but if these do not produce the desired concessions by the defender, he employs stronger and stronger measures until the goal is reached. 'Escalation persists until the aggressor either wins or gives up trying' (because the costs involved begin to outweigh the value of the goal involved).[20] In the 'structural change' model, parties to conflicts undergoing escalation experience the forms of social and psychological transformation discussed earlier. The effect of these changes is to produce rigid negative attitudes and perceptions of the adversary. Leaders are rewarded or re-enforced when they appear tough and unyielding.

Stage Three

The third model is the spiral of conflict. The logic of the spiral approximates mutual entrapment and involves situations in which the hostile acts of the adversary cause the other party to the conflict to respond in such a way as to cause the party making the initial move to take additional steps to advance its interest, which, in turn, elicits a more menacing response from the adversary. The parties trap themselves in a vicious cycle of conflict. Lewis Richardson's picture of the arms race between the Soviet Union and the USA illustrates the point. An arms build-up intended to enhance the security of one side in the Cold War has the opposite effect, because it causes the opposing side to respond in kind with weapons of its own, leaving both sides in a greater state of insecurity than at the beginning of the escalated spiral.[21]

Given the logic of escalated conflicts, it is hard to see how such encounters come to an end at all. But obviously they do. In some instances, the conflict ended when one party achieves an outright victory. The Second World War ended in September 1945 when the Japanese surrendered unconditionally to the USA and its allies. The Vietnam War ended in 1975 when North Vietnamese and Viet Cong forces entered Saigon and the US-supported regime in that city disintegrated. The American Civil War ended in April 1865 when Lee surrendered to Grant at Appomattox. In fact, the most common outcome of most civil wars is a military victory of one side over the other.[22] But outright victories may give way to subsequent conflicts, which, in turn, enter their own spirals of escalation. Prussia defeated France in 1870. France defeated Germany in 1918. Germany defeated France in 1940. France (or its allies) expelled the Germans from its territory in 1944 and so on.

In many cases conflicts undergo a process of de-escalation before they reach a conclusion. Schmid defines de-escalation as a 'lessening of intensity of armed conflict, with either fewer parties and/or states involved, fewer armed forces involved or less severe tactics and means of combat applied.'[23] Kriesberg and others mention the importance of timing in understanding the conditions that bring about the de-escalation of conflict. Opponents in conflicts that have become stalemated, especially if both sides are hurt by the continuation of the stalemate and neither side regards a victory as imminent, may be prepared to de-escalate.[24] The outcome of the October 1973 Arab–Israeli War comes to mind. (This view is not without its critics however.[25]) There is recognition that coercion is not working; that resources available for the conflict are becoming exhausted; and that the costs and risks of continuing along the present course are becoming too large. Under these circumstances a constituency in favour of de-escalating the conflict may appear, as did, for example, the peace movement during the Vietnam War in the USA. New leaders who are able to recognize that their side's involvement has become untenable or self-defeating may replace the intransigent figures whose conduct let the conflict spiral out of control. Old leaders may even undergo a change of heart and devise new policies as the result of failure, fatigue or the threat of imminent defeat at the polls.

De-escalation may be achieved through the formation or re-establishment of links between the parties in conflict. Just as there is often a reciprocal set of interactions that promote a conflict spiral, so too it may be possible to set in motion a set of actions and reactions that send the spiral cascading downward, reducing the conflict's range, scope and intensity. Goodwill gestures or small and concrete steps by one side showing that it is inclined to reduce the conflict may be reciprocated and the tit for tat process repeated until negotiations begin. The effort to promote de-escalation and seek a negotiated conclusion to the conflict is often aided by outside powers acting as intermediaries. At the international level, United Nations' agencies, various inter-governmental and regional organizations, the representatives of single countries and even such well-meaning individuals as former US President Jimmy Carter may play a role in promoting an end to violent conflicts.[26]

The path of de-escalation leading to a negotiated settlement and a mutually agreed accommodation is only one of the ways by which violent conflicts may end. Kriesberg identifies six alternatives. First, an outside party may intervene and impose a settlement. Kosovo, in the ex-Yugoslavia, currently 'enjoys' its autonomous status as the result of forceful intervention from outside. Second, one party may win and compel the other side to capitulate. Third, a more extreme version of winning, are the various cases in which one party eliminates the other by expelling it from its territory. Campaigns of 'ethnic cleansing', for example, are designed to achieve this outcome. A fourth alternative is the possibility of conversion. Important elements belonging to one party may become persuaded of the merits of the other party's case. In South Africa there were violent clashes and episodes of brutal repression to be sure, but apartheid came to an end only after a significant segment of the white population, including its elected leadership, persuaded itself that a continuation of the policy was untenable. In addition, a process of implicit bargaining may occur in which the parties involved take reciprocal steps to reduce the intensity of the conflict – without formal negotiations taking place, with the attendant possibility of one side or the other being accused of weakness by more intransigent elements within their own camp. Finally, one party may press its claims through violence against another, but meeting strong resistance may abandon the fight, at least for a while, and permit the conflict to go dormant.[27]

CONFLICT THEORY AND TERRORISM

Terrorism is a tactic which may be used in connection with inter-state, anti-colonial and internal wars as well as a means of achieving such less ambitious objectives as ending clinically provided abortions. Nevertheless, there is some agreement among those who study the phenomenon that, in terms of the number of incidents and casualties involved, terrorist violence has been more frequent and more lethal in conflicts within, rather than between, countries.[28] Of course, in cases involving 'surrogate warfare', or in the conflict between India and Pakistan over Jammu-Kashmir, it is sometimes hard to make a clear distinction between national and international campaigns. But, assuming for the moment a greater severity in domestic terrorism, it follows that terrorist campaigns would be less likely to end with negotiated settlements than violent conflicts in which terrorism is missing. This hypothesis is re-enforced when we consider the nature of terrorist violence. As Rapoport points out, acts of terrorism are sometimes carried out deliberately as a way of burning bridges. By attacking unarmed civilians in public places in particularly bloody ways, the perpetrators may hope they are making it nearly impossible for conflicts to end in a negotiated outcome.[29] The hatreds stimulated simply become too ferocious. The bus bombings carried out by Hamas and Palestinian Islamic Jihad in Israel after the Rabin assassination had just such a goal in mind. Based on this logic we should expect something other than mutually agreed accommodation to be the result of a terrorist campaign, though there have certainly been cases where the latter prevailed. Algeria achieved independence from France in 1962 after prolonged negotiations despite the persistent use of terrorism by groups on both sides of the struggle.[30]

Terrorism, of course, often occurs alongside other forms of violence.[31] There are some campaigns whose perpetrators rely exclusively on terrorism, such as the operations of Abu Nidal's Fatah Revolutionary Council during the 1970s and the Armed Islamic Group in Algeria during the 1990s. There are also an abundance of campaigns in which terrorism and other forms of unconventional warfare are conducted simultaneously. Peru's Shining Path and the Revolutionary Armed Forces of Colombia are examples of groups which wage guerrilla war in the countryside while staging terrorist attacks in the cities. There are also instances in which what begin as terrorist campaigns are transformed into full-scale civil wars. And in some of these cases – for example, the fighting presently underway in Sri Lanka – the terrorism persists along with other forms of violence, while in others it is superseded. We think of all the above as terrorist campaigns and incorporate their analysis into the general framework for understanding social and political conflict.

TERRORISM IN WESTERN EUROPE

Over the last couple of decades the countries of Western Europe have experienced four different types of terrorist campaigns none of which, to date, have been transformed into higher-scale conflicts or civil wars. Either as the result of a lack of sufficient popular support needed to sustain such transformations, the presence of state institutions strong enough to prevent such developments or the self-restraint of the commanders of the organizations committing the violence, the violence involved in all the campaigns we confront have been limited to small-scale terrorism.[32]

First, terrorism has been imported into various Western European countries – most notably, France, Italy, Germany and Greece – by groups from the Middle East who have found it advantageous to stage their attacks in a nearby region but one at some distance from the original site of the conflict. Next, many of the countries in Western Europe have had to confront terrorist campaigns waged by organizations seeking to promote the cause of communist revolution either in their countries of origin or on a world-wide basis. Some, like the Greek November 17 group, continue to be active to this day. Third, most notably in Northern Ireland and the Basque country of northern Spain, para-military groups have used terrorism on a protracted basis in order to achieve nationalist/separatist objectives: a merger of Ulster with the Irish Republic and an independent state for the Basques. Fourth, in Sweden, Germany, Austria, Italy and a handful of other countries, radical right-wing bands have carried out terrorist attacks with racist, anti-Semitic and xenophobic aims in mind. These bands hope, more specifically, to make life sufficiently miserable for Third World immigrants and asylum-seekers to bring about their repatriation to their countries of origin and thereby re-assert the racial and ethnic dominance of the majority European populations.

Western Europe has been the site of multiple campaigns of terrorism as the result of conflicts emanating from the Middle East.[33] Libya, Iran, Syria and Iraq have been accused of sending their agents or employed surrogates for the purpose of killing dissidents who have gone into exile. The publication of a single novel, *The Satanic Verses*, even prompted Iran to launch a public campaign to murder its author, Salmon Rushdie, while he was residing in the UK. The Kurdish PKK organization has repeatedly attacked Turkish targets on European soil. During the 1990s the violent conflict in Algeria between its military-supported unelected government and its Islamist enemies spilled over into Europe as members of the Armed Islamic Group carried out terrorist attacks in France and against French targets because of that country's evident support for the incumbent regime. The Middle Eastern conflict that captured the most attention has been that between the Palestinians (along with their various sympathisers) and Israel.

Given the variety of terrorist campaigns involved, to follow the cycle or cycles of violence employed is no easy feat. Nonetheless, some general comments make some sense. First, and most obviously, the developments we linked earlier to the first stage of a conflict, namely its emergence, had taken place not in Europe but in the Middle East. Middle Eastern terrorism typically enters the countries of Western Europe after the conflict has already escalated. In Europe, the conflict has spread, not only geographically but also in terms of the targets involved and, often, the intensity with which they are attacked. Thus, in the Middle East, Palestinian-related groups largely confined their attacks to Israeli targets on Israeli soil and to rival groups within their own camp. In the escalated context of the campaign in Western Europe, Jews in general – not simply Israelis – became fair game, as did the citizens and property of countries regarded as friendly to the Israeli cause. The intensity of the terrorist campaign also escalated in the sense that places of worship, embassies, consulates, travel agencies, commercial airliners and airports themselves came under attack. 'Struggle groups' emerged and were often able to find sanctuary and support among Middle Eastern immigrant communities in the various Western European countries.

Dennis Pluchinsky has plotted the annual frequency of terrorist attacks carried out by Middle Eastern groups between 1980 and 1989.[34] Bearing in mind that these incidents reflect multiple campaigns, the frequencies Pluchinsky reports resemble a normal distribution. The number of attacks increases from the early to the mid-1980s, crest in 1985, and then descend thereafter until the end of the decade. In numerical terms, Middle Eastern terrorism in Western Europe appears to go through a decade-long process of escalation and de-escalation. There was no conflict resolution and no negotiated settlement, although some tacit bargaining was no doubt at play. The terrorist attacks never completely stopped. In fact, there was a resumption or renewed escalation during the 1990s as the situation in Algeria unfolded and the struggle of the Kurds against the Turkish government intensified. But these were different causes and different conflicts.

But why the normal distribution between 1980 and 1989? Why the peak in 1985 and the decline afterward? Disentangling the various factors at work is not an easy task but a few developments stand out. The American bombing raids on Libyan cities occurred in 1986, after a long series of Libyan-backed attacks on American targets in Europe. These air strikes were followed by the decisions of a number of Western European governments to expel numerous Libyan students and diplomats from their territories and to shut down Libya's 'People's Bureaus' in their respective national capitals.[35] Furthermore, the European intergovernmental forum known as TREVI (Terrorism, Radicalism, Extreme Violence International) became significantly more active in promoting co-operation among the various police agencies in overcoming the terrorist threat from 1985 onward.

Middle Eastern terrorist operations in Western Europe during the 1970s were more clearly dominated by the various Palestinian groups and their violent struggle against Israel and its allies. It was a decade dominated by spectacular terrorist attacks: for example, the 1972 Munich Olympic massacre and a succession of airline skyjackings. For much of this period the terrorists operated in a relatively permissive environment. The French, Italian and other governments chose to look the other way if Palestinian terrorist groups tacitly agreed to carry out their attacks elsewhere. The arrest rate of those suspected of terrorist crimes was low, especially in the first half of the decade. And those who were arrested or detained were not uncommonly expelled from the country or given short terms in prison by governments not looking for trouble, particularly in the aftermath of the 1973 oil crisis.[36]

The Palestinian-dominated Middle Eastern terrorism that escalated in Western Europe during the 1970s and which caught the attention of a vast audience appeared to de-escalate by the end of the decade. This outcome, however, was not the result of a process of conflict resolution leading to an overall settlement. Instead, the strategic decisions on the part of some of the Palestinian groups to reduce terrorist operations in Europe seems to have been the result of a combination of factors. One factor at work was what Kriesberg and others have referred to as 'conversion'. Either in response to pressure from the Arab oil-producing states or on the basis of the violence itself, a forcefully imposed learning curve, states belonging to the European Community came to sympathize with the Palestinian side in the Israeli conflict. Expressions of goodwill by policy-makers, accompanied by both tacit and explicit bargaining between the PLO and the relevant states, along with improved domestic security measures, seem the most likely explanation for the waning of Palestinian terrorism in Europe by the end of the 1970s.

If we view the overall pattern of Middle Eastern terrorism in Western Europe over the last 30 years what we observe are a succession of waves. The first, dominated by the Palestinians, escalated and de-escalated; a second involving Libyan, Iranian and Syrian operations went through a similar cycle; followed more recently by the activities of Algerian and other Islamist groups along with the Kurdish PKK organizations. None of the terrorist campaigns ended their Western Europe phases through a negotiated settlement as described in the conflict resolution literature. This is no doubt the case because the principal parties engaged in the conflict were extra-European in origin.[37]

This is not the case with the terrorist campaigns of revolutionary organizations active in Western Europe during the 1970s and beyond. The sources of their conflicts were indigenous to the countries in which they were waged though they certainly benefited from material and moral support from behind the Iron Curtain. Despite the fact that the revolutionary groups who engaged in these conflicts shared the anti-capitalist and anti-imperialist vocabulary of Marxism-Leninism as well as a common commitment to the establishment of some version of a communist regime, we need to resist the temptation to think that their operations followed a single trajectory. Some of the conflicts were short-lived, for example, the struggle of Belgium's Fighting Communist Cells lasted a little under two years (1984–85), while others spanned over more than a decade, for example, Germany's Red Army Faction (RAF).[38] Some of the groups involved were responsible for hundreds of casualties, for example, Italy's Red Brigades, while others only inflicted a modest amount of damage, etc. Nevertheless, it does make sense to discuss their violent careers on the basis of the common framework.

Emergence

The fundamental distinction here is between early and late risers. Revolutionary terrorist activities appeared early in Italy and Germany, in the late 1960s or early 1970s. In Greece, with its Revolutionary November 17 Movement, in Spain, with its First of October Anti-Fascist Resistance Groups (GRAPO), and with France's Direct Action, the terrorist campaigns were initiated more than a half decade later. Experiences distinct to the countries involved seem to explain the variations in timing. The death of Franco and the end of his dictatorship, the subsequent transition to democracy, and ideological divisions within Spain's revived Communist Party provided the context for

GRAPO's emergence, while the mass student protest movements in West Germany and Italy from the middle 1960s to the early 1970s help explain the early initiation of terrorist campaigns in those countries. In spite of these and other national differences, there were a number of factors that the countries involved had in common. They were all democracies that had earlier suffered through periods of right-wing dictatorship or Nazi occupation. In a number of cases the revolutionary groups that emerged explained their own behaviour as an extension of the resistance movements that formed to oppose fascism. In Italy, for example, one of the first revolutionary organizations to surface called itself 'The New Resistance'. There was a central tendency to deny the democratic status of the states involved, to regard them as in some way extensions of the defunct dictatorships. Often the disaffected did this by linking the governments involved to the USA (through the NATO alliance and the operations of the CIA) and it's various imperialist transgressions, especially the Vietnam War.

Overall public opinion in the countries which became sites of revolutionary terrorist campaigns was not supportive of revolutionary violence. Nonetheless, the opinion surveys suggested that typically small percentages of respondents were sufficiently alienated from the prevailing order to endorse the use of violence against the State.[39] Four or five per cent of the public is a tiny minority, but expressed in whole numbers it may represent the views of thousands or, depending on the country's populations size, hundreds of thousands of individuals. In other words, West European terrorists had a constituency as well as a pool from which to draw recruits. In some of the countries involved – most conspicuously France, Germany and Italy – there had been a mass mobilization of students and young people more generally, in effect, a generational rebellion. Not all of these left-wing youth groups turned to terrorism but all of the larger terrorist groups emerged from the extreme elements of these broader mobilized populations.

The rebellion coincided with the appearance of 'New Left' movements in the Western European democracies, movements formed around the view that the 'Old Left' of Communist Parties and the Soviet bloc countries had abandoned their revolutionary vocations and had become revisionist collaborators of the USA and world capitalism. While the 'Old Left' confined its activities to the halls of parliament or the negotiating tables, the 'New Left' was committed to a politics of direct action and popular confrontations with the authorities. The national liberation struggles underway in the Third World, notably in Vietnam and over the question of Palestine, offered inspiration. Despite their criticism of the Stalinist incarnation of Marxism, the resilience of some of these larger and well-organized groups was fostered by their ability to find safe haven, occasional training and supplies in the Eastern bloc. The dislocation they caused with the western democracies, particularly Germany and Italy, was entirely in keeping with Marxist predictions, a fact which no doubt helped them to receive aid from the Soviet Union which in turn strengthened their abilities to wage war on capitalism.

Escalation

The transformation of popular protest into terrorist campaigns was promoted by a number of factors, some unique to individual countries, others common to most. The way in which the authorities reacted to New Left mobilization and protest played a role in a number of cases. The use of excessive force, even when unintended by those in command, convinced some protesters that they were dealing with 'fascists' with whom no compromise was possible. When the authorities were identified as 'fascists', processes of dehumanization and polarization were initiated that led to the conclusion that all forms of violence were appropriate. (Of course in at least one case, Italy, the revolutionary movements were literally dealing with fascists, or neo-fascists, who pursued a 'strategy of tensions' in collaboration with elements in the security services in order to repress the New Left groups.[40]). In Greece, the revolutionary November 17 movement took its name for the date in 1973 when the military junta sent riot police into the Athens Polytechnic to quell a student demonstration. The police killed 20 students and injured another 200. Twelve years later, November 17 circulated a communiqué justifying its assassination of a publisher which began: 'We must strike at the fascist CIA agents among the press who daily ridicule, poison and deceive the Greek people'.[41] The Spanish terrorist organisation GRAPO repeatedly addressed its communiqués 'To the working class, to all peoples oppressed by the Spanish fascist State' and defined itself as an anti-fascist resistance group at war with the country's 'socio-fascist government'. The communiqués to which we have referred were written more than a half decade after Franco's death and Spain's transition to constitutional democracy; and the 'socio-fascist' government to which GRAPO referred was headed by the Socialist leader Felipe Gonzalez.[42] The ensuing revolutionary terrorist campaigns could indeed be seen as largely imaginary wars against 'fascism' with real consequences. (It is a matter of some curiosity that the USA, which was largely responsible for the military defeat of real-life fascism, the Nazi and Fascist dictatorships in Western Europe, was often made to serve as a symbolic stand-in for the defunct regimes. The revolutionaries' representation of the USA in this way is consistent with the idea that as conflicts escalate, so do the adversaries' impulses to dichotomize and simplify. Anyone familiar with the reception accorded to Claire Sterling's *The Terror Network* in these years is aware of the same tendency on the other side, that is, the identification of all the revolutionary terrorist organizations with the Soviet Union and a KGB-initiated conspiracy.)

Although these 'wars' had in common their failure to mobilize large numbers of proletarians in the cause of revolution, they differed from one another in terms of their duration and the ability of the groups involved to recruit successive generations of members. The Greek November 17 has continued to operate on an intermittent basis into the twenty-first century, while Belgium's Fighting Communist Cells' life span was under two years. In addition to their duration, the campaigns differed in terms of how they began. In the Italian case, the Red Brigades first attacked property and then kidnapped hostages before they began to kill people. That is, the events displayed a mounting severity. But in other cases, for example, November 17, the revolutionaries began by assassinating individuals and continued this practice over time. If there is a common trajectory to the separate campaigns it appears to involve the frequency with which terrorist campaigns were launched over time. Of course, the pattern we detect requires empirical confirmation, but most, though not all, of the campaigns seem to follow this pattern. There is an increase in the number of terrorist attacks from one year to the next. In some cases, the Italian in particular, there is a rapid acceleration in a particular year, to a point where a peak was reached after which there was a rapid decline in the number of terrorist events committed. Or, escalation was followed by a precipitous de-escalation. Why?

De-Escalation

In general, the revolutionary terrorist campaigns did not come to a close on the basis of a negotiated settlement resulting in mutual accommodation. However, it does appear that a constituency in favour of de-escalation did develop within the terrorist organizations themselves. (The relationship between some members' desire to de-escalate the conflict may have been brought on by the opposite tendency on the part of the authorities for whom the groups' defeat may very well have taken on a life of its own.) Certainly in the Italian case, many revolutionaries living uncomfortable clandestine lives and despairing of ever reaching the organization's objectives sought a peaceful end to the conflicts they had either initiated or in which they had become entrapped. When government offers of amnesty were forthcoming, individuals seized them. In general, though, the revolutionary terrorist campaigns ended when the authorities were able to bring about the capitulation of the groups involved, either as the result of an outright victory (the arrest or elimination of group members) or as a consequence of internal changes, that is, de-moralization, disaffection and disintegration.

The two major terrorist campaigns in Western Europe in which the cause of nationalism/separatism was foremost, Northern Ireland and the Basque country of Spain, were the only ones to go through the full conflict cycle from emergence to escalation to de-escalation and then to a negotiated settlement outcome. In neither case can the negotiated settlement be considered secure, since in both cases extremist splinter groups have demonstrated their intent to continue the irredentist struggle.

IRELAND AND SPAIN

Emergence

In both the Irish and Basque cases the sources of the conflict are centuries old. At some times the conflicts were latent, at others they were expressed openly, often erupting into violence. But the parties to the conflicts never achieved a complete resolution. The pattern bears some resemblance to what Pruitt and Rubin refer to as the 'aggressor-defender' model of escalation. The aggressor party uses progressively stronger coercive tactics until the defender concedes, unless of course the defender proves too powerful. On various occasions over the course of these long conflicts, the British and Spanish governments were sufficiently powerful to cause the Irish and Basque struggles to become latent. But, as what Tarrow and others have labelled the 'structure of opportunity' changed, the conflicts resurfaced.[43] In the case of Northern Ireland, the Catholic civil rights protests of the late 1960s and the response to them by the Protestant-controlled provincial government provided the sparks needed to ignite the terrorist or para-military campaigns of both the IRA and the various Protestant bands.[44] In the Basque case, Basque Homeland and Liberty (ETA) committed itself to the path of violence in 1962 in the context of the Franco dictatorship but carried out relatively few attacks until the late 1960s. It was the

Burgos trial of 1970, involving the prosecution of 16 ETA militants by the Franco regime, which ignited or re-ignited the conflict. 'The trial was one of the most significant events in ETA's history. For the first time massive demonstrations, strikes, and occupations of churches in Euskadi took place in support of ETA's demands and its prisoners.'[45] From this point, ETA became the group differentiated for the purpose of waging an armed struggle on behalf of the Basque cause.

Escalation

In a numerical sense, there was a significant increase in the incidence of ETA violence in the years following Franco's death, despite, or perhaps because of, Spain's transition to democracy and the extension of the rights of local autonomy to the Basque provinces. ETA was responsible for killing more people in the three-year period 1978–1980 than it had from its commitment to violence in 1962 until the end of the dictatorship. The greater frequency and lethality of terrorist events occurred even though the French authorities became more willing to co-operate with a democratic Spain in detaining ETA suspects who had sought sanctuary in the Basque communities of Southern France. After the 1980 peak the rate of ETA killing declined somewhat but it never quite returned to its pre-democratic level until the early 1990s.

Following Franco's death, ETA violence escalated in other ways. It spread from the Basque homeland to other parts of the country. Madrid and Barcelona often became the sites of terrorist assassinations and bombing campaigns. Similarly, the range of targets expanded. Initially, and with the spectacular exception of the assassination of Franco's designated successor Admiral Carrero Blanco in 1972, ETA tended to direct its attacks against police officers, individuals who symbolized foreign occupation of the Basque country. As the conflict escalated, however, local and national politicians, journalists, industrialists, 'traitors', and ordinary citizens became more common victims.[46] Unlike the operations of the IRA or PIRA in Northern Ireland, ETA has not extended its terrorist campaign much farther afield. There have been incidents in southern France, but nothing comparable to IRA attacks in England or on the continent. The latter's operations have included, among a long list of attacks outside Ulster, attacks on British military installations in Germany, an attempt to assassinate former Prime Minister Margaret Thatcher, the successful assassination of Lord Mountbatten in the Irish Republic, a bombing attack on Harrod's department store in London, and a similar but more lethal effort at a pub in Birmingham.

The escalation of terrorist violence in connection with the troubles in Northern Ireland was the outgrowth of communal rioting in Belfast and Derry during the summer of 1969. The British government responded by sending troops to protect the Catholic population. It was clear that the Protestant police force was unwilling to do so. The consequences were far-reaching. Rather than providing protection, many Catholics came to see the British military presence as an army of occupation. On the other side, moderate Protestant politicians who favoured compromise over Catholic demands for improved job and housing opportunities were often drowned out by more militant figures. The IRA itself underwent a division, with the Provisional faction breaking away in order to wage an effective armed struggle for a united and socialist Ireland. The conflict escalated to a still higher level as the result of British miscalculations such as the policy of internment and 'Bloody Sunday' in January 1972, when British troops killed 13 unarmed Catholics attending a civil rights march. Add to this mix the formation of such Protestant para-military groups as the Ulster Volunteer Force (UVF), and the effect was a spiral of conflict entrapping the British government and both the republican and loyalist populations of Northern Ireland.

De-escalation

In Northern Ireland, there were repeated attempts to de-escalate the conflict over the years. *Inter alia*, a power-sharing plan sponsored by the British and Irish governments, the 1985 Hillsborough Agreement, aroused widespread Protestant resentment because, according to them, it went too far; while the PIRA condemned it because it did not go far enough. Two mothers, Catholic and Protestant, won the Nobel Peace Prize for their efforts to bridge sectarian differences. Pope John Paul II appealed for a peaceful settlement. From time to time various American political figures offered to mediate the dispute. This is to say that as the years passed, a substantial constituency in favour of de-escalation developed both inside and outside of Northern Ireland. By far the most important of these constituencies, however, emerged from those doing the actual fighting both within the PIRA itself and within the British security forces.

The conflict in the Basque country has not had the benefit of so much international involvement on behalf of a peaceful settlement. The decrease in the level of ETA violence was more the result of growing French co-operation with the Spanish authorities, the sometimes extra-legal operations of Spanish police agencies and the loss of support for the organization within the Basque community itself than as a result of foreign mediation. Nonetheless, the Spanish government and ETA representatives held discussions on and off in Algiers, beginning in 1987 and ending in failure in 1989. During part of this time ETA had been willing to abide by a truce. But after the talks failed, the terrorism resumed, though at a somewhat reduced level. Nevertheless, ETA leaders could not help but be aware that there was a growing constituency among Basques opposed to a continuation of the violence.

Negotiations and Settlement

In the case of Northern Ireland, negotiations among the various parties involved began in the mid-1990s and culminated in their signing of the Good Friday Peace Agreement in 1998. Extreme elements among both republican and loyalist followers have attempted to prevent the new power-sharing arrangement from taking effect. Despite some close calls, the Omagh bombing by the 'Real' IRA and the dispute over the de-commissioning of weapons, they have not succeeded. By most accounts the role played by outside negotiators was indispensable in reaching the outcome.

In Spain, leaders of ETA, following developments in Northern Ireland, declared a cease-fire in 1998 and resumed negotiations with the Madrid government. During these discussions the Spanish Prime Minister said he did not want outside parties to attempt mediation. The talks did not succeed. ETA declared an end to the truce and has resumed its terrorist campaign at a higher level than had been the case before it had begun.

CONCLUSION

Our investigation leads us towards two sets of conclusions. The first set refers to the specific cases in West European terrorism we have sought to sketch, while the second concerns the usefulness of the conflict theory framework for the analysis of terrorist campaigns in general. So far as the former is concerned, it seems to us that the escalation of an already emergent conflict into a fully fledged terrorist campaign was strongly influenced by the reaction of the authorities and the presence of other third parties to the violence. In Italy and Northern Ireland in particular (we have not included Turkey but it would have been included here had we done so), the violence was strongly influenced by the presence of neo-fascist bands, in the Italian case, and by the role played by the Protestant para-militaries in Northern Ireland. In both these campaigns, the presence of another, competing collection of 'struggle groups' promoted precisely the kind of spiralling effect mentioned in the literature. The reaction of the authorities also played an important role in determining the level of terrorist violence. The fact that Italian and Northern Irish authorities became linked, at least from the perspectives of the revolutionaries and republicans, with the violent right-wing groups made for a more rapid escalation of the conflict.

In thinking through the relationships between the aggrieved parties and the States they challenged, it strikes us that neither policies of repression nor concession were, by themselves, responsible for an escalation in violence. The Spanish government shifted from the former to the latter, a change which seemed to accelerate the terrorism, at least in the short run. The apparent willingness of the Greek government not to pursue November 17 has allowed the latter to continue as a minor annoyance for more than a decade. An over-reaction by police to popular protests seems to have promoted terrorism in some cases.[47] On the other hand, the creation of a permissive environment for Middle Eastern terrorists in Western Europe produced more violence. Stronger measures, coupled with tacit bargaining and the shifting sands of Middle Eastern politics, produced less violence, or so it seems. In the case of the very small groups, such as Belgium's Fighting Communist Cells, one government policy or another would not seem to have made much difference.

At the end of terrorist campaigns, the willingness of governments to engage in the tactics of de-escalation and negotiation or even tacit bargaining depended in large measure on the strength and endurance of their adversaries. When the adversaries had to be taken seriously, as in Northern Ireland and the Basque country, or in the case of Middle Eastern groups with state support of one kind or another they usually were. Nevertheless the states of Western Europe were in a better position than most to negotiate an end to the disturbances given the extensive layers of conflict resolution measures available, the stability and broad-based legitimacy of the States in question, and the mechanisms for international co-operation against terrorism.

What about the overall benefits of the conflict theory framework to the study of terrorist campaigns or terrorism-involved campaigns? Our sense here is that it has proven helpful in understanding the dynamics of these campaigns in Western Europe. However, it probably would be of greater assistance in conceptualizing or re-conceptualizing these dynamics in countries such as Lebanon, Sri Lanka, Algeria, Peru and Colombia, where the campaigns were transformed into large-scale and protracted conflicts with many participants. At the other end of the spectrum, it would also be valuable to find out if the framework would be beneficial in our understanding of the rise and fall of individual 'struggle groups' acting by themselves or terrorist bands in conflict with one another.

NOTES

1. For a discussion of the problems involved in developing theoretical constructs in the study of terrorism, see Michael Dartnell, *Action Directe* (London: Frank Cass, 1995), pp. 1–13.
2. Walter Laqueur, *Terrorism* (Boston, MA: Little, Brown & Co., 1977), pp. 133–74.
3. See, for example, Louis Kriesberg, 'The Development of the Conflict Resolution Field', in I. William Zartman and Lewis Rasmussen (eds), *Peacemaking in International Conflict* (Washington, DC: US Institute of Peace, 1997), pp. 51–77; Hugh Miall, Oliver Ramsbotham and Tom Woodhouse, *Contemporary Conflict Resolution* (Cambridge: Polity Press, 1999), pp. 1–5; Kenneth Boulding, *Conflict and Defence: A General Theory* (New York: Harper, 1962), pp. 1–2; see especially the 'Editorial' with which the *Journal of Conflict Resolution* 1/1 (1957), pp. 1–2 begins its publication.
4. Anyone who has witnessed a colleague walking along their university campus muttering to himself/herself with lips twitching has probably reached the conclusion some intra-psychic conflict is underway. But identifying its precise stage of development may take some doing. For one writer who did not abandon this effort, see Morton Deutsch, *The Resolution of Conflict* (New Haven, CT: Yale University Press, 1973), pp. 19–20.
5. A notable exception would be the work on social movements and cycles of protest undertaken by Charles Tilly, Sidney Tarrow, Donatella della Porta and others. See, for example, Sidney Tarrow, *Power in Movement* (New York: Cambridge University Press, 1994).
6. For a discussion, see Stuart Thorson, 'Introduction', in Louis Kriesberg, Terrell Northrup and Stuart Thorson (eds), *Intractable Conflicts and Their Transformation* (Syracuse, NY: Syracuse University Press, 1989), pp. 2–10.
7. Louis Kriesberg, *Constructive Conflicts* (Boulder, CO: Rowman & Littlefield, 1998), p. 52.
8. Ibid., p. 91.
9. Dean Pruitt and Jeffrey Rubin, *Social Conflict: Escalation, Stalemate and Settlement* (New York: Random House, 1986), p. 7.
10. See, for example, Max Heirich, *The Spiral of Conflict Berkeley 1964* (New York: Columbia University Press, 1971), pp. 2–15.
11. Terrell Northrup, 'The Dynamic of Identity in Personal and Social Conflict', in Kriesberg, Northrup and Thorson, *Intractable Conflicts*, pp. 55–82.
12. See, for example, Jagath Senaratne, *Political Violence in Sri Lanka 1977–1990* (Amsterdam: UU University Press, 1997), pp. 55–7.
13. See, for example, Edward Azar, *The Management of Protracted Social Conflict* (Aldershot: Dartmouth Publishing, 1990), pp. 15–17.
14. For a general discussion, see Lewis Coser, *The Functions of Social Conflict* (New York: The Free Press, 1956), pp. 87–110.
15. Pruitt and Rubin, *Social Conflict*, pp. 116–17.
16. Robert Taber, *The War of the Flea* (New York: Lyle Stuart, 1965), pp. 33–44.
17. See Alex Schmid (ed.), *Thesaurus and Glossary of Early Warning and Conflict Prevention Terms* (Leiden: Synthesis Foundation, 2000), pp. 40–1.
18. Joel Brockner and Jeffrey Rubin, *Entrapment in Escalating Conflicts* (New York: Springer-Verlag, 1985), p. 3.
19. See, for example, Richard Smoke, *War: Controlling Escalation* (Cambridge, MA: Harvard University Press, 1977), pp. 24–28.
20. Pruitt and Rubin, *Social Conflict*, pp. 89-90.

21. Lewis Richardson, *Arms and Insecurity* (Pittsburgh, PA: Boxwood Press, 1960), p. 15.
22. Roy Licklider, 'The Consequences of Negotiated Settlements in Civil Wars, 1945–1993', *American Political Science Review*, 89/3 (September 1995), pp. 683–4.
23. Schmid, *Thesaurus and Glossary*, p. 34.
24. Louis Kriesberg, 'Introduction', in Louis Kriesberg and Stuart Thorson (eds), *Timing The De-Escalation of International Conflicts* (Syracuse, NY: Syracuse University Press, 1991), pp. 3–5.
25. See, for example, Michelle Benson and Jacek Kugler, 'Power Parity, Democracy and the Severity of Internal Violence', *The Journal of Conflict Resolution*, 42/2 (April 1998), pp. 196–209.
26. Kriesberg, *Constructive Conflicts*, pp. 223–49.
27. Ibid., pp. 262–3.
28. See, for example, Peter Chalk, *West European Terrorism and Counter-Terrorism* (London: Macmillan, 1996), pp. 173–85.
29. David Rapoport, *Assassination and Terrorism* (Toronto, CA: CBC Merchandising, 1971), pp. 10–11.
30. See, for example, Martha Crenshaw Hutchinson, *Revolutionary Terrorism: The FLN in Algeria 1954–1962* (Stanford, CA: Hoover Institution Press, 1978).
31. For a discussion, see Leonard Weinberg, 'Initiation: The Decision to Wage Campaigns of Terrorism', a paper presented at the Annual Meeting of the American Political Science Association, Marriott Wardman Park, Washington DC (31 August–3 September 2000).
32. On the conservatism of the leaders of groups engaged in armed struggle, see J. Bowyer-Bell, *The Dynamic of the Armed Struggle* (London: Frank Cass, 1998), pp. 130–3.
33. For a general discussion, see Dennis Pluchinsky, 'Middle East Terrorist Activity in Western Europe in the 1980s: A Decade of Violence', in Yonah Alexander and Dennis Pluchinsky (eds), *European Terrorism: Today and Tomorrow* (Washington, DC: Brassey's Inc., 1992), pp. 1–29.
34. Pluchinsky, 'Middle East Terrorist Activity in Western Europe in the 1980s', p. 13.
35. For a discussion of the Libyan case, see Walter Laqueur, *The Age of Terrorism* (Boston, MA: Little, Brown & Co., 1987), pp. 280–8.
36. See, for example, J. Bowyer Bell, *A Time of Terror* (New York: Basic Books, 1978), pp. 78–93, 168–97.
37. In the case of the Palestinian–Israeli conflict, West European states, Norway for example, and institutions, have certainly played roles as third-party mediators.
38. Dennis Pluchinsky, 'Western Europe's Red Terrorists: The Fighting Communist Organisations', in Yonah Alexander and Dennis Pluchinsky (eds), *Europe's Red Terrorists* (London: Frank Cass, 1992), p. 47.
39. See, for example, Christopher Hewitt, 'Terrorism and Public Opinion', in Edward Moxon-Browne (ed.), *European Terrorism* (New York: G.K. Hall, 1994), pp. 69–94. See also Max Kaase, 'Political Participation, Political Values and Political Violence', in Raimondo Catanzaro (ed.), *The Red Brigades and Left-Wing Terrorism in Italy* (New York: St Martin's, 1991), p. 19.
40. See, for example, Richard Drake, *The Revolutionary Mystique and Terrorism in Contemporary Italy* (Bloomington, IN: Indiana University Press, 1989), pp. 2–3.
41. Alexander and Pluchinsky, *Europe's Red Terrorists*, p. 94.
42. Ibid., pp. 118, 120, 123.
43. Tarrow, *Power in Movement*, pp. 82–99. In the Basque case writers mention fears that the homeland was becoming an increasingly attractive destination to other Spaniards searching for better jobs. Many Basques may have felt they would lose their distinct culture and traditions as a result. See, for example, Raphael Zariski, 'Ethnic Extremism among Ethno-Territorial Minorities in Western Europe', in Moxon-Browne (ed.), *European Terrorism*, pp. 107–26.
44. See, for example, Tim Pat Coogan, *The Troubles* (London: Random House, 1996), pp. 70–95.
45. Goldie Shabad and Francisco Jose Llera Ramo, 'Political Violence in a Democratic State: Basque Terrorism in Spain', in Martha Crenshaw (ed.), *Terrorism in Context* (University Park, PA: Pennsylvania State University Press, 1995), p. 410–72.
46. Jon Lee Anderson, 'Home Fires', *The New Yorker* (12 February 2001), pp. 40–7.
47. For a discussion, see Donatella della Porta and Herbert Reiter, 'The Policing of Protest in Western Democracies', in Donatella della Porta and Herbert Reiter (eds), *Policing Protest* (Minneapolis, MI: University of Minnesota Press, 1998), pp. 1–32.

9

Breaking the Cycle:
Empirical Research and Postgraduate
Studies on Terrorism

FREDERICK SCHULZE

I N SPITE of the increasing relevance of terrorism in the conduct of political affairs and the subsequent growth of terrorism studies, if one had to characterize the current state of the discipline it would resemble a process of ossification. A quarter of a century ago, J. Bowyer-Bell noted, 'The academic response to terrorism had been ahistorical, exaggerated, and closely associated with congenial political postures.'[1] Notwithstanding some promising theoretical paradigms and a measure of increased professionalism, the gist of Bowyer's contention typifies the majority of terrorism research and analysis. The overriding deficiency of this state of stagnation is a dearth of empirically grounded research on terrorism.

This chapter focuses on the consequences caused by the absence of empirical data as experienced by the author in his pursuit of a doctorate. Beginning with a synopsis of the underlying effects caused by inadequate empirical research, the analysis subsequently explores the dynamics of empirical research emphasizing intensive field research among terrorists. Throughout the chapter, linkages will be delineated concerning cause and effect between empirical research and terrorism studies.

INFORMATION UNDERLOAD

The literature of terrorism is arguably in its nascent stage. According to
Schmid and Jongman, 'More than 85 per cent of all books on the topic
have been written since 1968'.[2] Over this time span a prodigious assort-
ment of books, monographs, articles, and other ephemera has emerged.
Relatively speaking, its track record is wanting and as Schmid and
Jongman critically note:

> There are probably few areas in the social science literature in
> which so much is written on the basis of so little research. Perhaps
> as much as 80 per cent of the literature is not research-based in any
> rigorous sense; instead, it is too often narrative, condemnatory,
> and prescriptive.[3]

In her analysis in *Terrorism Research and the Diffusion of Ideas*, Edna Reid
suggests an invisible college of terrorism researchers controlled to a
great extent by the 'diffusion of ideas that influence the positions
adopted by a wide range of actors, including government bureaucrats
and decision makers, legislative and corporate bodies, and the public.'[4]
Using a control group consisting of 32 prominent terrorism analysts,
Reid postulates that the information flow on terrorism and the research
process constitutes a cyclic arrangement.[5] Under such a paradigm,
terrorism studies – in spite of its transdisciplinary nature – is myopic,
restrained, and limits empirical research. Reid notes:

> The terrorism research process and the flow of information such as
> researchers' publications, government documents and media
> reports seem to constitute a closed system in which information is
> created, processed, published, and disseminated. Later the informa-
> tion feeds back into the circular research system to stimulate further
> creation, processing, publishing, and dissemination. Since the
> closed system indicates a static environment, the same hypotheses,
> definitions, and theories continued to be analysed, assimilated,
> published, cited, and eventually retrieved … Finally, the process of
> accumulation of a body of knowledge is slow and additional infor-
> mation must be discovered and related to the previous knowledge.
> Yet, this slow process of accumulating scientific information does
> not identify the most relevant information but accepts all the myths
> until empirical investigation proves otherwise.[6]

Unfortunately empirical investigation, with few exceptions, has been conspicuously lacking. Ted Robert Gurr concurs with this view, noting that:

> Careful gleaning of the literature turns up some sound quantitative, comparative and historical studies of terrorist phenomena. But the fact remains that the research questions raised in the literature are considerably more interesting than most of the evidence brought to bear upon them. With a few clusters of exceptions there is in fact a disturbing lack of good empirically grounded research on terrorism.[7]

Gurr goes on to say:

> I am convinced ... that many, perhaps most of the important questions being raised cannot be answered adequately with the kinds of information now generally available to scholars ... The ... problem is the lack of enough reliable data for the analysis of the entire range of questions about terrorism: etiology, process, and outcomes ...[8]

Terrorism studies are in an academic catch-22. It is illogical, unreasonable and irresponsible to continue in a manner that hinders the evolution of the discipline. One cannot test hypotheses or formulate models based upon secondary and tertiary accounts, especially when the lion's share of raw data is based upon media accounts. Variations in accuracy, analysis and investigative rigor make journalistic reporting problematic insofar as qualitative research is concerned. Moreover, primary source material is seldom examined and cited, defying the most basic tenet of social science research. A triumvirate composed of the media, government and academia has to a great extent proscribed the course of terrorism studies.[9] Although the origins of terrorism can be traced back throughout the course of written history,[10] the basis for this troika is understandable. The high-profile terrorist actions of the late 1960s and early 1970s, especially the spectre of aerial hijackings and hostage-barricade scenarios, galvanized liberal democracies into creating the foundation on which current terrorism research rests. An inevitable collusion of interests emerged designed to control information flow and content leading to an agenda focusing on prophylactic measures to counter the threat of international terrorism. Bruce Hoffman notes that most of the seminal works on terrorism came out of this period, penned by authors such as Paul Wilkinson, Walter

Laqueur, J. Bowyer-Bell and Brian Jenkins.[11] Hoffman points out that in spite of the increased attention focused on terrorism very few authoritative studies have emerged since these initial studies.[12] On the state of terrorism research *vis-à-vis* policy, Hoffman remarks that:

> In the area of policy relevance, however, terrorism research arguably had failed miserably. Nearly two decades of scholarly and policy-oriented research on terrorism has had little, if any, effect on either the incidence of terrorist violence or the organization in whose name these acts are perpetrated.[13]

The import of this observation corroborates both the failure of existing research approaches and warrants the construction of new research methodologies. Original systematic research then can be used to test existing theories, corroborating, modifying, or replacing them based upon data collection.

Ultimately, it is not that the academic community has failed to recognize problems associated with a lack of empirical and field research. Indeed, a number of researchers have done excellent work. However, these individuals were the exception rather than the rule. Consequently, while their research made valuable inroads, these efforts seemingly scratched the surface, opening up venues for subsequent analysis that other scholars failed to exploit.

ANALYTICAL AND METHODOLOGICAL FACTORS

Once the topic of the dissertation is chosen and approved by the appropriate monitoring bodies, the predominant factor, and by far the most important component of the dissertation, is the creation, development and refinement of the analytic question(s). Only after the analytic question(s) is/are formulated can a methodology be chosen or designed to facilitate the systematic ordering and ranking of information, permitting insight. Then the researcher can focus on the relevant data, its acquisition, application, and relationship to the structure of the dissertation.

In the case of this author, the principal emphasis of the dissertation was a case study of the Bruders Schweigen, more commonly know as The Order, an American white supremacist organization associated with the Christian Identity movement. Two overriding elements were incorporated: (1) an original analytical/theoretical and methodological framework; and, (2) data-gathering involving primary source material and field research. Enhancing the quantitative and qualitative acquisition of source materials, the methodological framework consisted of overlapping and interlocking theoretical concepts, providing variables to crosscheck and qualify the data while limiting induction particularly during the course of field research.[14] Concomitantly, this also addressed a deficiency in research on terrorism, expounded by Martha Crenshaw, that 'Too few researchers in the field build on the work of others. The quest for theoretical generalization should be balanced with attention to detail. Access to data will always be a problem, but not to the extent of curtailing inquiry'.[15] The overall goal was to provide a holistic analysis concentrating on the etiology of terrorism emanating from the extreme right.

Ted Gurr has argued that the causes of terrorism require more research attention. He noted that:

> Causes – structural, social, and individual – should receive as much or more attention. To draw an analogy from medicine ... it is as if medical researchers were to concentrate their efforts on the epidemiology and treatment of disease without studying its causes.[16]

Deciding to focus on the causation of American right-wing terrorism, the author determined that if etiological data could be ascertained and factors could be documented then potential preventative measures could be formulated.

Moreover, in surveying the case study literature on right-wing terrorist groups, it was found that a significant segment of the literature was in comparative format. This dissertation, however, departs from comparative analysis, asserting that more detailed analysis on individual cases is required for a fuller understanding of terror from the extreme right. The lack of empirically oriented, qualitative case studies on American right-wing terrorism, as well as on terrorism in general, limits meaningful quantitative research on the subject. Again, Crenshaw notes that:

> Even the most persuasive of statements about terrorism are not cast in the form of testable propositions, nor are they broadly comparative in origin or intent ... In general, propositions about terrorism lack logical comparability, specification of the relationships of variables to each other, and a rank ordering of variables in terms of explanatory power.[17]

Furthermore, as Paul Wilkinson explains:

> Context is all in analysis of political violence. In view of the
> enormous diversity of groups and aims involved, generalizations
> and evaluations covering the whole field of modern terrorism
> should be treated with considerable reserve. Oversimplified analy-
> sis of phenomena tends to induce simplistic and dangerous
> proposals for panaceas.[18]

RESEARCH STRATEGY AND APPLICATION

With these caveats in mind, equipped with my analytical question(s)
and methodological framework, research began in earnest. Depending
on the topic, analytical question(s), and methodological framework, the
researcher must formulate a comprehensive strategy suitable for the
dissertation. The author adopted an eclectic, syncretic research agenda
in accordance with the dictates of analytical framework. As the dissertation called for empirical research in different formats concomitant with
an emphasis on field research, this flexibility was required to deal with
any contingencies encountered. By adapting this approach the author
could focus on different avenues of data acquisition; however, if a
dissertation proposal embodies firsthand field research, various issues
come to the forefront.

For example, the issue of shared language and culture is important.
In selecting to focus on an English-speaking extremist group, the
author avoided considerable obstacles. Although it is possible to undertake a dissertation topic on groups whose language is unfamiliar, in
practice it is usually far from easy. The difficulties mount even further
if the proposed dissertation is to include field research. Travel, accommodation, translators, and acquisition of primary source material will
all be much more difficult. Furthermore, if access to extremists[19] and
terrorists is achieved, can the researcher implicitly trust his/her transla-
tor(s) when relaying questions and comments and be certain of their
veracity *vis-à-vis* respondents' answers? Moreover, if a translator is
assigned by an extremist organization, are organizational dictates going
to distort the quantitative and qualitative flow of information? A
researcher could find their hard work compromised by distorted data
and analysis. Most extremists are going to slant information to suit their
positions and viewpoints. This is to be expected when interacting with
individuals whose views are hostile to mainstream society. If prepared

sufficiently, a researcher can filter out or read between the lines during the process of discourse, or by an examination of notes or taped transcripts. There are risks then if the researcher is prepared to leave this in the hands of someone else.

Moreover, if the researcher is planning to interact with extremists in the field, outside sources of funding may play an important part of a research agenda. Regrettably, funding for postgraduate research on terrorism is quite limited and circumscribed. This incongruous state of affairs has impeded advancement in the discipline and discouraged potential scholars from engaging in terrorism studies. Furthermore, if a proposal entails field research, from the author's experience, depending on the topic, this can be more of a liability than an asset. The number of grants available for research dealing specifically with terrorism is miniscule. Those that are available usually fall between circumscribed parameters. Open-ended grants dealing with any aspect of terrorism are virtually non-existent. With the exception of small contributions from the University of St Andrews and the William R. Nelson Institute, the majority of research discussed in this chapter was self-funded and this is a common state of affairs for postgraduates who wish to research on this controversial subject. Ultimately, research on terrorism is overwhelmingly driven by the agendas of governments preoccupied with current policy concerns. Topic selection and research agendas can significantly affect potential funding.

If a researcher obtains funding from an organization or government entity with a known bias or agenda then his/her role as an impartial observer or when engaging in participant observation may be jeopardized. Because of the nature of terrorism studies, with its nexus between academia, the government, and other interested entities, this could still be acceptable to an individual researcher. However, the potential risk to the researcher may be increased significantly as a result. In some circumstances, a doctoral dissertation may be intended to become classified upon completion or geared toward distribution within a particular funding agency only. In itself this is fine; however, one must recognize that objectivity may be compromised to suit the mission of the funding agency.

DATA ACQUISITION AND NETWORK DEVELOPMENT

Empirical Data on American Right-Wing Extremism: A Sad State of Affairs

A major obstacle in preparing for this research was the lack of empirical quantitative data on US domestic terrorism. Criminologist Mark Hamm, in a review of social science research on US domestic terrorism and hate crimes, noted that 'The data necessary to conduct this research are in a sad state of affairs.'[20] The causes for this are numerous: the problem of defining terrorism; the lack of full exposure by certain governments to the problem of domestic terrorism; the merging of hate crimes and terrorism statistics under one rubric by watchdog groups and anti-extremists organizations; combined with the fact that 'There are actually no laws against domestic terrorism; that is, no federal (or state) statues to outlaw terrorism on US soil'.[21] What exists is a mishmash of figures and statistics that vary enormously according to the dictates of the issuing body.

Emblematic of this cyclic dependence on data based upon secondary and tertiary account is 'Project Megiddo', the Federal Bureau of Investigation's (FBI) highly touted report about domestic terrorism on the eve of the millennium. A supposedly authoritative report on the state of domestic terrorism, the research relied heavily on source material from the Anti Defamation League (ADL) and Southern Poverty Law Center (SPLC) in its analysis.[22] Both these organizations are antagonistic to the extreme right; hence the objectivity of their conclusions must be questioned. In scholarship on the American extreme right, both these organizations have produced voluminous amounts on the topic much of it factual and annotated, and just about every author on the subject has cited these organizations at one time or another. Taking these reports at face value, however, can lead the researcher to inaccurate conclusions distorting his/her analytical framework and the data generated from it.[23] The fact that the government utilized data from these organizations compounds this problem, while demonstrating the overall lack of raw data.

Conducting a literature review on the state of right-wing extremism, the author encountered deficiencies characteristic in the commentary associated with research on terrorism in general. Perusing the subject matter, other researchers who had conducted well-grounded empirical and academic analyses were identified. These individuals were contacted and apprised of my research. By initiating a dialogue and introducing myself, the foundation for an information and logistical network was established. This was useful because in-depth field research network development is essential.

Although I was in Scotland during this period of my dissertation, through research via the Internet, inter-library loans, and archival efforts, a significant amount of information was obtained and analysed. An examination of the major archival holding in the USA concerning Christian Identity and the extreme right determined their applicability *vis-à-vis* data procurement. Contacting the archives of one institution, I informed the librarians of the scope and objectives of the dissertation and made arrangements for an imminent visit. In response they generously forwarded a listing of their respective holdings. Moreover, they arranged a meeting with the curator of the collection, an individual whose expertise in the field enhanced the dissertation through valuable advice, and facilitated meetings with influential people in the movement.

The religion of Christian Identity is a locus of the white supremacist and white separatist constellations in the USA. In this preparatory stage prior to field research, I became a historian of the Christian Identity movement and its evolution to the present. By the time field research was undertaken, this status as a bona fide historian of Christian Identity was the avenue I pursued to get my foot in the door with Identity clerics, leaders and laymen. By thoroughly covering the ideology and theology of Identity, these individuals were convinced of my expertise in this field, and this became the first step of expanding a dialogue which eventually covered the thematic spectrum associated with Christian Identity. These initial forays via telephone conversations and written correspondence allowed entrance into the Christian Identity network: a network that touches the panoply of right-wing movements.

Networking: The Key Determinant in Empirical Field Research

Of all the lessons learned during the dissertation process, the centrality of networking was crucial. Starting from the onset of the dissertation, and continuing up to the present, networking through various channels – academic, governmental and media, as well as individuals connected to the movement – has not ceased. If optimal results are to be achieved, utilization of networks is essential. If not for the good offices of individuals met through this process, the insights, access to terrorists and extremists, and access to other forms of empirical data would have been extremely limited.

Networking should start once research is undertaken. For field research, establishing contacts or interacting with certain networks can take time and persistence. Once a dissertation topic, whose proposal includes interpersonal research with extremists, is approved, the researcher *must* immediately begin this process. During the initial stages a researcher's supervisor may be able to provide suggestions, leads, and potential contacts. In general, however, the researcher cannot expect a great deal of assistance in this endeavour. Empirical field research, especially that involving interpersonal contacts with political extremists and terrorists, is atypical – the exception not the rule. Additionally, no hard and fast rules, structured paradigms, or accepted codified procedures exist. In the author's case, extensive research, synthesized and guided by the parameters set down by the analytical and methodological framework, provided a schematic to follow during the course of research.

In establishing a network, I contacted a wide range of individuals whose knowledge or research was relevant to the dissertation. For example, by corresponding with a scholar whose research influenced the creation of the dissertation's analytical framework, arrangements were made to meet in Northern Ireland. Other scholars sent me copies of primary research material they had gathered during their own research on the topic. Most of this assistance came after the individuals were convinced of my sincerity and knowledge of the topic at hand. Numerous times, this came about by asking certain questions about their own research or views on a particular topic. Do not expect academics and other interested parties in the field just to send material as a result of one letter, phone call or email. As a researcher, you have to convince them that you are knowledgeable about the project and are trying to make a serious contribution to the scholarship. Once again, this ability to gain feedback from scholars who influenced my on-going research was a process of taking the initiative and starting a correspondence.

LEAVING THE IVORY TOWER

Initial Experiences in the Field

Field research is not for the irresolute or diffident scholar.[24] That being said, with the right approach, the dangers can be minimized significantly. Depending on the subject matter and analytical question(s), concomitant with the theoretical and methodological framework, a researcher can limit their immersion and participation. Still, the application and threat of violence is the essence of terrorism and researchers in this area must be cognizant of this reality.

Yet a researcher need not place him/herself in the murky terrorist subculture to provide valuable depictions and information on terrorism. One does not have to penetrate an active terrorist group – a dangerous prospect indeed – in order to enhance a dissertation while providing a foundation other scholars can follow up upon. In her work on the Red Brigades, Alison Jamieson not only interviewed imprisoned Italian terrorists, she augmented these interviews by interviews with government officials, security officers and other parties associated with the terrorist group.[25] Jamieson's research illuminates the importance and value that can be obtained by interacting with above ground individuals, sympathizers and other qualified persons. Family members, friends, teachers and former employers can all provide significant information on particular terrorists or even the group.

In spite of the preparations undertaken prior to taking a first step in the field, the researcher will encounter the visceral reality of entering unchartered territory. Although preparation can take a researcher so far, when their feet first hit the ground in the field, the realization quickly comes that this is a very different world in which one has to navigate. At times, the route may slide widely off-course.

Through contacts, I arranged to attend a conference in Colorado Springs dealing with right-wing extremism. The original plan was that if all went well, from there I would embark on my first tentative steps in the field. Numerous speakers in attendance had presentations, or so I thought, that would enhance this endeavor. It was my hope that people in attendance could further my research by providing leads to Christian Identity adherents which would be followed up at the end of the conference. To my disappointment – while I agreed with many of views of the conference participants toward Christian Identity – they neither shared nor encouraged my enthusiasm in meeting face to face with Identity adherents. In contrast they seemed to want me to disdain them from a distance – a position not uncommon to many people, as I would find during the duration of my research. Surprised and taken aback, and most likely through complaining about this state of affairs, I met two individuals who shared this viewpoint (or simply felt sympathy for this neophyte who wanted to meet Identity believers). Through the help of these newfound acquaintances, I found myself immersed in the militia movement. With a friendly warning about the abundance of firearms associated with militias, I found myself in Johnstown Colorado – home of the American Freedom Network, one of the premiere militia radio stations in the country. My host on the American Freedom Network was listed by the SPLC as one of the most prominent 'patriots' in America.

It was the first time I had been on a radio show and I knew I was getting somewhere when I realized the disc jockey carried a loaded 45cal. pistol in a shoulder holster. Previous research indicated that the Christian Identity movement had made significant inroads into the militia movement. While the people at the American Freedom Network went out of their way to distance themselves and the militia movement from Christian Identity,[26] they were still able to provide names and phone numbers of ex-Identity adherents (while lecturing to me on their beliefs and perceptions of the militia movement). This opened the path finally to conduct some face-to-face interviews.

The author's experience pertaining to the conference and its aftermath is illustrative of the complexities, contingencies, and flexibility required to achieve the desired goals of research. Field research is multifaceted: it can be analysed according to the parameters of various social science disciplines concomitant with diverse levels of inquiry. Furthermore, the dynamics, diversity, and context of terrorist movements requires adaptability both in the field as well as in methodological approaches. Each organization must be analysed and approached in a context-specific manner. The syncretic and eclectic theology of Christian Identity combined with its lack of an established hierarchy, clerical independence, and geographic dispersion virtually guaranteed that circumstances could arise which would require quick-fire decisions on how to approach and deal with potentially dangerous situations and people. The capriciousness of this course would become readily apparent during the course of three interviews with Christian Identity clerics.

The first interview was with one of the most radical Christian Identity pastors. Some members of the terrorist groups under study worshipped at his church and, more importantly, committed at least one terrorist act the day after they worshipped there. From information gathered at the conference, I was told it would be extremely difficult, if not impossible, to get an interview. I did not know whether this was an effort to dissuade me or if it reflected a genuine belief this was indeed the case. Through my militia contacts, however, I obtained the personal phone number of this pastor, a fact that caught his attention. However, I was not convinced that contacting him via his personal phone number was the best avenue for approaching him to arrange an interview. The number was not readily available and using it could possibly heighten his already keen sense of paranoia. Throughout the duration of my field research, my ulterior motives were always called into question, with numerous individuals assuming I was a government agent, informant or connected to a watchdog organization. When I did phone, the pastor suggested we meet for bible study and church on Sunday.

In light of his reputation, I grew increasingly nervous as the interview drew near. At first everything went well. I entered the church and introduced myself to the members of the congregation. They were inquisitive but friendly offering me coffee and home-made cookies and cakes. Some of the apprehensions I felt dissipated as conversations were struck up. At this point I was able to raise questions concerning Christian Identity, how they became involved, their perceptions of the religion and what it meant to them to be an adherent, their perceptions of society and government, as well as Christian Identity's relationship concerning these issues. Answers seemed honest and heartfelt. I felt I was getting a good insight into their beliefs and motivations, both individually and collectively, regarding this particular congregation.

Then the pastor came in and lived up to his reputation for being paranoid and radical. He instructed his congregation to refer all questions to him so that any additional interactions between myself and the congregation were effectively cut off. Sitting down for bible studies, I attempted to mitigate the rising unease inside me by asking questions. As I had forgotten to bring a Bible (a lesson learned for future interviews), the pastor chastized me, asking out loud how I was going to participate in bible studies without a Bible, and told the person next to me to share their copy. Some of the questions I raised during bible studies went over many of the congregants' heads, though they appeared to impress the leadership, perhaps to an unsettling degree. During the course of bible studies, I experienced the subjective, warped and paranoid worldview inhabited by the adherents. Mistrust of the government was manifest: fluoride in the water supply was a form of mind control; tonsillectomies were a government plot designed to sterilize the white race; etc. Members of the congregation offered anecdotes reinforcing these views, many times citing information I knew was factually erroneous. At times it was difficult to keep a straight face or not to interject on the subject matter.

Once bible studies ended, we proceeded to the church service. Although aware of Christian Identity's religious theology and the pastor's extremism, I was still taken aback by the content of, and virulence contained in, his sermon. Once again, the fanatical *weltanschauung* espoused by the congregation presented itself. In his sermon, the pastor expounded on the satanic influence of rock and roll music with its degenerative effect on society. At one point a cassette tape attributed to Colonel Jack Mohr, a Christian Identity demagogue, was played. In his exposition, Mohr described in lurid detail a relationship between the music of the Beatles to that of a hedonistic African tribal beat. He went into great detail about the debauchery associated with this primitive beat that the Beatles adopted. I had to control myself from laughing out loud. However, I was soon to become far more anxious than amused.

Throughout the service, certain individuals left and reappeared. Perhaps I was paranoid, but I had the impression they were trying to get into my rental car. The church was in a small converted fire station and on at least three occasions I saw individuals leave the building for extended periods of time. I became uneasy with this behaviour. Moreover, during the course of the service, I was implicitly threatened via biblical verbiage. After the service, I attempted to question the pastor, who refused to comply and reiterated to the congregation not to answer any questions and refer any queries to him. Upon leaving the church, but not before purchasing a significant amount of literature, I was a bit nervous. Reflecting back on my background research, however, I knew that other individuals who had been made welcome at this parish had later disparaged them in written exposés. So perhaps the hostility and suspicion I had felt from them was understandable. Still, I put in a lot of miles before I decided to rest.

The second interview went better. This cleric was an anti-Identity pastor, who lectured on the influences and penetration of the Christian Identity doctrine. Though not associated with the movement, his knowledge and insights were illuminating and were augmented by his own research and presentations on Identity. By reading through these materials, I gained further theological insight into the religion as well as documented biblical refutations of Identity theology. Once absorbed, this gave me knowledge and information that would significantly enhance future interviews with Identity adherents in a key area.

A third referral provided by the militia contacts was a real discovery. Through the aegis of the radio station I was put in personal contact with a former bodyguard of George Lincoln Rockwell, the infamous American neo-nazi leader. This individual, who was once heavily into Christian Identity, renounced his beliefs and was a major player in the militia movement. He was well connected within extreme right circles and provided a reference and a phone number to one of the original Identity founders.

After a couple of phone calls, the founder agreed to see to me on the condition that I had to have 'God in my eyes'. Since it was an 800-mile trip, I told him 'Well if I don't have it now I hope I have it when I arrive'. Upon arrival, my religiosity was acceptable and we proceeded to have a three-hour taped interview. Although the interview was a scoop, its true importance was not apparent for about a year. After the event, I found out that this individual was providing financing to the CSA, a hotbed of paramilitary training for right-wing terrorists. Members of the terrorist organization in my case study received training at the CSA, and CSA members actually joined the group. Also, shortly after the interview, the interviewee went to ground and I have not been able to trace him since. During the course of the interview, in spite of a benevolent tone, a theme of acceptance of violence for the cause was discerned. The thrust of the interview, however, was the creation of the Christian Identity theology and early pioneers in the movement. Once again, background preparation paid off handsomely as questions concerning another Identity theologian were raised, and preparations to interview the theologian in question had already been arranged. The information now gleaned concerning this individual enhanced both the questions and content of the upcoming interview. I found that many of the Christian Identity followers were willing to talk about other figures in the movement in detail, voicing their opinions quite explicitly. On numerous occasions, if an opening presented itself, I engaged in this line of questioning, which provided insights into the movement that were simply not available from the literature. Inside information gleaned from these encounters proved invaluable as I ventured deeper into the movement.

Although ostensibly practitioners of the same religious theology, the variations in approaches, ideology and viewpoints were striking. I expected this from my research; however, the intrinsic vicissitude of the movement which I observed in the field far exceeded my expectations (that were based on textual sources). Indeed, the next pastor I interviewed testified against the terrorist group under study. Much more polished and erudite than the previous interviewees, this individual's knowledge of the origins and evolution of Christian Identity combined with his firsthand experiences provided a composite of the Identity kaleidoscope. Moreover, at the church, I was able to interview two other Identity clerics. All three interviews were taped with their permission. Again, the full import of these interviews was not apparent until later, when an interfactional fight within the congregation caused a rupture, resulting in an acrimonious split. Since I had met both antagonists and recorded their thoughts on tape, the consequences and ramifications of the split were available for future research.

Summing up this initial venture into field research among extremists, many lessons were learned. Long hours of background preparation paid off. Besides providing an avenue to enter the field it also helped in understanding and assimilating new data. Initial networks were expanded allowing greater exposure to extremists, scholars and other parties. The friendships, acquaintances, and contacts an analyst nurtures should be treated in a respectful, ethical fashion. Prior to my ever using a name to gain greater access or open a door to a new contact, the original source was contacted and asked whether it was all right to use his/her name. Being compromised, or compromising another researcher, is an experience to be avoided at all cost. Not only may the researcher lose credibility, jeopardizing all the hard work expended; in certain cases it could genuinely place them or other colleagues in harm's way. This has happened twice in my own experience. Once my name was referred to by an individual who should have known better – although, had he contacted me, I would have been more than happy to try to help him out in his pursuits. In all fairness, this person did contact me after the event; however, had I been approached prior to his forays in the field, a potentially sticky situation could have been avoided. In the second scenario, an individual I have never met, nor corresponded with in any fashion, promulgated false information about me which could have placed me (and still might) in a dangerous and untenable situation. As more researchers venture out into the field, a code of conduct considering possible conflicts of interests needs to be sorted out for the benefit of all. Despite the fractious and sometimes antagonistic condition of US right-wing extremism, even where organizations are at odds with one another, they will still inform each other if they feel the person is associated with the government or watchdog agencies such as the ADL or the SPLC or other organizations which harbour a mission inimical to that of the extremists.

Upon returning to the University, all the data acquired was examined in detail. Interviews were transcribed, and much of the primary source data acquired from Identity pastors and adherents was analysed. Many of the interviews were enhanced by the fact that they were taped. Notes were also taken concurrently with taping. Sometimes I would put my own critique on tape after leaving the interview. Tape recordings of terrorists' and extremists' interviews are a touchy subject. There are pros and cons for and against the use of this medium. Throughout the duration of my field research, the issue of tape-recorded interviews was commonly addressed. Due to inherent suspicion, many times bordering on paranoia, interviewees were reluctant (or refused out-right) to have conversations taped. Moreover, critics of audio recording have noted that sometimes the presence of a recording device results in respondents answering in a less truthful or insightful manner than would be the case if written notes alone were taken. However, the author's own experience did not support this view. To their advantage, tape-recorded interviews provide a definitive record for both parties. Using this as my justification, I was able to tape numerous interviews. I informed the person that I would provide a copy if he/she desired, or they could also tape the interview with their own equipment (which happened on occasion). Then, if cited, both parties could resolve any issues or discuss if a comment was taken out of context. As an academic, objectivity (as much as is humanly possible) is paramount and verbatim recording enhances this goal. Insofar as surreptitious recording is concerned, it should be avoided. Again, academics in the field are not professional spies. Potential dangers far outweigh benefits, and if one should undertake such endeavours, one should realize the obvious ramifications of detection.

Empirical research and interviewing, especially in the field, is a specialized affair and, as far as terrorism studies is concerned, is still arguably in its incipient stages. Addressing deficiencies in terrorism research Andrew Silke notes:

> In only one per cent of reports are the interviews conducted in a systematic and structured manner. For all the rest the interviews are carried out on an *ad-hoc*, opportunistic basis, generally using only a semi-structured approached at best. This means that again there are concerns with the reliability of the data.[27]

While Silke notes there are advantages to unstructured interviews, primarily that the flexibility incorporated in the format allows the interviewer to follow promising avenues should they arise, the inability to carry out statistical analysis and the injection of a subjective bias remain causes for concern. Topic selection of the dissertation can be the deciding factor on how interview data is collated and utilized. In the author's case, the size of the terrorist organization under study, combined with heterodox theology and ideology emanating from Christian Identity, required a flexible format. Moreover, since I was attempting to ascertain causative factors inherent in the aetiology of religious right-wing terrorism, as well as trying to discern motivations for participation in the Bruders Schweigen, wholesale sampling was not an issue. Notwithstanding the flexible approach employed, I still structured all my questionnaires with generic queries relating to Christian Identity and its association with terrorism. In addition, the questionnaires were intended for specific individuals, focusing on what I felt were key issues pertinent to the dissertation. Each question was incorporated in a series: if the initial question hit a cord I had three or four more follow-up queries on the topic. In this fashion a wide range of issues could be addressed quickly depending on the interviewee response. From my first excursion into the field, I knew nothing was more frustrating than to hit on a key theme and then struggle to find follow-up questions. In the next round of interviews I hoped to avoid this.

Before returning for more advanced empirical research, work began on appropriate chapters of the dissertation and preparations began for another sojourn in the field. Follow-ups on new contacts established during the first trip were approached in preparation for a second trip, and again advice from individuals operating in the field concerning more in-depth research was sought. From this point forward, the research effort focused on acquiring primary source material, especially trial transcripts, primary source material from leading ideologues and theologians within the movement; and network expansion; as well as face-to-face interactions with extremists and terrorists. Keen to develop the latter sources in particular, I wrote to imprisoned terrorists asking for permission to interview them. The letters contained my reasons for an interview as well as self-addressed and pre-paid return postage. Through other sources, the phone number of the head of an intentional community was acquired whom I called concerning an interview. Once contact was established, this individual invited me to a compound for an unspecified number of days.

Another conference provided the impetus to return to the USA. In general, I try to pack as much activity as possible in to my research trips in order to minimize downtime and costs. Promisingly, I had received some positive responses to my request for interviews with inmates. At the conference, however, I received a major shock and setback. Attempting to schedule an interview with an incarcerated terrorist, I was told I had to contact the Justice Department and submit a research proposal. On the surface this does not sound unreasonable. However, considering the fact that the authorities were aware of the on-going research arrangements (I had already contacted the prison officials), in reality this news amounted to stonewalling. I was refused access to certain imprisoned terrorists even though they had agreed to interviews. Perhaps if I had been a little more diligent in my preparation, I would have heeded the words of Konrad Kellen who, in a 1982 RAND Report, noted 'The authorities in countries that held captured terrorists in prison showed little inclination to permit researchers to interview them'.[28] Throughout the remainder of field research, I had to strive mightily and persistently to see imprisoned terrorists. While I was ultimately allowed to interview some incarcerated individuals, there was no apparent rhyme or reason to the process. In the USA at least, the final decision lies in the hands of the warden. However, higher authorities can overrule wardens' decisions on interviews, though no one ever informed me that the Justice Department or other government agencies had intervened to prevent any interviews. Excuses for denied access ranged from the questionable to the ludicrous. For example, I was denied an interview with the leader of the Aryan Brotherhood in Oklahoma on the grounds that I was a motivational speaker for the movement!

Even now, I am still encountering opposition to conducting prison interviews. Once again, a framework should be established where bona fide scholars with proper credentials should be granted access to terrorists who agree to give interviews. With the current impediments to such work, it is not surprising that empirical research is very lacking in this regard. In due fairness to the Bureau of Prisons, certain facilities and employees have acted in a thoroughly professional manner concerning my requests. Unfortunately, such instances were the exception rather than the rule.

Although experiences between researchers vary, interviews with terrorists whether imprisoned or not should be approached with care. While the terrorist organization I was interested in is considered to be essentially defunct, their influence still permeates the extreme right. A phone call from one incarcerated terrorist could have put me in danger. Prior to my first prison interview (all of which were recorded on tape), over three phone calls were received by the residence at which I was staying, to check up on me. In all probability other queries concerning my research were made. This process, however, proved beneficial as the terrorists, their families, and sympathizers learned of my difficulties in gaining access, and were able to offer advice concerning this matter. For example, they suggested I obtain press credentials to help facilitate the interview process. While helpful, even press credentials did not guarantee interviews with the prisoners; I was still at the whim of the Justice Department, the Bureau of Prisons and the individual wardens and their executive officers.

INTO THE ABYSS

Total Immersion in an Intentional Community

Under stress one has to trust one's instincts and intuitions. At least this was what I was trying to convince myself, as my ride departed, leaving

me seven miles from the nearest paved road at an intentional community which one journalist had previously christened 'the holiday inn of
hate', given its well documented ties to terrorist and terroristic activity.
In this case my hunch was right. By entering the community with no
chance of escape, I implicitly placed my trust in the hands of the
community. This act of faith was appreciated and reciprocated in my
treatment, and the information gleaned from this encounter would
provide a holistic insight into extremists in their element. Repeated
trips to this intentional community would be the culmination of my
field research; an endeavour in which all the lessons learned and experience gained would be utilized. It also would be an emotionally draining
and potentially dangerous venture. Any mention or revelation of my
interest in terrorism could have deleterious ramifications. I made it a
point not to have any information concerning myself or my academic
interests on the St Andrews website.

Upon arrival, I was invited into the church service, after which
members of the community questioned me. My status as an academic
and expert on Christian Identity were accessed. Questions, however,
ran a broad gamut. 'Why was I here?' 'What is it like in Scotland?' 'What
is your religion and ethnic background?' 'Are you here as an objective
observer or are you going to write and publish disparaging accounts as
others have done previously?' Many eyed me with apparent suspicion
and mistrust; in some cases, bordering on hostility. After this initial
encounter, I was surprised to find myself living with the spiritual head
of the community. Our nightly conversations were academic sparing
matches that we both enjoyed. Discussion topics varied from Christian
Identity to current events. I was as honest as possible, my only significant omission was my interest in terrorism studies – a fact, which, if
revealed, could have had implications for both continuing research and
personal safety. Yet total immersion like this, even for limited periods, is
stressful. Two overriding concerns must always be present: (1) to limit
what personal information is revealed and to be careful not to expose
too much of oneself; and, (2) to remain aware that living in such a
subjective or slanted reality can have an impact on the objectivity of
your research and personal viewpoints.[29] Living in close proximity with
extremists can potentially lead to empathy or advocacy of their principles. Attempting to understand extremists' positions is one thing,
defending them is another. Depending on the situation a researcher
finds themselves in, a conflict of interests may arise. One way to
mitigate this is to stick to one's analytical and methodological framework. Admittedly, to be won over to a terrorist's cause is rare; however,
it can, and has, happened. The flip side of this coin is that even if your

objectivity remains intact, just the fact of interacting with extremists can lead some to question a researcher's motivations and mores.

After a week of interacting with the community, I was asked to leave. I later learned that I was on probation. Any time an individual spends time at the community he/she must be approved by the elders and the community at large. Disappointed – I had not been allowed to conduct a single interview – I asked if it would be possible to spend more time there in the future. My hosts informed me that it may be possible, but that, once again, the elders and the inhabitants would have to decide whether to grant me permission. Reflecting back on this first encounter, I realized that it was not the failure I initially felt; rather the opposite – by not asking too many questions, taking voluminous notes, or sticking a tape recorder in front of people, I had placed members of the community at ease, increasing their acceptance of me in the process. Moreover, by the end of my stay, I had started to immerse myself to a significant extent into the affairs of the community, getting a real sense of what it was like, and how they thought and acted in this environment.

From past encounters in the field, I had found that a researcher's appearance and background experiences could play an important part in trying to assimilate. Almost by accident, through the course of my field research, I found myself doing all sorts of things: lecturing, gardening, installing fences, construction work and welding to name a few.[30] Also participation in social activities, when possible, provided insightful off-the-cuff data as well as ingratiating myself to my hosts. If there was work to be done, I would be one of the first to volunteer. While helping a woman with her gardening, she casually mentioned that she and her husband had been questioned about conducting the surveillance on the Alfred P. Murrah building, the site of the Oklahoma City bombing. Moreover, she informed me that members of the Bruders Schweiegn had been at the compound. I doubt if this information would have came out during the course of an interview.

During my first stay, I interacted with people as much as possible, including certain individuals who kept to themselves. In particular, I was intrigued by one group of men who lived at the periphery of the compound. Each time I tried to interact with them or engaged in a dialogue, I felt uneasy and was treated with contempt. Returning to Scotland after my first visit, I discovered they were members of an active terrorist cell that had been robbing banks throughout the Midwest. When the news of their incarceration reached me, I realized that my limited interactions were probably a blessing in disguise.

This low-key, ready-to-lend-a-hand, posture paid off as the

community accepted my request to return. My subsequent visits were longer and more intense. Also the quality of my accommodations improved significantly. I took this fact to mean a measure of acceptance: I was actually living and cohabiting with the community, not just merely tolerated. Make no mistake though, from their perspective I was always an outsider to be viewed with some suspicion. This was only logical, considering that former terrorists and people with possible terroristic activities on their mind were living there. On one occasion a member of the community, whom I had a bad feeling about, questioned my religiosity during an interview with one of the leaders of the community. I responded that I did not see him in church that much. Taken aback by my response, which he perceived as a challenge, he immediately left. However, before the interview had concluded, he was back and handed the leader a $500 donation. Seeing this, I replied that it was a nice Christian thing to do. After this incident there was palpable tension concerning my presence. Earlier in the day, the leadership had said I was free to conduct interviews if individuals were willing. Despite this, the next morning they informed me I had only one day in which to conduct interviews and would have to leave the following day. A request to address the community concerning this abrupt change in posture at the daily church service was denied. Initially, I felt that interviews might be hard to come by, however, I did manage to interview a considerable segment of the leadership. Although I left in somewhat stressful circumstances, I have maintained contact with the community and will hopefully return, if allowed, to conduct further research on this developing experimental community.

CONCLUSION

Postgraduate students are in a prime position to break the cycle of dependency on secondary and tertiary accounts which plague terrorism research. In many circumstances, established researchers cannot venture out into the field. If they are working for government agencies or have published accounts on terrorism, access to extremists and terrorists may be severely constrained if not altogether impossible. Postgraduate students however are usually not bound by these constraints. This flexibility provides a real opportunity to venture out into the field to conduct research in new and challenging areas. Furthermore, depending on the nature of the research and future vocation, the possibility is there to expand existing networks, helping to continue the research process. Even if a researcher decides not to pursue face-to-face encounters, he/she should still aim to probe and access primary source materials. The lack of scholars doing this most basic and essential task is reprehensible. True, this may take longer and prove more difficult than simply relying on what is already out there, but no one said writing a dissertation should be a piece of cake. Rather, it should be seen as an intellectual challenge with the aim of making a genuine contribution to the scholarship. Without doubt, the current lack of empirical research and data on terrorism must be addressed in order for the discipline to advance. As Richard G. Mitchell warned:

> If social scientists fail to explore hostile research environs, their disciplines may be diminished, homogenized by ethics, routines and restrictions to the exercise of orthodox methodologies and standardized procedures, and directed into narrowed venues of application.[31]

At this point the progression of terrorism studies is perilously close to the condition described by Mitchell. Postgraduate students have a potentially large role to play if we are to avoid 'narrowed venues of application'. Increased qualitative data acquisition is vital for serious authoritative quantitative research. Failure to increase empirical data acquisition will only continue the current stagnation of terrorism studies. It is vital that as the next generation of scholars, teachers, and analysts of this discipline, we address this deficiency. If not, we are part of the problem currently blocking the advancement of terrorism research. Considering the prominence of terrorism in international and domestic affairs, correction of this problem is a moral and ethical imperative.

In light of the deficiencies currently facing the discipline of terrorism studies, this chapter concludes by offering a number of suggestions for postgraduate empirical research on terrorism:

- A major deficiency among researchers on terrorism is the common failure to become familiar with the history of terrorism. Terrorism did not start in 1968. The inability to appreciate and understand the breadth of historical motifs and motivations associated with terrorism impedes a holistic understanding of the phenomena. If a new researcher is unfamiliar with the long history of terrorism, reading one or two of the better histories of the subject will provide substantial reward.

- Terrorism studies, in most cases, is agenda-driven or oriented to what is in vogue at the time. Currently, a tremendous amount of attention has been focussed on Weapons of Mass Destruction (WMD) and Islamic Fundamentalism. While these topics have merit and are important, an overabundance of research is devoted to the 'in' topic at any time. This factor inhibits the gathering significant amounts of useful empirical data which in turn hinders a fuller understanding of the discipline.

- Finally, good theoretically grounded case studies, focused on the causation of terrorism, and which aim for an in-depth analysis of primary source material of terrorists, governments, and other principal actors, are badly needed. Such work adds immeasurably to terrorism studies and should be undertaken wherever possible.

NOTES

1. J. Bowyer-Bell, 'Trends on Terror: The Analysis of Political Violence', *World Politics*, 29 (April 1977), pp. 476–7.
2. Alex P. Schmid and Albert J. Jongman, *Political Terrorism: A New Guide to Actors, Concepts, Data Bases, Theories, and Literature* (New Brunswick, NJ: Transaction Books, 1988), p. 177.
3. Ibid., p. 179.
4. Edna O. Reid, 'Terrorism Research and the Diffusion of Ideas', *Knowledge and Policy*, 6 (Spring 1993), p. 17.
5. Ibid., p. 28.
6. Ibid.
7. Ted Robert Gurr, 'Empirical Research on Political Terrorism: The State of the Art and How it Might be Improved', in Robert O. Slater and Michael Stohl (eds), *Current Perspectives On International Terrorism* (New York: St Martin's Press, 1988), p. 115.
8. Schmid and Jongman, *Political Terrorism*, p. 174.
9. This is not to say there has not been independent academic research or media accounts. There have. However, few, if any social science disciplines exhibit a comparable symbiosis between the government, academia and the media.
10. Scholars argue over the origins of 'modern terrorism'. The author asserts that terrorism has been a historical fact and the so-called 'new terrorism' moniker is often an excuse to label deficiencies in forecasting the evolution of recent trends.
11. Bruce Hoffman, 'Current research on Terrorism and Low-Intensity Conflict', *Studies in Conflict and Terrorism*, 15, 1 (1992), pp. 25–37.
12. Ibid.
13. Ibid.
14. A crucial flaw in data acquisition and application is the tendency, many times unconsciously, to either select or shoehorn data to augment the methodological framework.
15. Martha Crenshaw, 'Questions to be Answered, Research to be Done, Knowledge to be Applied', in Walter Reich (eds), *Origins Of Terrorism: Psychologies, Ideologies, Theologies, States of Mind* (Cambridge: Cambridge University Press, 1990), p. 259.
16. Gurr, 'Empirical Research on Political Terrorism', p. 143.
17. As quoted in Schmid and Jongman, *Political Terrorism*, p. 41.
18. Paul Wilkinson, 'Fighting the Hydra: Terrorism and the Rule of Law', *Harvard International Review*, 7 (1985), p. 12.
19. For the duration of this chapter an extremist denotes an individual(s) who harbours extreme political and/or religious positions whereas a terrorist is an individual(s) who has been charged or convicted of a terroristic offense.
20. Mark S. Hamm, 'Terrorism, Hate Crime, and Antigovernment Violence: A Review of the

Research', in Harvey W. Kushner (ed.), *The Future of Terrorism: Violence in the New Millennium* (Thousand Oaks, CA: Sage Publications, 1998).

21. Hamm, 'Terrorism, Hate Crime, and Antigovernment Violence', p. 66.

22. See http://permanent.access.gpo.gov/lps3578/www.fbi.gov/library/megiddo/megiddo.pdf. See also the Fall 1998 edition of the Southern Poverty Law Center's Intelligence Report, 'Millennium Y2KAOS'. Anti-Defamation League, *Explosion of Hate*, p. 15. Kerry Noble, *Tabernacle of Hate: Why They Bombed Oklahoma City* (Prescott: Voyageur Publishing, 1998). See also Fall 1997 edition of the Southern Poverty Law Center's Intelligence Report, 'Rough Waters: Stream of Knowledge Probed by Officials'.

23. For improprieties concerning watchdog groups, see Laird Wilcox, *Crying Wolf: Hate Crime Hoaxes in America* (Olathe, KN: Editorial Research Service, 1996); and *The Watchdogs: A Close Look at Anti-Racist 'Watchdog' Groups* (Olathe, KN: Editorial Research Service, 1998).

24. While this chapter provides insights into my own personal experiences in the realm of field research, it is by no means a blueprint to follow. Although some of the lessons learned from my own endeavours will hopefully benefit future scholars in their efforts, there are no set rules in this arena. If I had to pass on one primary lesson, it would be to trust your gut instincts. If unsure about a situation pass it up no matter how attractive or important it may be to your research. No dissertation is worth jeopardizing your health or worse.

25. Alison Jamieson, 'Identity and Morality in the Italian Red Brigades', *Terrorism and Political Violence*, 2/1 (Winter 1990), pp. 508–20.

26. The penetration of Christian Identity into the militia movement has been well documented elsewhere. Through my interactions with militia members, however, I gained a greater insight into the nature of this phenomenon. While militia advocates tried to convince me that there was no linkage between the two, past research indicated this was inaccurate. The point is that, without going into the field, a more realistic assessment could not have been made.

27. Andrew Silke, 'The Devil You Know: Continuing Problems with Research on Terrorism', *Terrorism and Political Violence*, 13/4 (Winter 2001), p. 7.

28. Konrad Kellen, *On Terrorist and Terrorism* (Santa Monica, CA: RAND Corporation, 1982), p. 45. Available as Rand Note N-1942-RC.

29. Sherryl Kleinman and Martha A. Copp, *Emotions and Fieldwork*, Qualitative Research Methods Series No. 28 (Thousand Oaks, CA: Sage Publications, 1993), pp. 1–80.

30. If one says one can do something, expected to be tested. My experience in welding was put to the test. When I demonstrated my competency, my stock went up. On return trips I was asked to weld and repair various objects.

31. Richard G. Mitchell, Jr, *Secrecy in Fieldwork*, Qualitative Research Methods Series No. 29 (Thousand Oaks, CA: Sage Publications, 1993), p. 54.

10

The Road Less Travelled: Recent Trends in Terrorism Research

ANDREW SILKE

B Y FAR the most important review of research and researchers into terrorism to date has been that carried out by Alex Schmid and Albert Jongman.[1] The 1988 edition of their book, *Political Terrorism: A New Guide to Actors, Authors, Concepts, Data bases, Theories and Literature*, remains a key text for both new and established researchers alike. However, this unique source book is now over 15 years old and a great deal has happened in the intervening period. Yet there has been no systematic assessment of the research effort undertaken in the past decade. What then is the current state of research on terrorism?

Arguably the best way to identify trends and patterns in research efforts is to examine the published literature produced by active researchers. While the literature on terrorism is relatively young in academic terms – existing in a meaningful sense since only the late 1960s – Schmid and Jongman noted that by the time of their review it had nonetheless grown far beyond the scope 'of one single researcher [to] survey the field alone'. Indeed, the two writers pulled in the assistance of over 50 other researchers in order to complete their review.

The situation, however, is even worse today with the published literature continuing to expand at an impressive rate (a rate accelerated even further by the events of 9/11). This, of course, leaves anyone interested in reviewing research on terrorism facing a very onerous and disheartening task and it is unlikely that anyone would happily attempt to replicate Schmid and Jongman's review. However, one advantage a contemporary reviewer has which was not available in 1988 is the presence of two well-established journals which exist as the primary publishing outlets for research on terrorism. These journals are *Terrorism and Political Violence* (TPV) and *Studies in Conflict and Terrorism* (SICAT). At the time of the Schmid and Jongman review only one specialist journal existed in the field: *Terrorism: An International Journal*. In 1993, this journal was renamed *Studies in Conflict and Terrorism* following an amalgamation with another title. Taken together, and bearing in mind their different publishers, separate editorial teams and largely separate editorial boards (though there is some overlap on this last), the two journals can be regarded as providing a reasonably balanced impression of the research activity and interests in the field.

Recognizing this – and motivated by a desire to understand the patterns and trends in research activity and publishing in the field in recent years – this paper presents the results of a review of the published output of the primary journals in the area for the years 1990–1999. It is hoped that a review of this nature can be both of interest and of practical value to other writers and researchers on the topic, and that it may also help to establish the broader context in which individual research efforts occur.

THE NATURE OF THE REVIEW

Academic journals have a surprisingly diverse range of content. For the two journals under consideration here, this includes articles, research notes, editorials, book reviews, conference reports, review essays, database reports, and official documents and reports. The most immediate question facing a surveyor is how much of this material should be considered? In deciding this, the main criteria has to be which items are consistently the best indicators of significant research activity and effort? This current review follows the lead of the UK's national Research Assessment Exercise (RAE),[2] which posits that peer-reviewed journal articles provide a good measure of the broad quality of research work. Consequently, this review focuses solely on articles published in the journals during the time period.

This is a relatively stringent criterion and other reviewers may be willing to be more inclusive. For example, there is a case for considering the inclusion of research notes in a review such as this. They have not been included here, however, because of the considerable variation displayed in the items so classified in the journals. While some research notes were significant documents – both in terms of length and content – most were extremely brief and cursory. Indeed, it is something of a mystery as to why some papers were classed as research notes when they seemed in every respect to be comparable to articles published elsewhere in the same issue. It would be invidious, however, for one reviewer to subjectively select from among the other categories what he or she regards as equivalent to article standard. Rather than attempt this, this review simply excludes entirely from consideration all items which were labelled or described as other than an article. While this inevitably means that a few significant works are not considered, it means that overall the review is focused on what can be considered to be consistently the substantial research outputs of this ten-year period.[3]

The literature of terrorism is still young: something around 99 per cent of all books and articles on the topic have been written since 1968. An explosive growth in publications in the late 1970s has been followed by a less dramatic, but relatively steady, growth in the 1980s and 1990s, with a another dramatic outpouring of work in the wake of the 9/11 attacks. Schmid and Jongman, however, have noted that despite the fact that a very sizeable body of literature has accumulated, the substance of this writing is less than impressive. As they pointed out: 'Much of the writing in the crucial areas of terrorism research ... is impressionistic, superficial, and at the same time often also pretentious, venturing far-reaching generalizations on the basis of episodal evidence'.[4]

The study of terrorism is truly multi-disciplinary and no one discipline has been able to firmly take pre-eminence in research in the area. Researchers from fields such as political science, criminology, psychology, sociology, history, law, the military and communication sciences have all contributed to it. However, despite the diversity of research interest, research on terrorism remains plagued by a number of problems. Ariel Merari – a writer with a keen sense of the limitations of research efforts to date – had the following general point to make on the subject:

> Terrorism is a study area which is very easy to approach but very difficult to cope with in a scientific sense. Easy to approach – because it has so many angles, touching upon all aspects of human behaviour. Difficult to cope with – because it is so diverse. As terrorism is not a discipline, there can hardly be a general theory of terrorism ... There are few social scientists who specialize in this study area. Most contributions in this field are ephemeral. Precise and extensive factual knowledge is still grossly lacking.

Much effort must still be invested in the very first stage of scientific inquiry with regard to terrorism – the collection of data.[5]

In examining the quality of research on terrorism, Schmid and Jongman noted in their review that 'there are probably few areas in the social science literature on which so much is written on the basis of so little research'. They estimated that 'as much as 80 per cent of the literature is not research-based in any rigorous sense; instead, it is too often narrative, condemnatory, and prescriptive'.[6] Further, while the backgrounds of researchers may be relatively diverse, there has in general been a consistent lack of researchers to carry out investigative work in the area. Since it emerged as a clear and substantial topic of study, terrorism has suffered from a near-chronic lack of active researchers. Again, this is a point well recognised by Ariel Merari:

> Although political scientists have devoted considerably greater attention to terrorism than psychologists and sociologists, on the whole the scientific community has so far allocated a very small part of its research effort to this subject – a strange attitude towards a phenomenon that is clearly one of the most common forms of violent domestic and international political conflict in our time.[7]

The reasons for this general neglect are not difficult to imagine. Terrorism is a violent, emotive and dangerous activity, and terrorist groups are secretive, ruthless and very dangerous organizations. The risks involved for the potential researcher are considerable. Academic researchers have been threatened, kidnapped, attacked, shot and killed for attempting to research terrorism.[8] Clear obstacles exist for potential researchers and certainly many traditional methods of research struggle badly when attempts are made to apply them to the study of terrorism. As Merari has noted:

> On the practical side, terrorism is a very elusive subject for research … Collecting systematic, standardized, reliable information for the purpose of comparisons is next to impossible. Moreover, the customary tools of psychological and sociological research are almost always inapplicable for studying terrorist groups and their individual members.[9]

However, Merari did note that the physical manifestations of terrorism as well as public responses to it are, in principle, much more accessible to research than the psychology and sociology of terrorists. In practice, however, even this research is not easy. What shape did terrorism research then take in the 1990s? In particular, were there any signs that some of the traditional problems with the field were showing signs of improvement? The tables presented below attempt to provide some answers to such questions.

PATTERNS AND TRENDS IN RESEARCH

Table 10.1. Basic Trends in Publishing

Journal	Individual contributors	Contributors of two or more articles	Articles	Percentage of articles from one-timers
TPV	232	50	295	78%
Ter/SICAT	187	18	195	90%
Combined	403	69	490	83%

Table 10.1 gives some general information on the overall publishing trends.[10] It shows, for example, that in total 490 articles were published in the leading journals during the 1990s, and that these articles were written by 403 different authors. This gives a productivity ratio of 1:1.2, with on average each author writing 1.2 articles during the ten-year period. It is difficult to get a clear indication of what this says about the overall research trend in terrorism, but one interesting comparison can be made with criminology. As a subject discipline, criminology has a number of similarities with terrorism. The subject matter published in criminological journals focuses on various actors and activities involved in the criminal justice system and in the commissioning of crime. As a result, it often shares similarities with terrorism in terms of difficult research populations and real world relevance, as well as concerns with government responses, policing, human suffering and injustice. Thus, when compared to other areas within the social sciences, the criminology journals do seem to offer some legitimate comparison with the terrorism journals.[11] In 1997, two researchers looked at the publication trends in four leading criminology journals.[12] They found that in a five-year period, 497 articles were published in these journals and that these were written by a total of 665 authors. Comparing the criminology journals to the major terrorism journals we see that the author: article ratio is very different standing at 1:0.7 (i.e. one author accounts for 0.7 articles). This indicates that, at least compared to criminology, fewer authors are writing in the terrorism journals. Indeed, if the proportion

of writers to articles seen in the criminology journals was replicated in the terrorism journals, in the 1990s there should have been 656 individual writers published in the two journals rather than just 403!

Such a discrepancy in figures underlines the long-recognized problem that research on terrorism is relying on the efforts of too few researchers. This is the theme alluded to in the title chapter: engaging in terrorism research *is* the road less travelled. A constant problem in the field is that too few dedicated researchers take terrorism as their primary subject of interest. In the eyes of many of the more experienced researchers, what has been occurring in the past 30 years is that individuals, whose speciality and main interest lies elsewhere, see an application for their own area in terrorism, wade in, publish a paper or two and then depart, leaving the few dedicated researchers to wade through a continuous supply of material often espousing viewpoints and theories which serious researchers have rejected years ago, as what evidence was available consistently showed such approaches to be fruitless and/or fundamentally wrong.

The figures also indicate that terrorism research is rarely carried out by teams of researchers. Instead, the field seems to be almost entirely composed of individuals working on lone projects. In the 1990s, only 9.4 per cent of published research articles were the result of collaborative efforts. Over 90 per cent of the published work in the field was done by a single researcher working alone. Ultimately this indicates that the vast majority of research is being conducted with very limited resources. Research teams and partnerships are rare and the field is extremely dependent on the efforts of individuals who conduct research on terrorism in an independent and relatively isolated manner.[13]

Such problems are exacerbated further when it is also appreciated that of those who do carry out research on the subject, extremely few go on to publish more than once in the main journals. This is clearly seen in Table 10.1 which shows that a massive proportion (83 per cent) of the articles published in the 1990s were from one-timers (that is, authors who wrote only one article in the mainstream journals during the entire period). This appears to clearly reinforce Merari's view (stated in 1991) that terrorism research suffers not only from a lack of researchers in general but especially from a lack of researchers who take it as their main or major research interest. A field with such a high proportion of transient contributors can only but struggle to establish a solid conceptual framework.

In 1988, Schmid and Jongman attempted to answer the question 'Who are the leading authors in the field of terrorism research?' Their

Table 10.2. The most Prolific Authors in the Major Terrorism Journals, 1990–99

Ranking	Author	Articles	Schmid and Jongman 1988
1	Leonard Weinberg	10 (2)†	Jenkins
2	Bruce Hoffman	7	**Wilkinson**
3	William Eubank	7 (5)	**Bell**
4	**Paul Wilkinson★**	6	Alexander
5	**J. Bowyer Bell★**	5	**Crenshaw**
–	Peter Chalk	5	Laqueur
–	Alison Jamieson	5	**Schmid**
–	Jeffrey Kaplan	5	**Clutterbuck**
–	Dennis Pluchinsky	5	Mickolus
–	Andrew Silke	5	Friedlander
–	**Alex Schmid★**	5 (1)	Kupperman
12	Steve Bruce	4	Miller
–	Raphael Cohen-Almagor	4	Sterling
–	Raphael Israeli	4	Stohl
–	**Ariel Merari★**	4	Wardlaw
–	Robert White	4	Arendt
–	Max Taylor	4 (3)	Bassiouni
18	**Richard Clutterbuck★**	3	Carlton
–	Ronald Crelinstein	3	Ferracuti
–	**Martha Crenshaw★**	3	**Merari**
–	Michael Dartnell	3	Sloan
–	C.J.M. Drake	3	Thornton
–	Victor Le Vine	3	Wolf
–	Rachel Monaghan	3	Cline
–	Magnus Ranstorp	3	Cooper
–	Ehud Sprinzak	3	Crozier
–	Peter Alan Sproat	3	Dobson
–	John Horgan	3 (1)	Evans
–	Gus Xhudo	3 (1)	Gurr
–	Todd Sandler	3 (2)	Hacker

★ Cited as a leading author in the field of terrorism in Schmid and Jongman's 1988 review.
† Brackets indicate articles where writer was listed as second author (for example, Leonard Weinberg wrote eight articles as the first author, and two additional articles as second author: ten articles in total).

survey produced a list of 35 names. It is interesting to note that of these 35 names only a handful published articles in the leading journals in the 1990s. The most prolific writer in the primary terrorism journals in the 1990s was Leonard Weinberg.[14] A professor of political science based at the University of Nevada – and co-author of two chapters in this volume – Weinberg's work has focused particularly on the examination of right-wing extremism. His writing partnership with William Eubank (also based at Nevada) has been prolific, to say the least. Weinberg is the top author and Eubank is the third ranked author. Between them comes Bruce Hoffman as the second most prolific writer of the decade. Hoffman is distinctive for a further reason – he is the *only* writer who appears in the top 20 list for both TPV *and* for SICAT. Only one author has published more than Hoffman but no other researcher has divided their output between the leading journals at the level that Hoffman has.[15] A further interesting fact about these three leading writers is that none of them appeared in the 1988 list prepared by Schmid and Jongman. While the 1988 survey was unquestionably a measure of perceived *quality*, and this survey is essentially more a measure of *quantity*, the emergence of these other writers to the forefront of the field (at least in terms of output) does seem to indicate the arrival of new leading figures in the field. This conclusion certainly seems tenable when it can be seen that Paul Wilkinson and J. Bowyer Bell (two of the top three leading authors in the 1988 review) are listed as the next most prolific writers in the 1990s.

Table 10.3. The Professional Backgrounds of Authors

Ranking	Background	No. of authors	(%)
1	Political science	218	48.6
2	Government departments	43	9.6
3	Consultancy	27	6.0
4	Sociology	26	5.8
5	Psychology	24	5.4
6	History	19	4.2
7	Military personnel	15	3.3
8	Criminology	13	2.9
9	Lawyers	10	2.2
10	Law enforcement personnel	9	2.0
11	Academic law	8	1.8
12	Economists	7	1.6
–	Religious studies	7	1.6
14	Journalists	5	1.1
15	Anthropology	4	1.0
–	Media studies	4	1.0
17	Librarian studies	2	0.5
–	Medical personnel	2	0.5
19	Remainder	6	1.3
Total		449	100.0

Table 10.3 describes the backgrounds and specializations of the authors. Such information on the authors was gathered by examining the biographical notes provided in the journal issues or – where these were not available – by examining the correspondence address for the author. Usually, but not always, it was possible to describe the background and specialization of the author from such information. This information was compiled on the basis of individual articles as the details of authors could – and often did – change during the ten-year period. Information was unavailable about the author's background in the case of 81 articles (out of a total of 490).

Table 10.3 shows that, as a field, terrorism research is dominated by political scientists. This is not especially surprising. Schmid and Jongman in their review found exactly the same thing.[16] More interesting are the disciplines and backgrounds which emerge after the dominance of political scientists. Members of government account for the next largest group of contributors. This category includes quite a range of individuals including elected politicians, foreign ambassadors, senior civil servants and internal government analysts. Most of these individuals were involved with the US administration in particular.

Researchers working for consultancy organizations were the next most productive pool, with the US-based RAND corporation standing out as particularly productive. The mainstream social sciences followed next with sociology, psychology and history all contributing a significant level of articles. In comparison, criminology seems to account for a surprisingly low proportion of articles. It is also useful to see that counterterrorism professionals have also contributed a significant number of articles and, interestingly, those serving in the military have written more than those serving in law enforcement agencies.

Overall, Table 10.3 indicates that while most articles published in the journals have been by academics from a range of disciplines, a very substantial number have come from individuals working in a professional counterterrorism capacity. Indeed, of the top ten backgrounds listed, half are non-academic. This underlines the real-world and

Table 10.4. Trends in the Professional Backgrounds of Authors

Background	1990–94		1995–99	
	No.	(%)	No.	(%)
Political science	97	46.0	121	50.8
Government departments	30	14.2	13	5.5
Consultancy	12	5.7	15	6.3
Sociology	8	3.8	18	7.6
Psychology	8	3.8	16	6.7
History	5	2.4	12	5.0
Military personnel	6	2.8	9	3.8
Criminology	8	3.8	5	2.1
Law enforcement personnel	5	2.4	4	1.7
Lawyers	7	3.3	2	1.0
Academic law	5	2.4	3	1.3
Economists	5	2.4	2	1.0
Religious studies	5	2.4	2	1.0
Journalists	2	1.0	3	1.3
Anthropology	1	0.5	3	1.3
Media studies	2	1.0	2	1.0
Others	5	2.4	5	2.1
Total	211		238	

applied relevance that terrorism has and indicates, too, the type of audience that the journals are reaching.

The advantage of taking a ten-year-long period of review is that it also allows a meaningful opportunity to detect any existing trends. Table 10.4 indicates that the backgrounds of writers has not remained constant during the 1990s. Instead, the table indicates that there have been considerable changes in who is researching and publishing in the major journals. Table 10.5 below highlights those backgrounds where the major changes occurred.

Table 10.5. Significant Changes in Backgrounds of Authors

	The growth areas				*Losing ground*		
	1990–94	*1995–99*			*1990–94*	*1995–99*	
Political science	1	1	10%	Government depts	2	5	–56%
Sociology	5	2	100%	Criminology	5	8	–45%
Psychology	5	3	76%	Lawyers	7	14.5	–70%
History	11	6	108%	Economics	11	14.5	–58%
Anthropology	18	11	160%	Religious studies	11	14.5	–58%

Table 10.5 shows that the major growth areas were primarily in the academic disciplines. During the 1990s, political scientists actually increased their hold as the major players in the field with a ten per cent increase in the proportion of articles coming from that discipline. Sociologists also made a substantial increase in written output on terrorism in the latter half of the 1990s as did psychologists. Historians and anthropologists also began to play a more significant role. The growing role of these actors, however, was accompanied by a declining input from other sectors. In particular, the input of individuals working in government declined considerably in the latter half of the 1990s (dropping by 56 per cent on what it had been). Criminologists and lawyers also began to contribute considerably less to the journals; while there was also a drop in material being written by economists and those with a background in religious studies.

What do such trends tell us? It has always been lamented that the social sciences did not invest more effort into researching terrorism. The growth seen in the output from the social science disciplines may then be a cause for optimism that terrorism is receiving increased attention in these areas. The decline in writing from those in government (six articles a year until 1994, down to just two or three articles each year in the later years) raises some interesting questions. Is the decline an indication that government departments were losing interest in research on terrorism? Perhaps. Ultimately terrorism was not seen as a profoundly serious problem to western world governments and it is possible that the declining input from government sources is a reflection of this. No doubt 9/11 will herald a sea change here in the corridors of government (at least for a time) but it is interesting to note that the level of input from personnel in the military and in law enforcement agencies did not waver (and indeed actually increased very slightly in recent years). This seems to indicate that those at the coal-face of dealing with terrorism remained as interested and concerned as ever.

Table 10.6. Country of Residence of Authors

Ranking	Country of residence	Contributors	(%)
1	USA	268	57.4
2	UK	75	16.1
3	Israel	29	6.2
4	Canada	17	3.6
5	Australia	15	3.2
6	Republic of Ireland	10	2.1
7	Holland	9	1.9
8	France	6	1.3
9	Germany	5	1.1
–	Italy	5	1.1
–	South Africa	5	1.1
12	India	4	0.9
13	Spain	3	0.6
14	Austria	2	0.4
–	Denmark	2	0.4
–	Norway	2	0.4
–	Turkey	2	0.4
17	Brazil	1	0.2
–	Japan	1	0.2
–	Portugal	1	0.2
–	Romania	1	0.2
–	Russia	1	0.2
–	Singapore	1	0.2
–	Sri Lanka	1	0.2
–	Sweden	1	0.2
–	Switzerland	1	0.2
Total	26 countries	467	100

Examining the country of residence of writers provides an indication of those countries which are investing the most effort into researching and understanding terrorism and terrorists. Table 10.6 shows that the clear leader in this regard is the USA. More than half of all writers on the subject of terrorism in the 1990s were based in the USA. If journal publications can be taken as a loose indication of resources invested in research, then it is clear that the USA was investing nearly four times more than any other country. It is important to bear in mind, once again that these trends are from a time before 9/11. One may not be surprised at such activity in the wake of the most destructive terrorist attacks in recorded history, but the US dominance was already well established before 2001. As the leading journals are all English-language publications it is not surprising that English-speaking countries dominate the list. However, what is more surprising is that countries which – in contemporary terms at least – have had very limited terrorism problems (for example, Canada and Australia) nevertheless have produced many articles on the subject. A similar argument could be made (to a slightly lesser extent) with regard to the USA. Certainly, the number of articles emerging from the USA on the subject seems a little disproportionate considering the country's experience of terrorism in the 1990s. The high rankings of the UK and of Israel are much more understandable in light of the troubled experiences of both countries during this period.

Table 10.7 provides a comparative breakdown in the national locations of writers between the first five years of the 1990s and the second five years. As can be seen, the three leading countries remain the same for both periods, with the USA remaining the base for the clear majority of writers. This can be taken as a reasonable indication that the USA is also the base for the majority of terrorism research in the 1990s. Certainly, no other country even begins to approach the output of the

Table 10.7. Trends in the Country of Residence of Authors

1990–1994	Contributors	(%)	1995–1999	Contributors	(%)
USA	133	62.4	USA	135	53.1
UK	26	12.2	UK	49	19.3
Israel	11	5.2	Israel	18	7.1
Canada	9	4.2	Rep. of Ireland	10	3.9
Holland	7	3.3	Australia	9	3.5
Australia	6	2.8	Canada	8	3.1
France	5	2.3	South Africa	5	2.0
Italy	4	1.9	India	3	1.2
Austria	2	0.9	Germany	2	0.8
India	2	0.9	Holland	2	0.8
Rep. of Ireland	2	0.9	Norway	2	0.8
Spain	2	0.9	Turkey	2	0.8
Brazil	1	0.5	Denmark	1	0.4
Denmark	1	0.5	France	1	0.4
Germany	1	0.5	Italy	1	0.4
Russia	1	0.5	Japan	1	0.4
Singapore	1	0.5	Portugal	1	0.4
Switzerland	1	0.5	Romania	1	0.4
			Spain	1	0.4
			Sri Lanka	1	0.4
			Sweden	1	0.4
Total	213	100	**Total**	254	100

States – though in relative terms both the UK and Israel account for a consistent level of work.

While the USA arguably did not have as profound a terrorism problem as some other countries in the 1990s – for example, compared to that faced by countries such as the UK and Israel – its dominance here can largely be seen to reflect the fact that it is the major world research centre in general. The total US investment in research far exceeds that of any other developed nation. In 1995, the US spent over $170 billion on research, a figure nearly three times higher than its nearest rival (Japan at $70 billion). The UK's research budget in the same year was a much more modest $19 billion.[17] The heavy investment in research has paid off as US-based researchers by and large dominate the research world. The sheer volume of research papers emerging from the USA is staggering. It accounts for between 55–90 per cent of all journal output among the clinical, pre-clinical and social sciences.[18] As a result, its dominance of the terrorism journals is not surprising, though the fact that it dipped below 55 per cent of the output in the later stages of the 1990s may be indicative that US productivity was becoming disproportionately low compared to the nation's research environment. One assumes that 9/11 will reverse that trend at least in the short term.

Table 10.8. Significant Changes in Country of Residence of Authors

| | The growth areas | | | | Losing ground | | |
| | Rankings | | | | Rankings | | |
	1990–94	1995–99	(%)		1990–94	1995–99	(%)
UK	2	2	58	USA	1	1	–15
Israel	3	3	37	Canada	4	6	–26
Republic of Ireland	10.5	4	333	Holland	5	10.5	–76
Australia	6	5	25	France	7	17	–83
South Africa	N/A	7	N/A	Italy	8	17	–79

Table 10.8 shows that – as indicated with regard to the USA above – the relative productivity of countries has not remained constant. The table shows that there has been a considerable growth in research efforts in a number of countries. The UK and Israel accounted for an increasing share of research articles as the 1990s progressed. Likewise, in proportional terms, there have been dramatic increases from researchers based in the Republic of Ireland and South Africa, and a modest but noticeable increase from Australia-based writers. By and large, most of these growths are due to the activities of a relatively small number of

individuals. For example, the considerable increase seen from Ireland is due almost entirely to the work of four individuals who were all based in one university in that country, University College Cork (UCC). The work of these four people (one based in UCC's History Department, three in the Applied Psychology Department) saw a dramatic increase in Ireland's output, taking it to the fourth most productive nation in the latter half of the 1990s.

While a number of countries are experiencing increased research activity, others appear to be showing signs of decline. As already mentioned, the output from the USA appeared to be waning – even if only slightly. The USA still comfortably remained the dominant base for terrorism research but the second half of the 1990s witnessed a small but noticeable decline in output from researchers based there, and there was also a significant decline in output from Canada. However, it is in continental Western Europe where the decline has been most pronounced. Holland, France and Italy all showed a dramatic fall in publications. This is perhaps indicative that for many of the continental countries, terrorism was declining as a significant subject of research interest.

Table 10.9. Country Focus of Articles

Ranking	Country	Articles	(%)
1	USA	35	14.9
2	Northern Ireland	29	12.3
3	Israel	18	7.7
4	Italy	11	4.7
5	UK	9	3.8
–	India	9	3.8
7	Russia	7	3.0
8	South Africa	6	2.6
9	Germany	5	2.1
–	Spain	5	2.1
–	Sri Lanka	5	2.1
12	Cambodia	4	1.7
–	Canada	4	1.7
–	France	4	1.7
–	Iran	4	1.7
–	Japan	4	1.7
–	Columbia	4	1.7
–	Greece	4	1.7
19	Bosnia	3	1.3
–	Lebanon	3	1.3
–	Pakistan	3	1.3
–	Peru	3	1.3
–	Turkey	3	1.3
24	12 countries	2	10.2
36	29 countries	1	12.3
Total	64 countries	185	100

Table 10.9 shows those countries which were the focus of published articles. In order to qualify for consideration here, an article needed to be explicitly focused on one or at most two countries. In total, 235 of the 490 published articles had an explicit country focus (48 per cent). Considering that most terrorism researchers are based in the USA, it is not entirely surprising to find the USA is the country most focused on in the journals. Yet, how serious is the terrorism threat faced by the USA? After 9/11 one must conclude very serious indeed, but traditionally domestic terrorism in the States has been very limited. Tragedies on the scale of Oklahoma are extremely rare and while much attention has been focused on the extreme right, there is no sense of a serious coherent terrorism campaign emerging from this direction at any time in the near future. In contrast, threats from foreign sources have always been a more serious problem to US interests. A variety of terrorist groups from a range of backgrounds (particularly extreme Islamist groups) are content to attack what they perceive as US targets in their own countries or in nations which they can readily access. The two embassy bombings in Africa in 1998 present dramatic examples of the nature of this threat. While attacks such as these could not be described as common, they have represented the bulk of the terrorist threat facing the USA. Despite this, during the 1990s the vast majority of US-focused articles were primarily or exclusively about terrorism from domestic sources, and were not looking at the dangers posed by foreign groups such as al-Qa'eda.

A more understandable finding is that Northern Ireland is the second most discussed place on the planet in terms of the terrorism research literature in the 1990s. I have taken the liberty of distinguishing Northern Ireland from the rest of the UK to illustrate the distinctive prominence of this very small region. As Table 10.9 goes on to show, there are other articles about the UK which have nothing to do with Northern Ireland. Indeed, it is significant to note that even if the Northern Ireland problem did not exist, the UK would still account for a significant proportion of research articles. In proportional terms, Northern Ireland is the most intensely studied region on the planet. It accounts for only very slightly fewer articles than the world's most powerful country. Yet, just how much does Northern Ireland deserve such attention?

True, the terrorist problem in Northern Ireland is very significant and there can be no denying that the 1990s have been an exceptionally dramatic time for the Province. The declaration of the cease-fires, the splintering of established terrorist groups, the emergence of dissident campaigns, the formidable changes wrought by the peace process, prisoner releases, political groups associated with the paramilitaries now occupying government positions and so forth, all mean that it would be staggering if at least some interest was not focused there. But in relative terms there are other nations who have suffered comparable or even worse fates and yet the published literature on them has been far less. The terrorist experience of Spain or of Corsica are good examples here. The Spanish experience in the 1990s in particular has mirrored much of what has happened in Northern Ireland but far less has been written about it (only 5 articles as opposed to 29). Why?

There are probably a number of answers. To begin with, as part of the UK, the Northern Irish conflict is a conflict of the English-speaking world, and is thus more accessible to English-speaking researchers. Further, the Irish question has always had a special interest for the USA and many American researchers have taken the Irish conflict as their primary research interest. The interest of the Clinton administration has also helped to focus American interest. Combine that with a substantial level of research activity in the UK and a growing level in the Republic of Ireland, and it is not surprising that Northern Ireland

Table 10.10. Country Focus of Articles: Changes Over Time

1990–94	Contributors	(%)	1995–99	Contributors	(%)
USA	18	16.1	USA	17	15.2
Northern Ireland	13	11.6	Northern Ireland	16	14.3
Italy	7	6.3	Israel	13	11.6
Israel	6	5.4	South Africa	5	4.5
UK	6	5.4	Italy	4	3.6
India	6	5.4	Japan	4	3.6
Russia	4	3.6	Turkey	4	3.6
Spain	4	3.6	Cambodia	3	2.7
France	3	2.7	India	3	2.7
Germany	3	2.7	Iran	3	2.7
Armenia	2	1.8	Russia	3	2.7
China	2	1.8	UK	3	2.7
Greece	2	1.8	Bosnia	2	1.8
Holland	2	1.8	Burma	2	1.8
Indonesia	2	1.8	Columbia	2	1.8
Lebanon	2	1.8	Germany	2	1.8
Liberia	2	1.8	Sri Lanka	2	1.8
Namibia	2	1.8	Canada	2	1.8
Peru	2	1.8	Greece	2	1.8
Canada	2	1.8	Pakistan	2	1.8
Columbia	2	1.8	Others	18	16.1
Sri Lanka	2	1.8			
Others	18	16.1			
Total	112	100	**Total**	112	100

receives so much attention, while other more violent and destructive terrorist campaigns in the world receive extremely little.

Table 10.10 shows that the focus of research articles has changed over the decade. In the latter half of the 1990s there was a dramatic decline in interest in terrorism in continental Western Europe with far fewer articles focusing on Spain, Italy or France. There was also a decline in research on UK terrorism that was not connected to Northern Ireland. This is somewhat ironic as the Northern Irish conflict had entered its most subdued phase in three decades and yet was now the focus of more research articles than ever! As well as an increased interest in Ulster, there were even more dramatic increases in articles focused on other areas, and in particular on Israel and South Africa. Turkey and Japan also became sources of increased interest. In this sense, the changes seen here arguably reflect changes in what are perceived to be emerging hot-spots and trouble areas for terrorist violence.

While Tables 10.9 and 10.10 give a good indication of the geographic interests of terrorism research, a number of research articles were excluded because, while they had a discrete geographic focus, this extended to more than two countries. In order to take this into consideration, a more generalized system was used. This divided the world into nine separate regions as outlined in Table 10.11 and thus provided a very clear indication of where the terrorism research effort was being focused. The world region of most interest to terrorism researchers during the 1990s was clearly Western Europe. This was then followed by the Middle East. It is somewhat disconcerting though to note that regions such as Latin America – which are acknowledged to have relatively high levels of terrorist violence and where terrorists are much more serious threats to established regimes – have received such a paucity of attention.

Table 10.11. World Region Focus of Articles, 1990–99

Rank	Region	Articles	(%)
1	Western Europe	88	30.9
2	Middle East	50	17.5
3	Asia	46	16.1
4	North America	39	13.7
5	Eastern Europe	24	8.4
6	Africa	21	7.4
7	South America	8	2.8
8	Central America	6	2.1
9	Pacifica	3	1.1
	Total	285	100

Bearing in mind the growth of Australia as a base of terrorism research as described in Tables 10.6 and 10.8, it is a little surprising to note that extremely few articles are actually focused on terrorism in the Pacifica region. Indeed, as Table 10.12 below shows, as the number of research articles emerging from Australia has increased, the number of articles which focus on terrorism in Pacifica has actually decreased.

Table 10.12. World Region Focus of Articles: Changes Over Time

Region	1990–94	(%)	1995–99	(%)
North America	20	14.2	19	13.2
Central America	4	2.8	2	1.4
South America	5	3.5	3	2.1
Western Europe	53	37.6	35	24.3
Eastern Europe	11	7.8	13	9.0
Middle East	22	15.6	28	19.4
Asia	17	12.1	29	20.1
Pacifica	2	1.4	1	0.7
Africa	7	5.0	14	9.7
Total	141	100	144	100

As has generally been the case, Table 10.12 shows again that terrorism research has not been static during the 1990s. In terms of the regional focus of research, there have been significant changes in the areas which have attracted most interest. Western Europe accounted for nearly 40 per cent of articles prior to 1995, yet in the following five years it was down to nearly 20 per cent. As output on Northern Ireland actually increased during this time, this decline underlines a dramatic falling away of interest in terrorism in most of the other European countries. The Americas also witnessed a drop in interest, with Latin America being particularly badly affected.

With declining interest in terrorism generally in the Western World, the question is 'Where has the recent research effort been focused instead?' Certainly, the Middle East has received increased attention, but the real growth areas have been Africa and, more significantly, Asia. Neither of these latter two regions have ever really received the attention they deserved, so it is refreshing to see that there are some signs that the significance of their experience with terrorism is being recognized. Indeed, one indication that the research community was accurately sensing an emerging hot-spot was that in the latter half of the 1990s more research focused on Asia than on the Middle East.

Having considered how articles were focused in terms of geography, it is only natural to also enquire as to how they were focused in terms of actors. The criterion used here is that the article had to be primarily about one, or at most two, groups. It was not sufficient that a group was briefly mentioned or received discussion of a page or two. The group had to be clearly the major focus of the article. Under these conditions, 39 separate groups in total were the major focus of at least one article in the ten-year period.[19] The growing significance of al-Qa'eda appears to have been badly missed by the research community. In this ten-year period, only one article took the Islamist organization as its major focus (and even then this paper was not exclusively devoted to the group).[20] Doubtless history will record this as the single major failure of terrorism research activity in the 1990s. It is somewhat ironic that, in contrast, the terrorist group which received the most attention during this time was one becoming less and less of a threat with each year: the PIRA. Far more articles focused on the activities and structure of this organization than on any other terrorist group. The PIRA are widely regarded as one of the best-organized and most professional terrorist groups in recent decades, and they have been the focus of research attention from a large number of researchers both in the British Isles and in the USA. The US dominance of the research field is felt more obviously in the second most studied group: US-based militia groups. These have not been particularly active in terms of actually conducting terrorist campaigns and neither are they regarded as being as professional or as organized as

Table 10.13. Group Focus of Articles, 1990–99

Ranking	Group	No. of articles	(%)
1	PIRA	11	12.1
2	US militias	7	7.7
3	Branch Davidians	5	5.5
–	Loyalists (Northern Ireland)	5	5.5
5	neo–Nazis	4	4.4
–	PLO	4	4.4
–	Red Brigades	4	4.4
8	Hizbollah	3	3.3
–	Shining Path	3	3.3
10	Action Directe	2	2.2
–	Aum Shinrikyo	2	2.2
–	Earth First	2	2.2
–	ETA	2	2.2
–	FLQ	2	2.2
–	JDL	2	2.2
–	Khmer Rouge	2	2.2
–	Militant Islam	2	2.2
–	Red Army Faction	2	2.2
–	Revolutionary Organization November 17	2	2.2
–	FLN	2	2.2
21	Others	19	20.9
	Total	87	100

groups such as the PIRA, but the fact that they are the most significant domestic problem the USA faces means that they occupy wide coverage in the journals.

In joint third place, there is something of a surprise: the Branch Davidian religious sect. What is significant about the Branch Davidians is that this prominence in the literature is entirely due to one event: the siege at Waco, Texas which ended so disastrously in 1993. The Branch Davidians did not mount a terrorist campaign in any conventional understanding of the word. The siege itself was very much a discrete and self-contained affair, and the horrific destruction at its finale is now widely believed to have had more to do with the actions of the security forces than with the besieged Davidians. Nevertheless, this group and the events at Waco were among the most researched and discussed in the terrorism journals during the 1990s.

It is interesting to note that Aum Shinrikyo – a far more dangerous religious sect than the Branch Davidians ever were – account for only two articles in the entire decade. To date, Aum is the only terrorist group explicitly known to have invested substantial effort in developing both biological and chemical WMD, and to have followed this research and development by deploying these weapons in real-world attacks. Further, unlike the Branch Davidians, Aum continues to exist as a significant force both in Japan and elsewhere and, disturbingly, has regained much of the ground lost in the immediate wake of the Tokyo sarin gas attack. Yet, despite being a far more significant group in a number of respects, only two articles have been published which have Aum as their primary focus. Over twice as many articles focused on the Branch Davidians.

Occupying joint third place with the Branch Davidians are the loyalist paramilitary groups active in Northern Ireland. This, again, reflects the high overall level of interest in Northern Ireland in the research community. It is interesting to note though that twice as many articles have been focused on the PIRA as compared to the loyalists even though the loyalists have been much more active in the past decade (and are currently in the midst of bitter feuds).

Some of the same problems which applied when considering the geographic focus of articles were also an issue when attention moved to considering terrorist groups. Some articles considered several different groups which shared similar ideologies, backgrounds, activities, etc. However, if the article was examining more than two groups, it was not considered for Table 10.13 above. Table 10.14 then describes a more general assessment of the groups studied. This table describes all of the

Table 10.14. Terrorist-Type Focus of Articles, 1990–99

Ranking	Type	Articles	(%)
1	Nationalist/separatist groups	26	25.2
2	Islamic extremists	20	19.4
3	Marxist/communist	17	16.5
4	Right-wing extremists	13	12.6
5	Religious cults	8	7.8
6	Environmentalists	4	3.1
7	Criminal	2	1.9
8	State terrorism	2	1.9
9	Others	12	11.7
	Total	104	100

articles which were focused on discussing a particular group or particular set of groups. It gives an indication of the type of terrorists which were attracting the most research energy. The table shows that in overall terms the research focused primarily on insurgent terrorism – that is, terrorism committed by small, non-State groups.

As this table shows, the research effort was spread over quite a range of different types of terrorist. Nationalist/separatist groups such as the PIRA or ETA were the major targets of research effort in the 1990s. These were followed fairly closely by extremist Islamist groups, such as Hamas, Hizbollah and al-Qa'eda. Left-wing groups such as the old European terrorist organizations, like the Red Brigades and Red Army Faction, were the next most researched type. Following these, there were other discrete types of terrorists which were examined with declining energy. Significantly, a number of groups ultimately did not fit comfortably into the eight broad categories identified in the table. These black sheep terrorists were grouped together under the category 'Other' and included diverse groups such as the OAS, the Jewish Defence League and the Northern Irish loyalist groups.

Table 10.15. Terrorist-Type Focus of Articles: Changes Over Time

Type	1990–94	(%)	1995–99	(%)
Nationalist/separatist groups	11	25.6	14	23.3
Islamic extremists	6	14.0	14	23.3
Environmentalists	1	2.3	3	5.0
Religious cults	2	4.7	6	10.0
Marxist/communist	11	25.6	6	10.0
Right-wing extremists	1	2.3	12	20.0
Criminal	2	4.7	–	0.0
State terrorism	2	4.7	–	0.0
Others	7	16.3	5	8.3
Total	43	100	60	100

Table 10.15 shows that the focus on terrorist groups varied considerably over the course of the decade. As the 1990s progressed, more and more attention was directed into researching right-wing groups (both in Europe and, particularly, in the USA), religious cults and Islamist extremist groups. These attracted more and more attention in the latter stages of the 1990s. Nationalist/separatist groups continued to receive most attention (if only jointly with the Islamist groups in the past five years). In contrast, research interest in left-wing terrorism declined dramatically as the decade progressed, as did interest in state terrorism or 'terrorism' committed by criminal organizations. As with other tables, Table 10.15 shows that as a research field, the area is not static and there are very clear changes in the directions in which research effort and resources are being channelled. The increasingly strong concern with Islamist terrorism somewhat redeems the field, suggesting as it does that researchers were aware that this was presenting an ever-more critical threat, although more work on al-Qa'eda would have indicated greater verisimilitude.

SOME CONCEPTUAL ISSUES

A final issue, when considering the research output in the field, is to look at how conceptual issues are handled. It is generally agreed that terrorism lacks an agreed conceptual framework. The continuing failure to arrive at a widely agreed definition of terrorism and terrorists is the most obvious symptom of this missing framework. To many other areas of scientific research, the lack of such basic agreed concepts as definitions would be regarded as a massive obstacle to productive research, or to significant progress in the field. One might then expect that efforts to establish such a conceptual framework and work out acceptable definitions would occupy a considerable amount of space in the major journals in the area. However, this has definitely not been the case in the 1990s.

Of the 490 articles published in the ten-year period, just eight (1.6 per cent) could be regarded as primarily conceptual papers. These papers were all primarily concerned with addressing aspects of the definition debate. Nevertheless, a level of 1.6 per cent would not indicate to an outsider the profound lack of agreement on these issues which exist between terrorism researchers. Why then are such articles so rare?

The answer – at least initially – probably begins with the fact that there is a relatively low proportion of writers who contribute more than one article to the journals. All of the writers who have tackled the conceptual and definitional question head-on (with one exception) have been writers who have also contributed other more applied articles to the journals as well. It is probably reasonable to argue that those researchers most concerned about the conceptual state of the field are going to be those with the greater research commitment to the area. As Table 10.1 has already shown, very few writers appear to have taken terrorism as their major area of research interest, and as a result it is not entirely surprising to find that conceptual articles are thin on the ground.

Another factor which is probably also at work much of the time is that there seems to be something of a war-weariness among established researchers over the definitional quagmire. Everyone is by now very familiar with the huge difficulties faced by any attempt to achieve consensus, and, rather than continue to struggle for the nebulous goal of an agreed framework, researchers seem to have resigned themselves to accepting the current state of uncertainty and to allow everyone to work within their own more limited frameworks. On many levels this makes much practical sense. It means that valuable research work of applied real-world value is being done, and the somewhat wasteful definitional debate is not draining energy and time in the same way that it did in the 1970s and 1980s. That said, the current situation can only be a temporary stop-gap measure. Sooner or later, the conceptual confusion in the area must begin to severely hamper progress. It is likely that there is a ceiling of development which can occur with the current approach, but that when this ceiling has been reached, it will need wider conceptual agreement before further progress can be made.

How far away are we from this research ceiling? This is a difficult question to answer. As we have seen in this review, terrorism research is not evenly distributed across disciplines and topics. Instead it tends to periodically cluster in certain areas and on certain subjects before changing to new areas. It is probable that in some places terrorism research has already gone as far as it can go without a wider conceptual framework being in place. In other places, though, it is equally clear that productive research will still be possible for some time to come. The rather low number of committed researchers, if nothing else, at least appears to have bought some breathing space by ensuring that a considerable body of work remains open to constructive – and not overly controversial – enquiry.

However, there are also signs that the lack of conceptual/definitional agreement is having some damaging impact. As a whole, it has meant that the terrorism literature is extremely applied. This can be seen not only in the very small number of writers and articles which tackle conceptual issues full-on, but also in other respects. For example, the field is almost entirely focused on issues of immediate, real-world relevance. The papers are about terrorist groups which are currently active, about current or imminent threats, or are focused on regions with recent or current experience of terrorist violence. There is virtually no effort to set terrorism within a broader context. Only 13 articles (out of a total of 490) look at non-contemporary terrorism and only seven of these look at terrorism prior to 1960. We know that terrorism is not a recent phenomenon and that it has been occurring in some form or another for over 2,000 years. Yet this wider context is almost entirely ignored as terrorism research is driven by a need to provide a short-term, immediate assessment of current groups and threats. Efforts to establish coherent and stable guiding principles have been almost entirely side-lined. This is a serious cause for concern and is an issue which the more committed researchers will hopefully turn increased attention towards.

CONCLUSIONS

In reviewing the research literature for the 1990s, a number of conclusions can be drawn. First, compared to other relevant areas in the social sciences, terrorism appears to be continuing to suffer from an overall lack of researchers in general, and a near-chronic shortage of researchers who have taken the subject as their major research interest. The end result is that very few individuals have written more than one article on the subject in the leading journals.

In general, a small number of demographic characteristics dominate this small pool of researchers. Most are based in the USA and most also come from a background in political science. The dominance of the USA seems to have declined slightly as the 1990s progressed, and other countries appear to be investing increased resources into terrorism research. This is not to say that such research efforts are co-ordinated, coherent efforts: rather it merely indicates that certain countries appear to be producing more research into the subject than previously. 9/11 will no doubt lead to a refocusing of activity, with the USA – for a range of reasons – set to exert even greater dominance over the field. Conversely the 1990s saw other countries producing fewer research papers, indicating they were either not establishing new researchers with interests in the area, or were finding that the established researchers they do possess were diverting their energies elsewhere.

Political science remains by far the dominant, and hence most influential, discipline in the field. There is considerable growth in the input from other social science disciplines, with sociology, psychology and anthropology appearing to add more to the field as the 1990s progressed. In terms of developing a fuller conceptual understanding of terrorism this latter development is certainly encouraging. However, the declining input from government sources raises other questions. With some notable exceptions, articles from these sources have tended to lack the depth and wider conceptual appreciation of many other writers. However, the decline could be an indication that the government members (and especially the US administration) were becoming disenfranchised from the research effort. Is this the case? Hopefully not. It remains critically important that governments continue to appreciate the vital importance of good quality research on terrorism. Thankfully, it seems clear from the stable input from those in the military and in law enforcement that they at least continue to see the value in such research.

A major conclusion from this review is that, as a field, terrorism research has not been static in the last decade and instead clear changes in how the research effort has been channelled and focused have become obvious. It is extremely clear that the research effort is driven very much by issues of contemporary relevance. There is a bias towards topics of particular relevance to western democracies and in particular to topics of relevance to the USA. Whether the US focus was entirely deserved in the 1990s is debatable (particularly given the massive concern lavished on home-grown dissidents while groups such as al-Qa'eda were largely overlooked). But the USA, for its part, does support more research on the subject than any other country and it is only natural that there is some reflection of that in terms of what the field has focused on.

It seems clear that the research literature on terrorism is evolving and will continue to evolve. As new groups, threats and conflicts emerge, the focus of the literature will move to examine these – limited only by the current biases already described. The only concern is that the field appears to be overly applied. The research tends to look at immediate issues and search for immediate answers. We appear to be talking a great deal about the manifest symptoms of terrorism without ever really delving directly into the roots of the problem. The ability of this research to predict with any clarity or force is weak at best. In general, only rather feeble attempts are made to uncover the fundamental trends and patterns behind terrorism which cross organizational, national and temporal divides. These – it seems – are flaws which will only be addressed when the field can draw on the efforts of a much more substantial body of researchers. The current field, top-heavy as it is with transients, seems to face a formidable task in addressing what are the most substantial weaknesses in our knowledge and understanding of terrorism.

NOTES

1. Alex Schmid and Albert Jongman, *Political Terrorism: A New Guide to Actors, Authors, Concepts, Data bases, Theories and Literature* (Amsterdam: North-Holland Publishing, 1988).
2. The RAE has been used by the UK government as a way to measure the research performance of the UK's university sector. Performance scores in the RAE are directly linked to future government funding (that is, high scores result in more funding).
3. Each article which was published in the ten-year period was entered into a database based on 11 separate features. Coding was made for each author of each article on the following features:
   1. Author name
   2. Whether first, second or third author
   3. Journal title
   4. Journal Volume details
   5. Year of Publication
   6. Country where the author is based
   7. Occupation/background of the author
   8. Geographic focus of the article
   9. Temporal focus of the article
   10. Terrorist Group focus of the article
   11. Conceptual focus of the article
4. Schmid and Jongman, *Political Terrorism*, p. 177.
5. Ibid.
6. Ibid., p. 179.
7. Ariel Merari, 'Academic Research and Government Policy on Terrorism', *Terrorism and Political Violence*, 3/1 (Spring 1991) pp. 88–102.
8. However, some researchers have pointed out that the risks in researching terrorism have often been over-emphasized and exaggerated, and that it is actually possible to conduct considerable research work with little or no real personal danger involved. For more on this, see John Horgan, 'Issues in Terrorism Research', *The Police Journal*, 70 (1997) pp. 193–202.
9. Merari, 'Academic Research and Government Policy', p. 89.
10. Table 10.1 also shows that there were differences in the level of repeat writers between the two journals. Twenty-two per cent of the articles in TPV were written by authors who published other articles on terrorism in the period. Just ten per cent of the articles in Ter/SICAT were written by authors who also wrote at least one other article. It is not clear why this difference exists, but it does seem clear that *Terrorism and Political Violence* (*TPV*) seems to be attracting more articles from the consistent researchers. Interestingly, there also seems to be a very real divide in contributors to both journals. Just 16 writers out of the total number of the 403 individual contributors published in both of the main journals (four per cent of the total number of contributors). Even when we look at the 'regular' writers (two or more articles), only 23 per cent publish in both journals (the remaining 77 per cent reserve their material for just one of the main journals).
11. This paper is not attempting to argue that the comparisons are far-reaching or profound. Just simply that they are at least superficially sufficient to allow the descriptive illustration which follows. The standing of terrorism as a research field is debatable and as a research discipline even more so. It is not the intent of this chapter to attempt to tackle such issues and the comparisons made here should be taken purely in the context of the article.

12. Ellen Cohn and David Farrington, 'Changes in the Most-Cited Scholars in Major International Journals between 1986–90 and 1991–95', *British Journal of Criminology*, 38/1 (Winter 1998), pp. 156–70.
13. Considering this somewhat depressing situation, the growing number of research conferences on terrorism is an extremely welcome development. For a long time such conferences occurred only rarely, but in recent years there have been a growing number of them.
14. As the list below shows, Leonard Weinberg remains the most prolific contributor when all categories of material are considered (articles, editorials, research notes, conference reports, etc.). This list is broadly very similar to Table 10.2, though it is worth noting that two authors – Avishag Gordon and A.D. Harvey – rise significantly in the rankings based on the large number of research notes they have published in *TPV*. Apart from them, all the other names appear in Table 10.2.

Ranking	Author	Publications
1	Leonard Weinberg	11
2	Bruce Hoffman	10
3	Paul Wilkinson	8
–	Alex Schmid	8 (2)
5	William Eubank	7 (5)
6	J. Bowyer Bell	6
–	Peter Chalk	6
–	Max Taylor	6 (4)
9	Avishag Gordon	5
–	A.D. Harvey	5
–	Alison Jamieson	5
–	Jeffrey Kaplan	5
–	Dennis Pluchinsky	5
–	Andrew Silke	5
–	Peter Alan Sproat	5
–	John Horgan	5 (2)
17	Michael Barkun	4
–	Steve Bruce	4
–	Raphael Cohen-Almagor	4
–	Raphael Israeli	4
–	Ariel Merari	4
–	Robert White	4
–	Ronald Crelinsten	4 (1)

15. It is a distinct peculiarity of the field that the most productive writers do not seem to allocate their research papers evenly to both of the leading journals. Instead, it is clear that most of the more prolific writers publish almost exclusively in only one of the main journals and only rarely – if ever – publish in the other. As already stated, and as the list below indicates, the only notable exception to this trend is Bruce Hoffman who has shared out his writings more evenly than most. Why others have not followed suit is a little strange considering the relatively small size of both the research community and the research outlets.

TPV	Articles	Ter/SICAT	Articles
Leonard Weinberg	10 (2)	Dennis Pluchinsky	4
William Eubank	7 (5)	J. Bowyer Bell	4
Paul Wilkinson	6	Alison Jamieson	3
Alex Schmid	5 (1)	Benjamin Harrison	2
Bruce Hoffman	**5**	Brendan O'Shea	2
Jeffrey Kaplan	5	**Bruce Hoffman**	**2**
Andrew Silke	4	Carl Yaeger	2
Ariel Merari	4	Edward Badolato	2
Max Taylor	4 (3)	Gawdat Bahgat	2
Peter Chalk	4	George Klay Kieh, Jr	2

TPV	Articles	Ter/SICAT	Articles
Raphael Cohen-Almagor	4	John Arquilla	2
Robert White	4	Louis Rene Beres	2
C.J.M. Drake	3	Morris Busby	2
Ehud Sprinzak	3	Paul Diehl	2
John Horgan	3 (1)	Paul Henze	2
Michael Dartnell	3	Ralph Salmi	2
Rachel Monaghan	3	Robert Miller	2
Raphael Israeli	3	William Rosenau	2
Richard Clutterbuck	3		
Ronald Crelinstein	3		
Steve Bruce	3		
Victor Le Vine	3		

16. One difference between this review and Schmid and Jongman's is that the latter differentiated military/strategic studies from political studies producing two academic categories: political science and military. Following from Clausewitz's well-known axiom, this study, however, did not differentiate between the two. Writers described as having a background in strategic studies, war studies, etc., were classed here as political scientists. I freely acknowledge that other reviewers may disagree with this scheme and prefer Schmid and Jongman's approach.
17. National Science Board, 'US and International Research and Development: Funds and Alliances': http://www.nsf.gov/sbe/srs/seind98/access/c4/c4s4.htm; accessed 18 September 2000.
18. National Center for Education Statistics, 'Education Indicators: An International Perspective', http://nces.ed.gov/pubs/eiip/eiip.html; accessed 20 September 2000.
19. It is interesting to note that in the 1990s no article was focused on the possibility of terrorism committed by lone actors. It will be interesting to see if this changes over the coming years.
20. The article in question was: Gavin Cameron, 'Multi-Track Micro-Proliferation: Lessons from Aum Shinrikyo and al Qaida', *Studies in Conflict and Terrorism*, 22/4 (1999), pp. 277–309.

11

Redefining the Issues:
The Future of Terrorism Research
and the Search for Empathy

GAETANO JOE ILARDI

It is important to note that Americans have a difficult time in understanding extremist organizations with a religious orientation like al-Qaeda. It is essential that the agencies of our government involved in law enforcement and intelligence become intimately familiar with the culture of religious zealots whether of foreign or domestic origin. We must understand the nature of the threat before we can successfully confront it. In America, we also have fundamentalists such as Christian Identity, and other religious extremists who kill or maim in the name of God. Comprehending the danger and the mind-set of these groups is a first step to deterring the violence executed by the Osama Bin Ladens of the world. Unless we know what drives these religious extremists, who are willing to kill themselves in the performance of their violent acts, we will see days like September 11, 2001, repeated, perhaps with even greater casualties.

Testimony of Vincent Cannistraro before the House Committee on International Relations, 3 October 2001.

As a topic of debate, the purpose and direction of terrorism research has taken on a sense of urgency unseen in the last 30 years. The increasing frequency with which these matters are now discussed is a reflection of this contemporary sense of importance. This, of course, stands to reason. After three decades of intensive and prolific research, it is natural that the question, 'So what?', be posed more frequently. The persistent use of terrorism as a tool of political dissent, and at a level of intensity and ferocity previously unseen in modern times, urges such questioning attitudes. The strong prescriptive focus of terrorism research over the years, however, has for the most part failed to deliver the goods. In addition to its apparent failure to achieve its primary objectives – and there is little evidence to indicate the contrary – the prescriptive focus of terrorism researchers has also diverted attention from other critical matters, not the least of which is the development of a sound theoretical understanding of the dynamics of terrorism. One can also add to this a continued tendency to produce research whose methods are questionable, no doubt largely due to the perceived need to produce 'policy-relevant' material in a timely fashion; and, perhaps for the same reason, a widespread inability to identify and exploit original information sources. This notwithstanding, pressure remains on the field to continue to produce material, especially given events such as 11 September. The result has been a spiralling of the literature that in the end adds little to our overall understanding of terrorism.[1]

While the appeal of producing material capable of influencing decision-making in a concrete and immediate sense is undoubtedly real, the cost of pursuing such a course with almost single-minded determination has become too great. There exists a clear and present need for terrorism researchers to focus their collective energies upon the critical goal of understanding the dynamics of terrorism, including its root causes, taking into particular account the role of culture and history in explaining contemporary behaviour and motivations. In other words, adopting an empathetic approach to the analysis of terrorism by acknowledging the interconnectedness and true complexity of events. This process calls for the addition, rather than the reduction, of variables in the study of terrorism.

The need for such an approach is important not only to advance the terrorism discipline, which is becoming increasingly stagnant, but also for the purpose of fulfilling the even greater external need of providing government, law enforcement and the public with a greater *strategic and tactical* awareness of the issues surrounding terrorism. The ultimate purpose of this must be to dispel notions that find their roots in simplified and overly restricted assessments of terrorist behaviour. The importance of adopting this approach was made particularly evident in connection with the tragic events of 11 September 2001. Not only did these events reveal an intelligence failure of sorts, but also exposed a more profound intellectual failure, a failure of the mind. Furthermore, the debate that followed these events, more than ever, highlighted the need for an injection of realism, one capable of serving as a practical and reasonable guide to thought and action. It is to this end that terrorism research must commit itself.

In the wake of the terror attacks upon New York and Washington in September 2001, much of the world was aghast. The audacity of the attackers and magnitude of the attack created a true sense of disbelief. 'Surreal' was a term frequently used to describe the events on that fateful and most horrible of days. The actions of the terrorists, at least in the initial stages after the attacks, were simply too shocking to comprehend. Inevitably, Americans sought answers. Most questions, however, were determined and shaped by an unfamiliar sense of vulnerability and outrage at having been violated. How was an attack on this scale possible without it being detected in its planning stage by US intelligence? How were the attackers able to bypass airport security? How could similar attacks be prevented in the future? Americans became preoccupied with restoring some sense of security and certainty in what was previously the most secure and confident of societies. The creation of a Cabinet-level position within the US government of the aptly named Office of Homeland Security was intended to ease these fears and restore confidence. This inward-looking focus, while natural under such tragic circumstances, reflects a broader historical inclination on the part of Americans, and other nations with occidental roots, to adopt a worldview bordering on the parochial. At a time when a deep and meaningful understanding of terrorism is crucial to the world's ability to develop suitable counter responses and effective defences against groups such as al-Qa'eda, we are instead witnessing the use of language and behaviour that encourages simple universalism and parochial tendencies. While many may take comfort in embracing such views, they do nothing to aid the practical business of defending one's self from the scourge of terrorism.

Indeed, the atmosphere that prevailed after the attacks left little room for pluralism or diversity of thought and opinion. President Bush was left unhindered to set the agenda, and the nature and tone, of America's response to international terrorism. The digest of congressional developments, *CQ Weekly*, captured the power of an invigorated President Bush:

> The entire agenda of the President and Congress, all the usual political plots and calculations, has been swept aside. Issues and arguments that a week ago seemed crucial now seem almost

insignificant. For the present, there is only one issue, one agenda. It is for the President to set that course ... and it is for Congress to close ranks behind him. After months without a mandate, President Bush has almost universal public support to do what he considers necessary, and, with few reservations, law-makers seem ready to agree ...[2]

The same environment that empowered President Bush also served to discourage dissenting points of view. As is usual during times of 'war', views that diverge from those of the government of the day, or those that can broadly be construed as aiding and abetting the enemy, are considered disloyal. This was particularly evident in the aftermath of the attacks, where with the notable and predictable exception of people such as Noam Chomsky, dissenting perspectives, including those among the media, academia and other social observers, were few and far between. Efforts to understand the terrorists' grievances, including their historical roots and the function of US foreign policy in shaping these grievances, were paid scant attention. To demonstrate any degree of empathy, regardless of how slight, was to place one's credibility in harm's way. To empathize implied conceding some validity to the act by acknowledging the existence of a legitimate cause or motive. To empathize was to sympathize. To sympathize was unimaginable, and unforgivable.

This environment did little to encourage the development of a more sophisticated and considered analysis of terrorism, its roots and motivation. President Bush was instrumental in encouraging this thinking, with his constant references and arguments revolving around simplified notions of good *versus* evil. President Bush frequently referred to terrorism and terrorists as evil and evil-doers, while Osama bin Laden was described as 'the evil one'. In one speech alone, on 11 October 2001, Bush managed to use the word 'evil' 11 times. This rhetoric found a receptive audience and soon spread to other high-level administration officials, including Secretary of Defence, Donald Rumsfeld.

This rhetoric has, and continues to have, a damaging effect upon efforts to achieve meaningful and constructive empathy. Such language serves to invite ignorance by providing a rationale that does not encourage understanding. In denouncing bin Laden and his cohorts as evil, the USA and its Western allies are absolving themselves of the need to understand them, to ascertain those forces that ultimately led to that terrible day in September, including the role their own decisions and policies may have played. This rhetoric also extended to the systematic and carefully orchestrated use of the term 'terrorism', which has taken on even greater connotations of evil in the post-11 September period. Its use has done little to encourage rational and dispassionate debate and has the potential, in the current climate, to undermine efforts to achieve empathy in two important ways. First, the term 'terrorism' has a levelling effect. It reduces all the different types and motivations, and all the other idiosyncrasies that define a group or act as unique, to virtual irrelevance. Instead of encouraging debate, such terminology encourages fear, prejudice and bias, while also serving to obscure the roots of the problem. Second, it is effectively being used to deny the perpetrator even the slightest degree of legitimacy, so that their grievances are at best incidental. Terrorist motivation is lost and smothered by the act itself and how it comes to be defined. While this has always been true in the past, the intensity of feeling in the post-11 September world has made an abomination of anything even remotely associated with terrorism. The word itself has become a political tool of immense power, capable of providing a rationale for a range of actions, including war.

This levelling became evident in other areas, as the USA and its Western allies invoked their trust in basic values such as law, democracy, freedom and peace.[3] Whilst these are core values upon which the occidental world operates and thrives, their continued use as universal values that have relevance and application to people everywhere fails to acknowledge cultural and historical differences. This presumption, that people are essentially alike, is a further indication of the contemporary practice of reducing essentially complex events to their most basic of levels. Collectively, this is not an environment that encourages systemic thinking, or one that has a true appreciation for the interconnectedness and dynamics of events. Before the dust was able to settle on the World Trade Center (WTC) and Pentagon, it was clear that the world's ability to empathize would emerge as one of the first intellectual casualties.

The question of empathy, or more precisely, its absence, was also apparent with regard to the debate centring on US intelligence. In the discussion that followed 11 September, the most frequently raised question concerned the failure of US intelligence to provide adequate warning. How could the US intelligence community, with its massive budget and high-tech gadgetry, fail to detect an attack involving so many terrorists, against a target that had been singled out in the past, and which had been in the planning, quite possibly, for years? The extent of the surprise, and its impact upon an American public who rightly felt violated by the attacks, inevitably led to comparisons with Pearl Harbor. The subsequent debate then centred on the need for more money and resources, greater co-operation, and modifications to those laws which have served to stifle the intelligence community's creative juices, including a review of the 1976 executive order signed by President Ford outlawing assassinations.

The subsequent examination of US intelligence revealed just how ill-equipped it was to achieve a level of empathy necessary to make realistic assessments of terrorist motivations and possible intentions. It was soon revealed that at the time of the attacks, the CIA possessed only one Afghan analyst, despite the central role this country was known to have played in its support for al-Qa'eda. Similarly, there was, and continues to be, a chronic shortage of Arabic, Farsi and Pashto translators within the US law enforcement and intelligence communities. Likewise, the number of Arab-American FBI agents has been estimated at fewer than 25.[4]

These deficiencies reflect a broader failure on the part of the US law enforcement and intelligence communities to develop the type of empathy that is crucial to understanding the motivation, intentions and mind set of terrorists generally, and those motivated by religion in particular. Empathy requires that the observer accept that the world of the terrorist, and the world from which the terrorist is drawn, is complex. To achieve real empathy, the observer must consider those non-operational aspects of intelligence relating to the potential target, including the seemingly irrelevant details of the target's culture, history, religion, traditions and language. Only then can understanding of the target group be truly appreciated to the extent that it is possible to see the world through the eyes of the target. Among other things, the ability of US intelligence to achieve this level of empathy has also been undermined by its excessive reliance upon technical intelligence. The use of technical intelligence collection methods has well and truly asserted its dominance within the US intelligence community, with the result that human intelligence has been permitted to fall by the wayside. It has been estimated that 90 per cent of the annual $35 billion intelligence budget is spent on technical spy equipment.

An appreciation for the importance of cultural understanding and its accompanying subtleties upon the practical aspects of counterterrorist work was rarely acknowledged in the post-11 September attacks. The nexus between culture, history and contemporary events is elusive within a society that has demonstrated an increasing impatience for, and some may say ignorance of, history and foreign cultures. The Chairman of the US House Permanent Select Committee on Intelligence was one of the rare exceptions, as reflected in his comments on the need for quality intelligence analysts:

We don't have enough analysts. We are hopelessly underinvested in analysts. These are again, the language people, the people familiar with the culture, the people who have actually been on the street in Khartoum or wherever you want to go, who understand a little bit what this means. Sitting in a chair one way might mean something to one person; it might be unremarkable to somebody else. If you know the culture and see the way a person is gesturing with his hands or his feet or something, you get a message that you might not get if you don't understand the culture. So it is critical that we have those people. We're horrendously underinvested in them.[5]

In the operationally and tactically focused world of the law enforcement and intelligence communities, such journeys into the target's background have traditionally shown to be a relatively low priority. It has recently been revealed that the CIA's Counter Terrorism Centre (CTC) had only five analysts assigned full-time to al-Qa'eda, while the FBI had one.[6] The operational focus of agencies such as the FBI was also made abundantly clear during the investigation into the activities of the US intelligence community in the lead up to 11 September:

At the FBI, our review found that, prior to September 11, 2001, support for ongoing investigations and operations were favored, in terms of allocating resources, over long-term, strategic analysis. We were told, during the course of our FBI interviews, that prevention occurs in the operational units, not through strategic analysis ... We were also told that the FBI's al-Qa'ida-related analytic expertise had been 'gutted' by transfers to operational units.[7]

But to argue that matters of culture, religion and history can make little contribution to the practical aspects of counterterrorism work merely reveals the limited extent to which these issues have been considered. Take the ancient practices of *ketman* and *taqiya*, in which the hiding or disguising of one's Islamic faith is sanctioned to protect oneself from hostile forces. This simple technique, steeped in history and religion, is central to any understanding of present-day Islamic covert action and counterintelligence. Its extension to contemporary terrorist behaviour and planning is evident. The al-Qa'eda training manual, *Military Studies in the Jihad against the Tyrants*, is replete with instructions on the importance of concealing one's Islamic beliefs. 'Brothers' are instructed to 'have a general appearance that does not indicate Islamic orientation' (no beards, toothpicks, long skirts or copies of the Koran).[8] Similarly, who could forget that image of Mohammad Atta captured on an airport surveillance camera in Portland, Maine, as he was about to board a flight to Boston, where he and his associates would hijack American Airlines Flight 11. Atta, clean-shaven and wearing a vibrant blue open-collared shirt with a bag slung over his shoulder, hardly conformed to the popular Western image of an Islamic extremist moments away from executing one of the most devastating terror attacks in modern history.

It would seem that the events of 11 September and the insights they have provided offer a rare clarity of vision and purpose for terrorism researchers. The need for a voice of reason defined by impartiality, and a body of knowledge capable of enhancing our understanding of the nature of terrorism itself, has emerged post-11 September as one of the key priorities facing not only the terrorism research community but also any government's response to the threat of terrorism. Historically, however, the terrorism research community has shown itself largely incapable and unwilling to adopt this most crucial of roles.

For years, terrorism researchers have churned out enough material to fill a small library. Anyone even vaguely familiar with the field is aware that one of its most noticeable and defining features is the size of its literature. Of this literature, the overwhelming majority of it has a prescriptive focus. Indeed, from its earliest beginnings, terrorism research has pursued a course largely determined by the perceived need to create a body of knowledge characterized by practicality and timeliness. The rationale for the flurry of works generated in the earliest stages of the discipline's development stemmed from the belief that terrorism was an important policy problem in need of *urgent solutions*. Ever since, works relating to the prevention, control or response to terrorism have, to varying degrees, dominated the field. The *1999 Social Science Index* reveals that of the 24 entries[9] under the headings *'Terrorism'* and *'Terrorist'*, at least 14 of these have a prescriptive focus. These have included journal articles or editorials on matters as diverse as combating terrorist use of WMD, to coping strategies for bus commuters in Israel. The underlying purpose of many such studies has been to advise policy-makers on how best to counter and cope with the terrorist threat.[10] Attempts to provide operationally focused guidance are often at the heart of this advice to the extent that terrorism research has virtually ignored non-contemporary terrorism and history in general. This state of affairs has led one observer to comment that some of the most prominent authors' writings has at times come dangerously close to 'counterinsurgency masquerading as political science'.[11]

Attempts to influence decision-making in this way have been a cause for concern to numerous terrorism scholars over the years. There is a popular belief that the study of terrorism has suffered from a focus on remedies to the detriment of efforts designed to understand the phenomenon itself.[12] According to Ted Gurr, the discipline's prescriptive focus has 'subtly but persistently' distorted the research process in general. It is Gurr's contention that this has led to a situation in which researchers have shied away from the careful study of the causes and dynamics of terrorism. Instead, the preoccupation has been with the study of trends, effects and responses. The collective result is research that treats terrorist groups and incidents as independent, rather than dependent variables.[13]

Other commentators have described this prescriptive fixation in similar terms:

> The perception of political terrorism as a practical problem requiring urgent solution has led to poorly defined, ideologically biased, conceptually skewed research ... policy-oriented research tends to impede sound theoretical work because of the urgent social need ... to achieve concrete results in the real world.[14]

Of course, this prescriptive focus is understandable. The allure of forming close relationships with government, including the ability to influence the direction of counterterrorist policy is real. Conversely, self-preservation has also encouraged a prescriptive approach to the study of terrorism while simultaneously discouraging an approach capable of promoting empathy. The danger with presenting research designed to encourage empathy is that it may very well be interpreted as sympathy (one might add that this is particularly true in the current climate). Research has indicated that terrorism experts who cannot be relied upon to present a pro-Western view have found themselves on the periphery, denied the status of 'terrorism expert'. Thus, prevented from giving expert testimony before Congress, or making presentations before terrorism conferences and other like venues, they have largely been unable to define the issues.[15] It is precisely these individuals, however, who should be encouraged to pursue their research interests, especially if they are capable of providing insights and perspectives which mainstream terrorism researchers have been unable or unwilling to provide. There is also, of course, the not insignificant question of money. As Martha Crenshaw has observed, ' ... in a field of research so heavily subsidized by government as is terrorism, the temptation to adopt the government point of view is strong'.[16]

The net result is that analyses of terrorism that emerge from areas such as academia, research centres and think-tanks are almost entirely presented from a Western perspective. The ability to gain insight into the historical and cultural workings of terrorist organizations whose origins are not typically occidental, while not impossible, has traditionally shown itself to be limited. This limitation has been compounded by the fact that the vast majority of terrorism researchers hail from North America, Western Europe or some other corner of the globe where terrorism is considered an abomination.[17] The major motivation for terrorism researchers therefore derives from their own belief or value system where the preservation of the peace and the defeat of terrorism are key priorities. Offering prescriptive advice therefore comes naturally to many terrorism researchers, especially those with occidental roots and values.

The nature of terrorism research itself has also encouraged a less than empathetic approach. Largely methodologically driven, terrorism research has come to rely upon quantitative analysis as the favoured research method, no doubt due primarily to the shortage of raw data. The media continues to be the principal source of data for terrorism researchers, and forms the basis of many of the world's terrorism incident databases. This statistical treatment of terrorism, by its very nature, is not conducive to an analysis of terrorism that is likely to promote empathy. Analyses of this nature have shown themselves to be dispassionate, unappreciative and indifferent to those essentially human elements such as history, culture and tradition that are so fundamental to any insightful and meaningful understanding of terrorism. After all, how does one capture on a database those elements and variables that define who a terrorist is?

Adda Bozeman, in her classic study of intelligence, captured the essence of the opposing nature of quantitative analysis and efforts to achieve realistic empathy through the study of the human condition:

> Just how does one quantify pride, prestige, prejudice, moral outrage, insistence on survival, vanity, and vengeance? What does one do with killing in obedience to spirits of the earth or living ancestors? Where in the theoretician's charts and models is there a place for hatred of the enemy or love of country?[19]

While it may be true that greater empathy may have made little difference to the outcome of events culminating in 11 September, the exposure of this inadequacy within the US intelligence community and elsewhere reveals a significant opportunity for terrorism researchers, one which calls for a break from those persistent habits of the past. Instead, researchers must concentrate their efforts on those matters on which they can provide insight not readily available to policy-makers and counterterrorist officials. Acknowledging the limitations and restrictions imposed upon the ability of counterterrorist professionals to achieve realistic empathy, terrorism researchers are well positioned to fill this most significant and glaring of voids for three critical reasons.

1. Terrorism researchers, relative to their counterparts within government counterterrorist circles, have traditionally been time-rich. Scholars and other researchers, generally speaking, have the unique advantage of being able to immerse themselves in their subject matter to an extent largely unknown within government. Empathy in itself implies a level of understanding that can only be attained through a process of immersing oneself in the culture and history of the research target over a period of years rather than months. Indeed, researchers often spend a lifetime developing the depth of knowledge necessary for the attainment of empathy. Government agencies, on the other hand, are simply not geared toward the development of empathy. The attainment of empathy is not a process characterized by speed. Intelligence services, and their analysts, however, do not have the luxury of time.[20] Within this environment, the ability to spend years researching the complexities of a target group's history, culture, religion and traditions, and relating this to practical counterterrorist advice can be elusive, not to mention impractical.

2. Researchers have demonstrated a preparedness to adopt a multi-disciplinary approach to problem-solving and research generally. This multi-disciplinary approach, with its tendency to draw upon areas such as history, anthropology, political science, psychology, and sociology is precisely the type of systemic thinking required to achieve real empathy. What policy-makers and counterterrorist officials find difficult to achieve, should come naturally to most researchers.

3. Open source exploitation. While material obtained directly from practicing terrorists will always remain highly prized within research circles, the infrequency with which this material is obtained cannot in itself sustain the terrorist discipline should this continue to pursue its current prescriptive obsessions. It is this type of material, original, direct from the source, and of potential operational value that will

always interest government elements most. Operationally focused prescriptive advice, which has served as the principal focus for terrorism researchers to date, is rarely based upon access to terrorist sources. Research efforts intended to promote empathy, however, have the advantage that they are less dependent upon such elusive information sources. Instead, readily accessible open sources in the form of histories, political analyses, and religious texts serve as the basis for much of this type of research. This is especially true with regard to Islamic terrorism, where the nexus between history and contemporary events is particularly prominent and revealing. Islamic religious texts, for example, have consistently served as comprehensive and powerful secular guides.

It is on the basis of these strengths and opportunities that terrorism researchers need to promote and encourage empathy within the government, and other domains. It may be the case that high-level decision-makers will largely be beyond the reach of the vast majority of terrorism researchers. It has been frequently said that such decision-makers simply do not have the time or the inclination to consider the largely theoretical, and arguably not particularly policy-relevant, research that is the hallmark of the discipline. If that is the situation, and I think that most researchers involved in the field would recognize this as the case, then a different target audience needs to be considered. It is my view that intelligence analysts, such as those employed within the CIA's Directorate of Intelligence, would be the ideal audience, providing significant opportunities to shape the *strategic and tactical direction of counterterrorism without compromising the integrity, quality and efficacy of the research product*. Several reasons can be provided for this.[21] First, intelligence analysts are more receptive than their political masters to the variety of research that has traditionally emerged from academia and think-tanks. Customarily, analysis is the more cerebral, open-minded area of the intelligence community. Many practicing analysts have extensive research experience and attained higher degrees (the CIA's economic intelligence division, for example, is believed to have the largest percentage of PhDs of any US government department).

Second, analysts are far more accessible to terrorism researchers than are policy-makers. Terrorism researchers are far more likely to reach analysts through journal articles and seminars than they are to reach policy- makers, who must juggle their interest in terrorism with a multitude of other issues that compete for their time and attention. Terrorism research is therefore more likely to influence the direction and content of the intelligence product, than it is the direction and content of government policy.

Finally, terrorism analysts have the type of access to policy-makers of which the vast majority of terrorism researchers can only dream. The CIA's Directorate of Intelligence, for example, counts the President, Vice-President, Cabinet and the National Security Council as consumers of its intelligence products. While using an analyst as a surrogate for conveying messages and ideas to policy-makers may not hold the glamour that terrorism researchers sometimes crave, it nevertheless remains an important means of reaching policy-makers and influencing, perhaps in imperceptible ways, their thoughts and decision-making processes.

In the last 12 months, terrorism research has arrived at a fork in the road. It can choose to proceed down that path which it has travelled with monotonous regularity during the past 30 years. This well-worn path, with its emphasis upon *specific* prescriptive advice, has produced few tangible benefits. The lack of progress in original research capable of providing fresh insights into the causes and dynamics of terrorism is an obvious manifestation of the limits inherent in continuing to tread this path. Alternatively, terrorism researchers may choose to explore that path which calls for a more impartial, comprehensive and empirically based assessment of the facts for the purpose of raising the level of understanding of terrorism and terrorists. Such research has a better chance of influencing decision-makers, albeit indirectly, by allowing them to more realistically judge the effects of their policies upon the emergence, growth and endurance of terrorist behaviour. The choices made now, during this critical period, will determine whether or not terrorism research and those engaged in it are relegated to a position of intellectual and political irrelevance. As the events following 11 September amply demonstrate, an injection of realism into the terrorist debate is desperately needed. The pressure, however, to conform to the typically occidental interpretation and analysis of terrorism has likewise never been greater. This represents the real challenge facing those engaged in terrorism research today.

Perhaps the final comments should be left to Schmid and Jongman and their renowned 'firefighter' analogy. Although 14 years old, their words now have greater relevance, meaning and urgency than at any other time during the last three decades of terrorism research:

> The researcher should not confuse his roles. His role is not to 'fight' the terrorist fire; rather than a 'firefighter', he should be a student of combustion ... Such a neutral researcher might be less

popular with political parties attempting to win allies to bolster their perspective. However, the quality of his research might improve and ultimately his prescriptions for dealing with terrorism might be more valuable if they are not built on the ideological foundations of one or another party to the conflict.[22]

More than ever, there is a need for terrorism researchers to study combustion with a degree of impartiality and sophistication seen too infrequently in the past, and to leave the fire fighting to the fire fighters. In time, one can only hope that a more universal understanding of combustion will ultimately improve the effectiveness of the fire fighter's ability to prevent, control and respond to fire.

NOTES

1. I believe that the attacks upon New York and Washington and the subsequent 'War on Terrorism' will be an exception. American seizure of vast amounts of al-Qa'eda documentation in Afghanistan, the capture of dozens of al-Qa'eda members throughout the world, and other intelligence collected along the way will represent a treasure trove of original material for terrorism researchers to pore over during some time in the future. In fact, some of this material is already making its way into the public domain.
2. Cited in House of Commons Library, Research Paper 01/72, '11 September 2001: The Response', p. 14.
3. Secretary of State Colin Powell, for example, in one of his statements following the events of 11 September said: 'As we join to end the scourge of terrorism, let us also unite to seize the opportunities we share to build a world of peace, prosperity and democracy'. Similarly, President Bush's State of the Union address to Congress, in January 2002, is replete with references to the law and peace.
4. Joby Warrick, Joe Stephens, Mary Pat Flaherty and James V. Grimaldi, 'FBI Agents Ill-Equipped to Predict Terror Acts', *Washington Post*, 23 September 2001.
5. Interview with Porter Goss: http://www.pbs.org/wgbh/pages/frontline/shows/terrorism/interviews/goss.html
6. Eleanor Hill, 'Joint Inquiry Staff Statement, Part 1', 18 September 2002, p. 18.
7. Ibid., pp. 28–9.
8. Full version in author's possession.
9. Excluding reviews and letters.
10. Edna O.F. Reid, 'Evolution of a Body of Knowledge: An Analysis of Terrorism Research', *Information Processing and Management*, 33/1 (1997), pp. 91–106; Ted Robert Gurr, 'Empirical Research on Political Terrorism: The State of the Art and How it Might be Improved', in Robert O. Slater and Michael Stohl (eds), *Current Perspectives on International Terrorism* (London: MacMillan, 1988), p. 143; Dennis Pluchinsky, 'Academic Research on European Terrorist Developments: Pleas from a Government Terrorism Analyst', *Studies in Conflict and Terrorism*, 15/1 (1992), pp. 13–23. The seminar held at the School of American Research in Santa Fe, New Mexico, in October 1986 to discuss terrorism research and public policy had as its goal 'To go beyond discussion of research to focus on the problems and prospects of putting research on terrorism to *work in the formation of public policy*' [Own emphasis].
11. Alex P. Schmid and Albert J. Jongman, *Political Terrorism: A New Guide to Actors, Authors, Concepts, Databases, Theories and Literature* (Amsterdam: North-Holland Publishing, 1988), p. 182.
12. Martha Crenshaw, 'Current Research on Terrorism: The Academic Perspective', *Studies in Conflict and Terrorism*, 15/1 (1992), pp. 1–11.
13. Gurr, 'Empirical Research on Political Terrorism', p. 143.

14. Cited in Schmid and Jongman, *Political Terrorism*, p.180. On p. 179, they have also described the absence of even-handedness in the study of terrorism as 'the chief deficiency of the literature of terrorism'.
15. Edna O.F. Reid, 'Evolution of a Body of Knowledge', p.104.
16. Martha Crenshaw, 'How Terrorism Declines', in *Terrorism Research and Public Policy* ... p. 72.
17. Reid, 'Evolution of a Body of Knowledge'.
18. Ibid., p. 98
19. Adda Bozeman, *Strategic Intelligence and Statecraft* (Washington, DC: Brassey's, 1992), p. 52.
20. Dennis Pluchinsky, 'Academic Research on European Terrorist Developments: Pleas from a Government Terrorism Analyst', *Studies in Conflict and Terrorism*, 15/1 (1992), pp. 13–23.
21. Dennis Pluchinsky has also sought to encourage the terrorism research community to customize its products for the benefit of terrorism analysts. See Pluchinsky, 'Academic Research on European Terrorist Developments', pp. 13–23.
22. Schmid and Jongman, *Political Terrorism*, p. 179.

Index

11 September 2001, xvii, xviii, 2, 9, 12, 19, 20, 24, 25, 27, 75, 77, 78, 79, 80, 86, 101, 108, 113, 116, 119, 121, 125, 134, 186, 196, 197, 200, 209, 215, 216, 217, 220, 221, 223, 226; 11 September, research failure, 22–5; post-11 September, 7, 26, 111
17 November terrorist group, 139, 150, 152, 153, 158
1950s, 52, 65, 139
1960s, 108, 139, 141, 150, 151, 154, 163, 186
1970s, 3, 73, 106, 110, 115, 138, 141, 146, 149, 150, 151, 163, 188, 208
1980s, 3, 52, 73, 94, 121, 122, 148, 188, 208
1990s, 3, 22, 23, 68, 74, 84, 106, 113, 122, 129, 146, 147, 148, 188, 190, 191, 192, 193, 195, 196, 197, 198, 199, 200, 202, 203, 204, 205, 206, 207, 209, 210; in Spain, 201
1999 Social Science Index, 221

A Review of Recent Trends in International Terrorism and Nuclear Incidents Abroad, 74
A.T. Kearney/Foreign Policy™, 97
Aberswyneth, MSc, 26
Abu Nidal, 146
Abu Nidal Organization, 5
academic: analyses, 168; community, xix, 25, 44, 74, 109, 163, 164, 225; conferences, 91; analyses of terrorism, 223; disciplines, 9, 195; dissenting perspectives, 217; *see* researchers
accuracy, 62
Adams, James, 53
aerial hijackings, 8, 9, 120, 121, 123, 124, 125, 131, 149, 163 *see also* bin Laden, Osama
Afghan analyst, 219
Afghanistan, 23, 78, 119
Africa, xviii, 23, 203; embassy bombings *see* Kenya; North, 101; Sub-Saharan, 101
agricultural targets, 86
AIDS, 92
airline industry, 119
airports, 131, 148; security, 134, 216; US, 120, 124, 131
Al Khubar Towers, 121
al-Aqsa conflict, 16 *see also* Intifada
Alexander, Yonah, 73
Alfred P. Murrah building, 181 *see also* Oklahoma
Algeria, 146, 147, 148, 159

Algerian Armed Islamic Group (GIA), 122, 146, 148
Algerian groups, 150
Algiers, 157
al-Qa'eda, xvii, 5, 12, 22, 23, 77, 78, 79, 80, 85, 100, 124, 136, 200, 204, 206, 207, 210, 214, 216, 219, 220; al-Qa'eda hijackers, 24; training manual, *Military Studies in the Jihad against the Tyrants*, 220
ambassadors, foreign, 194
ambient danger, 13
America *see* USA
America's Achilles Heel, 76
American: allies, 144; Civil War, 144; American embassies, 1998 bombings of *see* Kenya; extreme right, 168; public *see* public; researchers *see* researchers; revolution, 95; right-wing extremism/terrorism, 165, 168
American Airlines Flight 11, 221
American Freedom Network, 171, 172
American National Criminal Justice Reference Service (NCJRS), 108, 112, 114
American White Supremacists, 164
Americanization, 94
Americans, 216
Americas, the, 95, 203 *see also* Latin America, USA
Amnesty International, 17, 94
An Garda Síochana, 40, 48 *see also* Gardai
An Phoblacht, 36
analysis(es): academic, 168; empirical, 168; level of, 12
analysts, 20, 162, 176, 183; Afghan, 219; government, 224, 225; intelligence services, 215, 224; policy/ies, 91; shortage of, 220; terrorism, 162
Angola, 100
Angry Brigade, 138
anthrax, 82
anthropologists, 13, 195
anthropology, 210, 224
Anti Defamation League (ADL), 168, 176
anti-extremist organizations, 168
anti-Semitic, 147
anti-Tamil rioting, 141
anti-terrorism initiatives, 135
apologists, 21
appeasers, 20, 21
applied research, 58

Appomattox, 144
Arab oil-producing states, 149
Arab–Israeli conflict, 16, 144
Armenian population, 95
Armenian Revolutionary Federation (ARF), 95
articles: country focus, 199–200; country focus, changes, 201–2; group focus of, 204–6; terrorist-type focus, 206; terrorist-type focus, changes over time, 206–7; US-focused, 200; world region focus, 202–3; world region focus, changes in, 203
Aryan Brotherhood, 179
Asia: 203; Central, 23, 139; South East, 23
Asian capitals, 23
assassination(s), 125, 126, 152, 155; outlawed, 219; series, 131
Associated Press, 128
Athens Polytechnic, 152
Atta, Mohammad, 221
attack(s): mass-destructive, 81; prevention, 216; punishment, 78; small-scale tactical, 81
audience context, 63
Aum Shinrikyo: 22, 74, 75, 77, 79, 80, 81, 83, 205; biological weapons programme, 77
Australia, 95, 197, 203
Austria, 147
authors: country of residence, 196, 197; countries of residence, changes in, 198; countries of residence, trends in, 197; professional backgrounds of, 193; specializations, 193; trends in professional backgrounds, 194
Avenging Israel's Blood *see* DIN
Aviation Week, 106, 114

Bangladesh, 100
Barcelona, 155
Basque: community, 157; country, 147, 154, 155, 156, 158
Basque Homeland and Liberty *see* ETA
Basques, 147
Bass, Gail, 74
Beatles, 173–4
behaviour: deviant, 21; patterns of, 11; political, 10; terrorism, 215; terrorist, 12, 34, 35; rules of, 21
Beirut TV, 94
Belfast, 13, 37, 49, 156
Belgium, 150, 153, 158
Bergen, Peter, 94
Berkeley, 141
Berlin, West, 132
bias, 62, 64
biased sample, 65
bible study, 172–3
bin Laden, Osama, xvii, xviii, 23, 77, 214, 217
biological: attacks, 120; weapons, 24, 74, 76,

80, 81, 82, 85, 86; weapons of mass destruction, 205 *see also* CBRN
bio-terrorism, 108, 120
Birmingham, 155
'black' propaganda, 39 *see also* fundraising
Black September, 132 *see also* Israeli: athletes, Munich Olympic Games
Blanco, Admiral Carrero, 155
Bloody Sunday, 156
bombings, 9, 126, 127, 128, 135, 155; bombings and threats, 126; bus, 146 *see also* Kenya
books, 91; number of, 25
Bosnia, 23
Boston, 221
Bowyer-Bell, J., 31, 32, 33, 34, 35, 161, 164, 193
Bozeman, Adda, 223
Branch Davidian, 205
Brewer, J., 14
British Isles, 204 *see also* England; UK
British Psychological Society, 26
British: government, 154, 156; jails, 32; miscalculations, 156
Brockner, Joel, 142–3
Brophy-Baermann, Bryan, 132
Bruce, Steve, 31, 52
Bruders Schweigen, 164, 177 *aka* The Order
Burgos trial, 155
Burundi, 100
Bush, President George, 119, 216, 217; 11 October speech, 217; agenda of, 216; proposed budget, 120

campaigns: dissident, in Northern Ireland, 200–1; terrorism, 202; of violence, 1
Canada: 95, 197; decline in research output, 199
Cannistraro, Vincent, 214
capitalism, 151, 152
capitalist ideas, 93
Capitalist State, the, 95
Carter, President Jimmy, 75, 145
case studies, 57
Catholics, 156
CBRN (chemical, biological, radiological or nuclear) weapons, xvii, 72, 79
cease-fires, in Northern Ireland, 200
Center for Nonproliferation Studies, 77
cesium-137, 83
charities, 26
Chechnya, 23
Chemical Weapons Convention and Australia Group, 83
chemical: attacks, 120; and biological (CB) weapons, 74; 'recipes', 83; weapons, 24, 74, 76, 80, 81–2, 83, 85, 86; weapons of mass destruction, 205; *see also* CBRN, chemical and biological weapons

Chile, 95
chlorine, 81
Choice-Theoretic Model of Terrorism, 123–8
Chomsky, Noam, 217
Christian Identity: 164, 169, 172, 180, 214; adherents, 169, 171, 176; anti-Identity pastor, 174; association with terrorism, 177; beliefs, 80; clerical independence, 172; clerics/pastors, 169; doctrine, 174; early pioneers of movement, 175; ex-adherents, 172; geographic dispersion, 172; hierarchy, 172; ideology, 176; leaders, 169; Rockwell, George Lincoln, 174; theology, 172, 173–6
CIA: 151, 219; Counter Terrorism Center (CTC), 220; Directorate of Intelligence, 225, 226; economic intelligence division, 225; shortage of analysts, 220
civil: rights march, 156; servants, senior, 194; war(s), 141, 142, 146, 147
civilians, attacks on, 6, 8, 155 *see also* public, the
clinical sciences, 198
Clinton administration, 201 *see also* US government
Clinton, President Bill, 23
Cold War: 73, 93, 143; post-Cold War era, 93, 129; post-Cold War terrorism, 129
collaborators, alleged, 17
Colombia, 146, 159
Colorado Springs, 171
Combat 18, 13
combatants, 17
commercial airliners, 148
Commission of the European Union, 94
communication: sciences, 188; targets, 86
Communist Manifesto, 93
Communist Parties, 150, 151
comparative politics, 113
conceptual: conceptual/definitional agreement, 208; confusion and disagreement, 58; development, 30; frameworks, xviii; issues, 207–9
Conference on Contemporary Research on Terrorism, 70
conferences, 26
conflict: different categories of, 139; international, 139, 140; intra-personal, 139, 140; new discourse, xviii; new era, xviii; resolution, 140; theory, stage one, 140–1; theory, stage two, 141–3; theory, stage three, 143–5
Congress *see* US, Congress
conservative weapons, 80
consulates, 148
control: and punishment, systems of, 21; groups, 66
conventional: terrorist violence, 9; weapons, xvii, 79
conversion, 149
Conybeare, John, 132

Coogan, Tim Pat, 31
Cork, 40, 45
Corsica, terrorist experience, 201
Countering Suicide Terrorism, 24
counterterrorism, professional background, 194
counterterrorist officials, 224
CQ Weekly, 216
Crenshaw, Martha, 8, 12, 30, 33, 165, 222
crime, commissioning of, 67, 190
criminal: justice, departments/schools of, 27; justice, system(s), 13, 21, 67, 190; organizations, 207
criminological perspectives, 31
criminologists, 195
criminology: 21, 67, 68, 113, 188, 190, 194; departments/schools of, 27
CSA *see* The Covenant, the Sword, and the Arm of the Lord
CTC *see* CIA, Counter Terrorism Center
culture, 220
Current History, 114
cyanide, 81
cyber targets, 86

Daily Reports see Federal Bureau of Investigation
Dallas Morning News, 94
Dallas, 94
data: accessible sources of, 15; collection, 58; empirical, 183; lack of distinct and quantifiable, 11; methods of gathering, 59; 'noisy', 66; primary, 30, 62; produced by others, 60; raw, analysis of, 61; raw, gathering of, 61; secondary, 60, 63; secondary, analysis of, 61; uncontrolled gathering, 66
databases: computerized, 115; ERL, 108; event, 10
Davies, Norman, 73, 96
decision-makers, 225, 226
de-escalation, 144–5, 153–4
degree of risk, 12, 13
deLeon, Peter, 74
della Porta, Donnatella, 31
democracies, third-wave, 100
democracy, 92, 218
democratization: 91; definitions of, 91; level of, 98–9; process of, 100
deregulation, 93
Derry, 156
description, 138
Designations of Foreign Terrorist Organisations, 5
Deutch, John, 75
Dhahran, 121
DIN ('Avenging Israel's Blood'), 80
Direct Action, 150
Director of Intelligence for the Official IRA *see* Irish Republican Army

dirty bomb, 83
Dissertation Abstracts online *see* UMI
Druze militiamen, 94
Dublin, 36, 37, 38, 39, 41, 50, 95
dynamite, 96

East European countries, 122
Easter Rising, 1916, 50
Eastern bloc, 152 *see also* Soviet bloc
economic: deprivation, 140; impact of
  terrorism, 27; status, 140
economists, 195
Egypt, 122
Ellison, G., 13
embassies: 125, 148; bombing of *see* Kenya;
  personnel, 126; US, 132
Emergency Medical Teams, 120
Enders, Walter, 125, 130, 131, 132, 133
Engineering, 105
England, 155 *see also* British Isles; UK
environmental degradation, 93
ESRC, 26
ETA: 5, 154, 206; cease-fire, 157; demands
  and prisoners, 155; leaders, 157; militants,
  155; representatives, 157; suspects, 155;
  violence, 156
ethnic: affinity, 140; cleansing, 145
Eubank, William, 192
Europe: 23, 78, 79, 96, 148, 150, 155;
  American targets in, 149; right-wing
  groups, 207; waning of Palestinian terror
  in, 149
European: countries, 95; imperial expansion,
  97; nations, 132; successor states, 95;
  terrorists, 206; voyages of discovery, 93
European Community, 149
European Union, 100, 122
Euskadi, 155
extradition problems, 8
extreme right *see* right-wing
extremists: 23, 166, 176, 178, 180, 181; access
  to, 182; interpersonal research with, 170;
  political, 170

failures: 4; academic, xvii, 22–5; in
  intelligence, xvii; intellectual, 215
Falkenrath, Richard, 76
Falls Road, 49
fanaticism, 124
fanatics, 20, 47
fascism, 95
fascists: 152; dictatorships, 153
Fatah Revolutionary Council, 146
Faultlines, 109
Federal Bureau of Investigation (FBI): 5, 81;
  Arab-American agents, 219; *Daily Reports*,
  128, 135; 'Project Megiddo', 168; shortage
  of analysts, 220
field research *see* research

Fighting Communist Cells, 150, 153, 158
Finland, 95
First of October Anti-Fascist Resistance
  Groups *see* GRAPO
First World War, 95, 96
Flanagan, Ronnie, Chief Constable of
  Northern Ireland, 19
Ford, President Gerald, 219; outlawed
  assassinations, 219
Foreign Broadcast Information Service
  (FBIS), 128
forensic psychology *see* psychology
France, 122, 144, 146, 147, 148, 150, 151, 202;
  decline in research output, 199; Southern,
  155
Franco, General Francisco: 150, 152, 155;
  dictatorship, 154
freedom: 218; fighters, 8
French: authorities, 155; government, 149;
  intellectuals, 94; Revolution, 94, 95; targets,
  148
Friedman, Thomas, 94
From Beirut to Jerusalem, 94
FSU, nuclear leakage, 84
fundamentalists, 130
funding: from government, 18; from law
  enforcement agencies, 18; from military,
  18; large-scale projects, 25; terrorism
  projects, 26

Gamat al-Islamiya, 122
Gardai, 40, 41, 42, 48, 51
Gearty, Conor, 7
Geneva Conventions, 8
Germans, 80
Germany: 95, 122, 144, 147, 150, 151, 152;
  West, 151; in 1960s, 150
GIA *see* Algerian Armed Islamic Group
Gibbons, E., 3
globalization: 91, 92, 96; backlash against, 100;
  definitions of, 91; and international
  terrorism, 99–100; level of, 98–9
Goldwater, Barry, 141
Gonzalez, Felipe, 152
Good Friday Peace Agreement, 1998, 157
Gordon, Avishag, 27, 69
government(s): 13, 20, 65, 163, 195; agencies
  and activities, 26, 58, 176, 179, 182, 224;
  counterterrorist circles, 224; departments,
  195; funding, 24; interest in research,
  224–5; internal analysts, 194; members of,
  194; mistrust of, 173; national, 139;
  officials, 171; policy, 226; primary source
  material, 184; responses to nuclear
  terrorism, 73, 190; Western world, 196
GPO *see* US, Government Publication Office
  database
Grant, General, 144
grants, open-ended, 167

GRAPO, 150, 151, 152
Greece, 135, 147, 150, 152, 153
Greek government, 158
Green Book see Irish Republican Army
Green Peace, 94
groups: apocalyptic, 78; culture, 224;
  experimental, 66; history, 224;
  nationalist/separatist, 207; religion, 224;
  religiously motivated, 76; Russian
  revolutionary, 95; secularly motivated, 76;
  'traditional' terrorist, 81; traditions, 224
Guelke, Adrian, 13
guerrilla warfare, 8
Gurr, Ted Robert, 163, 165, 222

Hacker, Fred, 138
Hague Regulations, 8
Hamas: 5, 6, 122, 124, 206; bus bombings, 146
Hamm, Mark, 168
Harrods, 155
hate crimes, 168
Herman, Edward, 15
highly enriched uranium (HEU), 84
hijackings *see* aerial hijackings; *see also* bin
  Laden, Osama
Hillsborough Agreement, 1985, 38, 156
historians, 195
history, 188, 194, 220, 224
Hizbollah, 5, 122, 139, 206
Hoffman, Bruce, 23, 47, 74, 76, 92, 122, 163,
  192, 193
Holland, decline in research output, 199
Holocaust, 80
Holy Terror, 77
Horgan, John, 13, 15, 31
hostage-barricade scenarios, 163
hostage-taking, 10, 127
household production function (HPF), 125,
  126; summary of, 127–8, 130, 131, 133,
  135, 136
human: aggression, 138; suffering, 190
Huntingdon, Samuel, 92, 95, 97, 98, 100

Iceland, 95
ICT *see* International Policy Institute for
  Counterterrorism
ideology: left-wing, 78; nationalist/separatist,
  78
imperial: conquest, British, 96; conquest,
  French, 96; expansion, European, 97
India, 101, 109; Institute of Conflict
  Management, 109
Indonesian authorities, 13
industrialists, 155
industry, responses to nuclear terrorism, 73
inferential analysis, 68
injustice, 190
Inner Macedonian Revolutionary
  Organization (IMRO), 95

intellectuals: 91; French, 94
intelligence: analysts, 224, 225; gathering, 138;
  personnel, 47; services, 224, 226; US, 216,
  218, 219, 220, 223
interdisciplinary, 30
inter-governmental organizations, 145
international: relations, departments of, 27,
  106; response to terrorism, 4
International Atomic Energy Agency (IAEA),
  84
International Monetary Fund (IMF), 92, 93
International Policy Institute for Counter-
  Terrorism (ICT), 16, 17, 24; ICT Report,
  2002, 16–17
International Task Force on the Prevention of
  Nuclear Terrorism, 73
Internet, 115, 169
internment, 156
interviews/ing, 30, 60, 63–5; procuring, 31–4
Intifada, 16
IRA *see* Irish Republican Army
Iran, 122, 147
Iranian operations, 150
Iraq, 147
Ireland: 33, 95, 154–7; anti-terrorist police,
  51; increase in terrorism research, 199;
  researching terrorism in, 34; united and
  socialist, 156 *see also* Northern Ireland;
  Republic of Ireland
Irish: -based research, 31; government, 156;
  terrorism affairs, 35
Irish Dynamiters, 95
Irish Republic *see* Republic of Ireland
Irish Republican Army (IRA), 12, 35, 37, 39,
  40, 41, 48, 154, 155; Army Council, 42, 46,
  52; attitudes to crime, 33, 39; attitudes to
  drugs, 33; attitudes to social problems, 33;
  bombs, 34; command structure, 35, 44, 46,
  50, 51, 52, 53; criminal activities, 35, 44;
  Director of Intelligence for, 34; financing,
  49 *see also* fundraising; former members, 50
  see also members/membership; functional
  structure, 35, 46, 50; fundraising, 37, 39, 44,
  49, 51, 52, 53; *Green Book*, 34, 51; interviews
  with, 35–6; leadership, 33;
  members/membership, 38, 42, 46, 48, 51;
  'mini-manual', 51; money laundering, 44;
  organizational structure, 44; personnel, 33;
  prisoner, 48; Provisional break away, 156 ;
  'Real', 157; rebirth in 1970s, 40; recruits, 34;
  splinter group, 122 *see also* Omagh bombing
Iron Curtain, 150
Islamic/Islamist: countries/states, 6; covert
  action, 220; extremists, 23, 32; extremists,
  Western image of, 221; faith, 220;
  fundamentalism, 184; (extremist) groups,
  23, 150, 200, 206, 207; Islamists, 147;
  militants, 94; revolution, 122; terrorism,
  207 *see also* jihad

Islamic Jihad, bus bombings, 146 *see also* jihad
Israel: 16, 17, 132, 136, 148, 149, 197, 198, 202; allies of, 149; bus bombings, 146
Israeli: actions, 17; athletes, 132 *see also* Black September, Munich Olympic Games; attacks, 132; conflict, 149; government, 16; military, 16; raids against PLO, 133; society, 17; targets, 148; victims, 17
Israelis, 16, 148
Istanbul, 81
Italian: authorities, 158; government, 149; terrorists, 171
Italy: 95, 147; 150, 151, 152, 153, 154, 157, 158, 202; decline in research output, 199; in 1960s, 150
ITERATE (International Terrorism: Attributes of Terrorism Events): 15, 128, 135; ITERATE III, 97

Jamieson, Alison, 31, 171
Jammu-Kashmir, 139, 146
Japan, 198, 202, 205
Japanese, 144
Jenkins, Brian, xviii, 2, 19, 73, 74–5, 164
Jewish Defence League, 206
Jews, 148
jihad, 6, 23, 122 *see also* Islamic Jihad; religious groups
Johnstown, Colorado, 171
Jongman, Albert, 3, 10, 58, 59, 65, 70, 112, 162, 186, 187, 188, 189, 191, 193, 194, 226–7
Journal Citation Reports (JCR), 109
journalistic: approach: 11; reporting, 163
journalists: 32, 35, 41, 52, 53, 91, 155, 180; British, 49–50
journals: 25, 65, 67, 70, 91, 110, 113, 117, 187, 208; academic, 187; articles, 225; audiences reached, 195; criminology, 190, 191; leading/main/major, 190, 191, 193, 195, 197; primary, 61; readership, 25; specialist, 107; terrorism, 191, 198, 205
Juergensmeyer, Mark, 122

Kaplan, David E., 77
Kashmir, 23
Kellen, Konrad, 74, 178
Kenya: 22; 1998 bombing of US embassies in, xvii, 22, 121, 200
ketman, 220
KGB, conspiracy, 153
Khartoum, 220
Khobar Towers, 1996 attack on, 22
knowledge growth: 104–18; and research methods, 117
Koran, 220
Kosovo, 145
Kriesberg, Louis, 14, 140, 149
Kuperman, Robert H., 73

Kurdish Workers' Party *see* PKK
Kurds, 148, 150 *see also* PKK
Kyklos, 110

La Bell Discothèque, West Berlin, 132
Lacquer, Walter, 20, 75, 95, 138, 163–4
Lakenheath, 132
Landes, William, 123–4
Latin America, 202, 203 *see also* Americas, the
law: 188, 218; departments/schools of, 27; process of, 21
law enforcement: agencies, 196; US, 219
lawyers, 195
Lebanese: civil war, 94; resistance, 6
Lebanon, 159
Lee, General, 144
leftist groups, 130
left-wing: terrorism, 207; terrorist groups, 206; youth groups, 151
Leitenberg, Milton, 77
Leventhal, Paul, 73
liberal democracies, 163
Liberation Tigers of Tamil Eelam (LTTE), 81
Library of Congress (LC), 109
Libya: 129, 147; 'People's Bureaus', 149; US bombing raids, 132, 133, 149
Libyan: diplomats, 149; operations, 150; students, 149
life histories, 30
Life Science, 105
Linz, Juan, 92
literacy, 96
literature: 11, 54, 116, 165; focus of, 210; growth of, 104, 106–8; holes in, 9; integrators of, 60, 61; lopsided, 9; Northern Ireland, 200; poor quality, 9; psychologically based, 47; social science, 60, 162, 189; spiralling of, 215; still young, 188; terrorism, 72, 74; weapons of mass destruction, 72, 74, 85
Lombroso, Cesare, 138
London, 155
loyalist paramilitaries *see* Northern Ireland, paramilitaries
LTTE *see* Liberation Tigers of Tamil Eelam

McCulloch, Lesley, 13
Macdonald, Keith, 63
McVeigh, Timothy, 139 *see also* Oklahoma
Macedonian population, 95
madness, 20
Madrid, 155, 157
Major Crimes as Analogs to Potential Threats to Nuclear Facilities and Programs, 74
Malaysia, 6
Manila: 23; Israeli embassy in, 22–3; US embassy in, 22–3
Marshall, Andrew, 77
Marxism, 122, 152

Marxism-Leninism, 150
mass: casualties, xvii, 20, 21, 76, 78, 79, 82, 130; communications, 109, 113; destruction, 72; participation in political life, 96; political movements, 138; social movements, 138
Masters courses, 25
Médecins sans Frontières, 94
media: 9, 44, 163; accounts, 163; agencies, 52; American-dominated mass, 94; dissenting perspectives, 217; Irish, 41; outlets, 62
Medline, 108
mental: illness, 1; issues, 10; state of terrorists, 20
Merari, Ariel, 4, 53, 58, 69, 188–90, 191
methodological issues, 54
methodologies: 59–61, 70; limited, 69; perceived difficulties, 9
Mickolus, Edward, 11
Middle East: 23, 101, 147, 202, 203; conflict, 148; countries, 122; delegates, 6; groups, 148; politics, 158
Midwest, the, 181
militants, 23
Military Studies in the Jihad against the Tyrants see al-Qa'eda
military: 188; attacks on, 8; bases, 125; strategists, 20, 21; departments of, 27; personnel, 126, 196
militia: groups, USA, 204; movement, 171, 172, 174; radio stations, 171
millennium: 122; movements, 121
Minnesota Patriots' Council, 82
misconceptions, 2
misquoting, 37
Mitchell, Richard G., 183
Mohr, Colonel Jack, 173
morality, 19
Motivations and Possible Actions of Potential Criminal Adversaries of US Nuclear Programs, 74
Mountbatten, Lord, 155
multidisciplinary bridging organizations, 26
Munich Olympic Games, 1972: 132; massacre, 149 *see also* Black September, Israeli athletes
myths, 20, 21

Nairobi, 123
National Defense Authorization Act, 119–20
National Security Council, 226
national: identity, 140; liberation struggles, 151; self-determination, 96
nationalism, 44 *see also* groups: nationalist/separatist; ideology: nationalist
NATO, 122, 151
Nazi: occupation, 151; dictatorships, 153
NCJRS *see* American National Criminal Justice Reference Service
negotiations, 157

neo-fascist bands, 158
neo-Nazis *see* Combat 18
New Left, 151, 152
New York, 24, 25, 116, 216
New York Times, 128
New Zealand, 95
Newman, Robert D., 76
newspapers: 91; reports, 53
Nobel Peace Prize, 156
non-combatants, 17
Non-Governmental Organizations (NGOs), 94
North America, 23, 223 *see also* USA
North American nations, 6 *see also* USA
North Vietnamese, 144
Northern Ireland: 9, 13, 19, 32, 33, 38, 39, 44, 49, 52, 122, 147, 154, 155, 156, 157, 170, 200, 201, 202, 203; cease-fires, 200; dissident campaigns, 200–1; paramilitaries, 201, 205; paramilitaries, loyalist, 13, 158, 205, 206; paramilitaries/terrorists, Protestant, 13, 154, 158, 201, 205, 206; peace process, 201; political groups, 201; prisoner releases, 201; splintering of groups, 200; terrorism in, 200; Ulster Volunteer Force, 156 *see also* Ireland; Republic of Ireland; Southern Ireland
Northern Irish: authorities, 158; conflict, 201, 202; terrorism, 53
November 17, 147
Nuclear Terrorism: Defining the Threat, 73
Nuclear Theft, 72
nuclear: building of weapons, 72; facilities, 72, 73; materials, theft of, 73; programme, US, 73; proliferation by states, 73; terrorism, 73; weapons, 76, 84, 85 *see also* CBRN
Nuremberg, 80
Nye, Joseph, 93

OAS, 206
objective understanding, 20
objectivity, 11, 58, 177, 181
observers, non-Republican, 44
occidental: interpretation, 226; world, 218
Occupied Territories, Israeli actions in, 6
Office of Homeland Security, 119, 216
Official IRA's Director of Intelligence *see* Irish Republican Army
OIC *see* Organization of the Islamic Conference
oil crisis, 1973, 149
OIRA, 51
Oklahoma City: 9, 123, 179, 200; bombing, xvii, 122, 157, 181; bombing of the Murrah Federal Building, 121 *see also* McVeigh, Timothy
open: access, 61; sources, 33; sources, exploitation, 224
Operation Enduring Freedom, 119

opportunity sampling, 64
Oregon, 80
Organization of the Islamic Conference
  (OIC), 6
organized crime, 27
O'Sullivan, Gerry, 15
Ottoman Empire, 95

Pacifica, 203
Pakistan, 121, 146
Palestine, 151
Palestinian: delegates, 6; fatalities, 17; groups,
  149; lives, 16; -related groups, 148;
  resistance, 6; struggle, 6; terrorism/
  terrorists, 132, 149
Palestinians, 17, 148, 150
paramilitaries, 32, 34, 158 *see also* Northern
  Ireland
paramilitary: activity, 37; groups, 35; offences,
  42 *see also* Northern Ireland: paramilitaries
paranoia, 20
Paris, 134
peace studies, 109, 113, 140
peace, 218
Pearl, David, 121
Pearl Harbor, 218
Pentagon, 119, 218
People's Will organization, 95
personal safety, 9, 12
personality: disorders, 20; types, 138
Peru, 146, 159
Philippines, 23
Phoenix Park, 95
PIRA *see* Provisional Irish Republican Army
Pisacane, Carlo, 95
PKK, 5, 81, 147, 150
places of worship, 148
plague, 82
PLO: 149; camps, 132; Israeli retaliatory raids
  against, 133
Pluchinsky, Dennis, 148
plutonium, 84
Poland, James, 3
police: 11, 13, 35, 36, 47, 49, 51, 120, 155;
  London, 13; Protestant, 156; Spanish, 157
police–public relations, 13
policing, 190
policy/ies: 20, 21, 59; analysts, 91; anti-
  terrorism, 120; communities, 74; concerns,
  58; editorial, 70; public, 93
policy-makers, 2, 138, 149, 221, 224, 224, 226
policy-relevant material, 215
Polish socialists, 95
political: behaviour, 10; milieu, 86; science,
  106, 188, 209, 210; scientists, 194, 195;
  sensitivity, 9; terrorism, 139; violence, 8
political science, 221, 224
*Political Terrorism: A New Guide to Actors,
  Authors, Concepts, Databases, Theories and*

Literature, 59, 112, 186
politicians: 20, 63, 155, 194; non-republican,
  35; Protestant, 156
politics, departments of, 27
Pope John Paul II, 156
pornography, 3
Portland, Maine, airport, 221
post-11 September, 7, 26, 111, 218, 219, 221
  see also 11 September 2001
post-Cold War: era, 93, 129; terrorism, 122 *see
  also* Cold War
postgraduate: research, funding for, 167;
  students, 182, 183
post-trauma treatments, 108
potassium cyanide, 80
pre-clinical sciences, 198
prejudices, 2
primary: data, 30, 162; research material, 170;
  source material, 163, 166, 178, 183, 184
prisons: 9, 32; authorities, 32; prison
  psychiatrists, 9
private industry, 26
privatization, 93
professional organizations, 26
Project Megiddo *see* Federal Bureau of
  Investigation
Propaganda by Deed, 95
propaganda: 63; state-sponsored, 19
property, destruction of, 8
Protestant: paramilitaries/terrorists *see*
  Northern Ireland; police, 156; politicians,
  156
Provisional Irish Republican Army (PIRA),
  23, 31, 34, 49, 155, 156, 204, 205, 206 *see
  also* Irish Republican Army
Pruitt, Dean, 143, 154
Prussia, 144
psychiatrists, 138
psychological approaches: 30; factors, 30;
  methodologies, 53; perspectives, 31;
  polarization, 142; transformation, 143
psychologically deviant, 21
psychologists, 53, 138, 195
psychology: 188, 194, 210, 224; forensic
  psychology, 67–8, 113
psychopathy, 1
public, the: 20; American, 218 *see also* civilians
purpose of research: descriptive, 57, 58;
  explanatory, 57; exploratory, 57, 58
Purver, Ron, 74

qualitative approach: 11; data, 12; data
  acquisition, 183; research, 163, 166;
  research methods, 57
quantitative research, 11, 166, 183

R & D investment, 115
Rabin, Yitzhak, assassination, 146
racial: discrimination, 140; supremacy, 96

racist, 147
radical right *see* right-wing
radioactive weapons, 24; ('dirty bomb'), 83 *see also* CBRN
radiological terrorism, 86
Radlauer, Don, 16
Rajah, Tariq *see* Reid, Richard
Rajneeshees, 80
RAND: Corporation, 73, 77, 92, 194; Report, 1982, 178; RAND–St Andrews' Database of International Terrorism, 77, 97, 135
Rapoport, David, 75, 76, 95, 96, 146
Red Army Faction (RAF), 150, 206
Red Brigades, 150, 153, 171, 206
regional organizations, 145
Reid, Edna, 162
Reid, Richard, 134 *aka* Tariq Rajah
Reinstedt, Robert, 74
religion, 220
religious: belief, 140; bigotry, 140; cults, 207; fanatics, 139; groups, 121–2, 130; milieu, 86; studies, 195; zealots, 214
Reporter's Guide to Ireland, 51
reporting, bias in, 18
Republic of Ireland, 38, 44, 48, 50, 51, 147, 155, 198, 201 *see also* Ireland; Northern Ireland; Southern Ireland
Republican: Easter Commemorations, 50; fundraising parties, 40, 50; history, 34, 40; meetings, 44; movement, 37, 43, 48; movement, shift towards peace, 52; prisoners, 37; respondents, 47; sympathisers, 40; terrorist groups, 35 *see also* Irish Republican Army; Provisional Irish Republican Army
Republican Convention, 141
Republicanism, 39
Republicans, 32, 38, 43, 50, 52
research: 26; actor-based, 9; agendas, 167; articles, 191; Canada, decline in output, 199; centres, analyses of terrorism, 223; communities, 60; dissertations, 69–70; empirical, 161, 164, 166, 170, 178, 183; empirical, networking, 169–70; exploratory, 65; fads, 59; field, 161, 164, 172, 176, 178, 181; field, dangers/dangerous, 39, 170; field, firsthand, 166; firsthand, xviii, 54, 30–56, 166; function of, 57ff.; funding, 18; influence, 225–6; initial experiences: 170–9; lack of original, 226; literature, 209; methods, 12, 57; methods, empirical, 112; methods, weak, 11; multi-disciplinary approach, 224; need for, 2; network, 169; on terrorism, 196; overall trends in, 190; papers, decline in, 209; patterns/trends, 190; policy-relevant, 225; primary, 54; populations, difficult, 67, 190; qualitative, 163; quantitative, 183; teams/partnerships, 191; US, decline in output, 199; US,

dominance of, 204; US, investment in, 198; Western Europe, decline in output, 190
researchers: 224, 226; academic, 35, 189, 194; advice, 225; attacked, 12, 189; American, 200, 201; countries of origin, 223; occidental origin, 223; postgraduate, 69; reluctance to enter violent field, 30; review of, 70; shortage of experienced, 1, 12, 30, 69, 191, 208, 209; teams of, 191; threat of violence to, 170, 189; US dominance, 197
Research Assessment Exercise (RAE), 187
Reuters, 128
Revolutionary Armed Forces, 146
Richardson, Lewis, 143
ricin, 82
Right, the *see* right-wing
right-wing: American, 168, 176; American militias, 13; dictatorship, 151; extreme right: 168, 169, 174, 179; extremism, 168, 171; movements, 169; radical bands, 147; radical right, 82; Right, the, 93; rioting, 156; tackling, 16; terrorists/groups, 165, 175, 207
Roberts, Adams, 3, 4
Robson, Colin, 57
Rockwell, George Lincoln: 174; Christian Identity founder, 174 *see also* Christian Identity
rogue states, 84, 139
Rubin, Jeffrey, 142–3, 154
Rumsfeld, Donald, 217
Rushdie, Salman, 147
Russia, tsarist, 96 *see also* tsarist autocracy
Russian Empire, 95

Saigon, 144
salmonella, 80
Sandler, Todd, 125, 130, 131, 132, 133
Sands, Amy, 77
sarin attack, Tokyo, xvii, 74, 79, 81
Saudi Arabia, 22, 121
Schmid, Alex, 3, 7, 10, 58, 59, 65, 70, 112, 144, 162, 186, 187, 188, 189, 191, 193, 194, 226–7
Schulze, Fred, 15
Science, Medical and Technical (STM) disciplines, 108, 114
scientific organizations, 26
Scotland, 169, 180, 181
Scott, G., 3
Second World War, 144
secondary accounts, 163
security: forces/services, 13, 20, 35, 46, 50, 65; Irish, 40; officers, 171
self-imposed constraints, xvii
seminars, 26, 225
Sengupta's Law of Bibliometrics, 105–6, 115
settlement, 157
Shafritz, J., 3

Shining Path, 146
Shouf Mountains, 94
SICAT, 192
Silke, Andrew, 177
Sinhalese, unfair treatment of, 141
Sinn Fein: 32, 35, 37, 39, 46, 48, 51;
    members, 41; publicity officers, 48, 50
Sinn Fein National Headquarters: 36, 37, 38;
    Head of, 36–7; Prisoner of War
    Department, 36
situational danger, 13
skyjackings *see* aerial hijackings
Small, Stephen, 13
smallpox, 82
snowballing/snowball sampling, 39, 47
social: justice, 96; milieu, 86; polarization,
    142; transformation, 143
social science: community, 26; disciplines, 2,
    25, 36, 65, 108, 109, 138, 194, 198, 210;
    literature, 162, 189; research, 11;
    researchers, 66
social scientists, 91, 183
Sociological Abtract database, 111–12
sociologists, 195
sociology, 188, 194, 210, 224
soldiers, 17
Somalia, 100
source material: secondary, xviii, 30, 31;
    primary, 30, 54, 61, 62, 184; tertiary, xviii,
    30
South Africa: 145, 198, 202; apartheid
    government, 13
Southern Ireland *see* Ireland; Republic of
    Ireland
Southern Poverty Law Center (SPLC), 168,
    171, 176
Soviet bloc, 151 *see also* Eastern bloc
Soviet Union: 75, 80, 143,152, 153; collapse
    of, 84; ex-, 97
Space Technology, 106, 114
Spain: 122, 147, 150, 154–7, 202; Communist
    Party, 150; in the 1990s, 201; terrorist
    experience, 201
Spanish: authorities, French co-operation
    with, 156; fascist State, 152; government,
    154, 157, 158; police agencies, 157; Prime
    Minister, 157
spiral of conflict model, 143
spiralling: effect, 158; of the literature, 215
SPLC *see* Southern Poverty Law Center
Sprinzak, Ehud, 75
Sproul Hall, 141
Sri Lanka, 141, 146, 159
Sri Lankan Army, 81
Sri Lankans, 141
S-Shape Growth Curve Theory, 110–11
St Andrews university: 70, 77, 167; website,
    180 *see also* RAND, RAND–St Andrews'
    International Database of Terrorism

Stalag 13, 80
statistical: analysis, 66, 68; methods, 11;
    procedures, 11
statistics: 65, 113, 168; descriptive, 10, 11, 66,
    68; inferential, 11, 66, 67; probablistic
    arguments, 11; relationships and patterns,
    11; terrorism, 168; use of, 68
Stepan, Alfred, 92
Sterling, Claire, 153
Stern, Jessica, 76
Stiglitz, Joseph, 93
Straits of Gibralter, 132
structural change model, 143
struggle groups, 158, 159
students, mobilization of, 151
Studies in Conflict and Terrorism, 61, 113, 187
Studies in Nuclear Terrorism, 73
substitution effect: 119–37; policy
    implications, 134; shortcomings, 135–6
suicide: assault, on USS *Cole*, 22; bombers:
    17, 139; bombers, Palestinian, 6; terrorism,
    Lebanese, 24; terrorism, Palestinian, 24;
    terrorism, Tamil, 24
Sushi bars, 92
Sweden, 95, 96, 147
Switzerland, 95
Symbionese Liberation Army, 138
sympathisers, 20, 21
Syria: 147; PLO camps in, 132
Syrian operations, 150

tactical attacks, 76
Taliban regime, 119
Tamil protests, 141
Tanzania: 22; 1998 attacks on US embassies,
    xvii, 22, 121
taqiya, 220
Taylor, Max, 31, 72, 73
technologically conservative, 76
technology, upgrades in, 134
Tehran, takeover of US embassy, 129, 130
television programmes, 91
terrorism: academic discipline, 105; American,
    right-wing, 165; analysts, 162; assessment
    of, 113; behaviour, 215; causes of, 7, 222;
    comparative studies of, 163; concepts of,
    78, 210; criminal organizations, 207;
    culture and history, 215; definition, under
    American law, 92; definitions, 6, 7, 91, 207;
    definitions, academic, 92; definitions,
    conflicting, 2–3, 4; definitions, growth in,
    111–12; definitions, legal, 92; definitions,
    quagmire, 208; dissident campaigns in
    Northern Ireland, 200–1; domestic sources,
    200; dynamics of, 215, 222; economic
    impact of, 27; émigré, 101; events, peak
    years, 115; experts, 222; financing of, 53;
    focus of, 215; high-incident states, 133;
    historical studies of, 163; history of, 183,

221; insurgent, 9; international, 163; Islamist, 207, 225; journals, 198; journals, prolific authors, 192; modern, 96, 97; motivations, 19, 21, 30, 215; nineteenth-century, 96; non-contemporary, 221; occidental interpretation, 226; patterns, 210–11; perceptions of, 19–20; prediction, future terrorism, 10, 11; prediction, reliable, 23; published output on, 25; quantitative studies of, 163; religion-based, 129–35; research, 12, 26, 164, 165, 191, 194, 202, 203, 209; research, direction of, 25; research, empirically grounded, 161; research, field, 190; research, increase in Ireland's output, 199; research, leading authors in, 191; research, unevenly distributed, 208; research community, 221; researchers, lack of agreement, 207; researchers, mainstream, 222 *see also* research; researchers; root causes, 215; state, 207; state sponsorship, 73, 207; states, destabilized by terrorism, 27; states, low-terrorism, 133; statistics, 168; stratified, 99; studies, 11, 12, 18, 26, 27, 86, 161, 163, 167, 180, 183, 184; successes against, 4; symptoms of, 210; transnational, 121–3; trends, 210–11; trends, long-term, 23; UK, 202; understanding of, 226; understanding, weaknesses in, 211
Terrorism: An International Journal, 187
Terrorism, Radicalism, Extreme Violence International (TREVI), 149
Terrorism Act 2000, 5
Terrorism and Political Violence, 61, 113, 187, 192
Terrorism Research and the Diffusion of Ideas, 162
terrorist(s) groups/organizations: 5, 6, 9, 36, 58, 170, 178, 189, 200; access to, 182; activities of, 9, 10; attacks, 9; background life histories, 10; behaviour of, 12, 34, 35; campaigns, 9, 202; definitions of, 207; events, 10, 11; former, 182; grievances, 217; historical background, 12; historical origins, xviii; how equipped, 11; how organized, 11; how trained, 11; incidents, internal dynamics, 10; international, 24; interviews with, 179; left-wing, 206; loyalist *see* Northern Ireland; membership of, 9, 11; negotiations, 135; networks, 135; primary source material, 184; problem, authorities' view of, 16; proscribed, 5, 6; psychology of, 190; recruitment, 135; right-wing *see* right-wing, terrorists; small non-state, 206; sociology of, 190; subculture, 171; tactics, xviii; 'traditional' type, 78; understanding of, 226; use of WMD, 221
tertiary accounts, 163
Texas, 205
Thatcher, Prime Minister Margaret, 155
Thayer, Bradley A., 76

The Covenant, the Sword, and the Arm of the Lord (CSA), 80, 81, 175
The Cult at the End of the World, 77
The Dalles, 80
The Economist, 96, 113
The New Resistance, 151
The Nonproliferation Review, 77
The Order *see* Bruders Schweigen
The Red Hand, 52
The Satanic Verses, 147
The Secret Army, 34
The Terror Network, 153
The Terrorism Industry, 15–16
The Threat of Nuclear Terrorism: A Reexamination, 74
The Ultimate Terrorists, 76
think-tanks: 225; analyses of terrorism, 223
Third World, 22, 151
threshold autoregressive (TAR) model, 133
Timothy McVeigh, 121 *see also* Oklahoma
Tipton, Colin, 63
Tokyo, 75, 79 *see also* Sarin
total immersion, 179–82
tourism industry, 119
Toxic Terror, 76
translators: 166; shortage of Arabic, 219; shortage of Farsi, 219; shortage of Pashto, 219
TransWorld Airlines, 135
travel agencies, 148
tsarist autocracy, 95 *see also* Russia
Tucker, Jonathan, 76, 77, 85
Turkey, 158, 202
Turkish: air force base, 81; government, 148; targets, 147
Twin Towers *see* World Trade Center

UK: 4, 5, 6, 25, 95, 122, 138, 147, 197, 198, 200, 201; airbases, 132; government, 4, 6; interests, 132; terrorism in, 202 *see also* Northern Ireland
Ulrich's Guide to Periodical Literature, 109–10, 117
Ulster: 13, 19, 147, 202; British military installations, 155; Ulster Volunteer Force (UVF), 159 *see also* Northern Ireland, paramilitaries
UMI, 112
United Nations: 93; agencies, 145; Terrorism Prevention Branch, 7
United Press International, 128
Universal Decimal Classification (UDC), 109
University College of Cork: 41, 199; Applied Psychology Department, 199; History Department, 199
University of Nevada, 192
university: courses, 25; departments, 26
Upper Heyford, 132
US: administration, 194, 201, 210; Clinton

administration, 201; Congress, 217; Congress, agenda of, 216; Department of State, 5; domestic terrorism, 168; embassies, 132 *see also* Kenya; Federal Aviation Administrative data, 124; focus on, 210; foreign policy, 217; government, 15, 26, 135, 216; government departments, number of PhDs, 225; Government Publication Office database (GPO), 108, 114; interests, 132, 136; intelligence community, 216, 218, 219, 220, 223; Justice Department, 178, 179; law enforcement community, 219; National Defense Authorization Act, 134; Navy, 22; Patterns of Global Terrorism, 97, 100, 115; right-wing extremism, 176; Senate, 77; Senate, Chairman of House Permanent Select Committee on Intelligence, 219–20; Senate, House Committee on International Relations, 214; Senate, misinformation, 77; Senate, report, 77; targets, 200; trans-Pacific flights, 23; troops, in Yemen, 22
USA: 5, 6, 15, 22, 23, 26, 79, 95, 101, 119, 120, 121, 132, 134, 136, 138, 143, 144, 151, 152, 169, 178, 179, 196, 197, 198, 201, 204, 209, 210, 214, 217, 218; anthrax spores, 92; decline in research, 199; domestic terrorism, 205, 210; militia groups, 204; poisoning of urban water supplies, 80; radical right, 82; right-wing groups, 207; terrorism researchers, 200; terrorist threat facing, 200; Western allies, 217, 218; white separatist/supremacist, 169 *see also* North America; North American Nations
USS *Cole*, 22

validity, 11
vector autoregression (VAR) analysis, 131
Veterans of Foreign Wars of the United States (*VFW Magazine*), 109
victims: elderly, 17, 18; female, 17, 18, 19; Israeli children, 18; Palestinian children, 18; young, 17, 19
Viet Cong, 144
Vietnam, 151
Vietnam War, 144, 151

Waco, 205
Wall Street, 119
War on Terrorism, 25, 120
war(s): 7, 121, 143; anti-colonial, 145; crimes, 7, 8; criminals, 7, 8; internal, 145 *see also* civil war; inter-state, 145; legitimate acts of, 7; rules of, 8; surrogate, 146; unconventional, 138
Washington Post, 128
Washington, 24, 25, 116, 216
watchdog: agencies, 176; groups, 168
weapons of mass destruction (WMD): 24, 59, 72–90, 184, 205; research, biological/medical, 26; state sponsorship for, 85; terrorism involving, 73, 75, 76, 77, 78, 84, 86; terrorist use of, 221; weapons'-usable equipment, 82–3 *see also* CBRN
Web of Science, 109
Weinberg, Leonard, 192
West Bank, 139
Western: countries, 3; democracies, 210; policy-makers, 8; world, 9, 203
Western Europe: 6, 147, 148, 153, 154, 158, 159, 202, 203, 223; continental, 202; continental, decline in research output, 199; Middle Eastern terrorism in, 148, 149, 150, 158; terrorists, 151
Western European: governments, 149; terrorism, 157; world, 95
white separatist/supremacist, USA, 169
White, Robert, 31, 34, 35, 39, 52, 53
Wilkinson, Paul, 27, 163, 166, 193
William R. Nelson Institute, 167
World Bank, 93
World Catalogue, 112
World Trade Center, 1993 bombing, xvii, 91, 119, 121, 218
World Trade Organization (WTO), 93

xenophobic, 147

Yemen, 22, 100
young people, mobilization of, 151
Yugoslavia: 145; ex-, 142

Zelikow, Philip, 75

Printed in the United Kingdom by
Lightning Source UK Ltd., Milton Keynes
139411UK00001B/22/P